SELF AND WORLD

SELF AND WORLD

AN EXPLANATION OF AESTHETIC REALISM

ELI SIEGEL

DEFINITION PRESS, NEW YORK, 1981

Library of Congress Catalog Card Number 75-44647

ISBN (cloth bound edition) 0-910492-27-1
ISBN (paperback edition) 0-910492-28-x

Printed in the United States of America
by the Haddon Craftsmen

Contents

Introductory Note

Self and World is the prose companion to Eli Siegel's great poetic work, beginning with "Hot Afternoons Have Been in Montana" in 1925 and continuing throughout his life. *Self and World* is the expression and explanation of Aesthetic Realism, which he taught in classes and in lessons to individuals from 1941 to almost the time of his death in November 1978. I believe *Self and World* is the greatest book ever to have been written. If you think I am saying greater than the Bible or Shakespeare—yes, I am.

Eli Siegel's greatness was in three fields, the famous three: truth, beauty, and kindness. He had a mind the size of which I never saw equalled, and it had also speed, depth, dexterity, and brilliance beyond any other I know. His ability to make relations was sheerly astonishing. It was a joy to see his mind in action: to see him announce a subject, describe it, define it, explore it, explain it, show its relations. The effect of his teaching was extraordinary. Those of us who studied with Eli Siegel felt our selves were understood as they had never been before in this world, and that the world, too, was new for us—it opened up, and things were clear that had never been clear before. I felt this. How can I describe it? It was as if the shutters were taken off the windows of my soul.

Eli Siegel had the ability to see truth; he saw new truth about mankind: us, our minds and feelings. This is the rarest knowledge, and he had it. He saw beauty in a new way and made it plain, able to be seen by others. He said: "All beauty is a making one of opposites, and the making one of opposites is what we are going after in ourselves." I think this is one of the kindest, loveliest sentences ever written. It gives a beautiful motive to every human being ever born.

As a book, *Self and World* is not difficult; it is rather easy to understand. One of its beauties is, so much is said, of such depth, and said so clearly. The writing is vivid, compact, humorous, and in a prose so musical that phrases stay in one's mind and recur and recur.

It is curious that *Self and World* has almost no quotations from other books, other writers. Eli Siegel remarked on the absence of quotations himself. I think the reason was, he wanted this to be an expression of Aesthetic Realism that was "pure," classic, in the sense of uncluttered, like an outline free of ornament, or a most perfect vase.

Self and World is about the subject of its title. Nothing can be more grand or all-embracing—nor more precise. *Self and World* gives us the power to understand ourselves and to like ourselves. It often seems that if we understand ourselves, the exact opposite of liking will be the result. Eli Siegel said the greatest desire of the self is to like the world with the facts present, and that if we like the world, we will like ourselves.

Self and World was written in 1942–43, essentially; some things came later—the Frances Sanders Lesson is of 1945, and the chapter on dreams is from a lecture of 1950. Two chapters, "The Aesthetic Method in Self-Conflict" and "Psychiatry, Economics, Aesthetics," were printed as pamphlets in 1946, and the rest of the book was mimeographed during the forties and fifties for the use of students; but all these years the book as such was not published.

When, in the last months of his life, the publication of

Self and World was talked of, Eli Siegel said he wanted the first form of it to be preserved as much as possible, and where this made for inconsistencies of spelling or punctuation, let them be, for they show its history. So does the repetition of the story of the devil and the painter. This was first written, I believe, for a short Summary of Aesthetic Realism (Aesthetic Analysis then) which he gave to Donald Kirkley, who wrote an article about him for the Baltimore *Sun* in the autumn of 1944. Later, Eli Siegel incorporated the story into the "Guilt Chapter." It seems to belong in both places, and so, since the Summary is now part of *Self and World* (being the introduction to "Psychiatry, Economics, Aesthetics," Chapter Ten), it appears twice.

The story makes its ethical point; I believe it also tells something about the author and came from deep in his experience. Eli Siegel could, with very little effort on his part, have become very famous. This was especially true when he won the *Nation* Poetry Prize for "Hot Afternoons Have Been in Montana" in 1925; but it was true later, too. All he had to do was be a little tactful, refrain from certain criticisms, not tread on certain toes, be a little more praising here and there. This is what everybody knows and what everybody does. People expect it. Eli Siegel's refusal to be part of this chain of flattery and contempt was his strength and his glory; it is why we loved and trusted him beyond anyone, and it also made him envied and hated.

II

Eli Siegel had generous respect for other thought and for other thinkers and writers, and his ability to be affected by others was not in conflict with his originality. He was boundlessly influenced by what he read, saw, and heard; and he was boundlessly original.

He read enormously during his high school years in Baltimore, and often spoke of reading in the Enoch Pratt Free Library in Baltimore and in Druid Hill Park, and of his literary conversations with his friend, Adolphus Emmart, later of the Baltimore *Sun* and later not so friendly, but whose early companionship was much valued by Eli Siegel.

He read the English and French poets and everything he could pertaining to literature. He cared for Hazlitt, for Tennyson, for Coleridge of course, and for Hugo and Mallarmé. When he spoke of his favorite authors, one of the first he mentioned was the tremendous critic, George Saintsbury.

One of his earliest published writings was "The Scientific Criticism" which appeared with a companion essay, "The Complete Socialism," in the first number of *The Modern Quarterly* in 1923. He was not quite twenty-one. These two essays represent two of Eli Siegel's lifelong interests, two aspects of his thought, two opposites: beauty and justice. They were always together in his mind.

Eli Siegel was, first, vastly interested in reality; he wanted to know and be affected by all that was not himself; and, too, he was most original, most independent and unforgettably individual. The more he was affected by otherness, it seemed, the more he became richly and outstandingly himself. People, most of us fiercely carving out our individualities, envied him this proud, effortless uniqueness.

Eli Siegel was the kindest person I have ever known. He wanted to know what I felt and he spent hours trying to find out—this even after we had been married for thirty years; he never took for granted he knew what I felt already. This was his ethics, it is how he was to people, and that is why many others besides myself felt the same way I did: that he was the kindest person they ever knew.

This is true. Why, then, in the year 1981, are Eli Siegel and his work still not known as they ought to be? The answer is, Eli Siegel's honest goodness, his unmatched genius, his unequalled intelligence makes people angry. The most shameful thing in my life is, it made me angry. I thought he was the greatest man who ever lived; and he honored me with his love and even married me. I had the largest reason in the world to be grateful, but I thought my great feeling for him made me less. I was ashamed I thought so much of him. Oh, Eli, forgive me. I loved you so much it made me angry.

How could Eli Siegel be in the world and the world not know it? How could we have let this happen? Eli Siegel was put in a situation very, very cruel. I sometimes wondered how he could praise a world which had put him in such a cruel position. That is, it gave him the finest mind that had ever been, a mind able to apprehend it, the world, in all its subtleties and in its greatness and hugeness and might; and it gave him this power, but not one thing to help him have it welcomed. With all this, he remained sweet and kept his humor.

When we see how much he was able to do without recognition or acclaim, imagine what he might have done if he had had them! He thought, for example, if he had been able to work with doctors, he could have found the cause of cancer. I think this is likely true. I am quite sure that when his work is known, no one will ever again become insane.

Knowledge of his work has been available to the world since 1946. That it has been kept from the world by the anger, the mortified conceit of the press, the literary and academic world, is a crime against health and beauty which must stop now. *Self and World* has the power to end the terror of respect.

Despite all the forces against it, Eli Siegel's work continues. At the Aesthetic Realism Foundation in New York, classes are given, and there are consultations in which people talk about their lives with honesty and respect. New knowledge is present. The basis of it is in *Self and World*. It makes people happy and kind. Oh, world, it is what you have waited for.

March 1981   MARTHA BAIRD SIEGEL

Preface: Contempt Causes Insanity

THE FIRST QUESTION

Is it true, as Aesthetic Realism said years ago, that man's deepest desire, his largest desire, is to like the world on an honest or accurate basis? And is it true, as Aesthetic Realism said later, that the desire to have contempt for the outside world and for people and other objects as standing for the outside world, is a continuous, unseen desire making for mental insufficiency?

The large difference between Aesthetic Realism and other ways of seeing an individual is that Aesthetic Realism makes the attitude of an individual to the whole world the most critical thing in his life.

Aesthetic Realism in 1941 first said that it was one's way of seeing the world which caused mental mishap or difficulty. And it was in the same year, 1941, that Aesthetic Realism said the useful way of seeing mind was to look upon it as a continual question of aesthetics.

In 1941, no interest was shown by press or academy in the question whether the world was seen right when a person suffered mentally; and no interest was shown by press or academy in the aesthetic way as perhaps the most useful

This Preface is taken from five issues of *The Right of Aesthetic Realism to Be Known* (TRO): numbers 177, 178, 133, 134, 180, published in 1976 and 1975.

way of seeing mind. At this time there is more of a disposition to see these two questions as they deserve to be seen.

Nevertheless, what is true and untrue in the field of mind needs to be clearly and effectively seen. Therefore, what was said in *Self and World* which, as book, began in 1942, should be looked at after thirty and more years of busy life, with enough suffering, injustice, pain, to show that a world unwisely seen was still the world people were using.

I imply in an early chapter of *Self and World*, "The World, Guilt, and Self-Conflict," that mental distress begins with a putting aside by a person of what the world truly is or may be. I wrote, in 1942, this:

> In every instance of a guilt feeling, there is evidence pointing to the fact that the cause is *a feeling of separation of oneself from reality as a whole.*

I must say, the possible truth of this sentence is as large a matter in the lives of men and women, everywhere, as can be thought of. There has been some feeling, certainly, in history that a living being, knowing that he is alive, has some obligation to see truly where he is alive and through what he is alive and what he is meeting every day. This obligation, Aesthetic Realism says, must be seen as well as one can see it.

We do not have the obligation, at the beginning, to approve of the world or to disapprove of it. We do have the obligation, however, to see the world as well as we can. No such obligation is recognized by the present inhabitants of earth. Nor is this obligation recognized by the diverse mental practitioners in the various lands of the present world.

Aesthetic Realism states that ethics begins with the human obligation to see everything, living and not living, as well as one can. Where we get away from this obligation or don't see it, or diminish its meaning, it is rather clear that contempt is showing its strength; indeed, is winning.

The first victory of contempt is the feeling in people that they have the right to see other people and things pretty much as they please. For this reason, the viewpoint of Aesthetic Realism that we have an obligation to see everything as well as we can, is a critical matter.

The fact that most people have felt there is no such obligation, that they had the right to see other people and other objects in a way that seemed to go with comfort—this fact is the beginning of the injustice and pain of the world. It is contempt in its first universal, hideous form.

IS CONTEMPT PREVALENT?

I have implied before that the having of contempt is easy. All you have to do is to stop thinking about something before you really know it—even think that you know it—and contempt has won. We have to see, then, and we can't see it too often, whether there is the obligation to know what is different from ourselves; and, of course, ourselves too. In the matter of knowing what is different from ourselves and ourselves likewise, obligation is joy. The desire to know, as Aristotle once implied, is an obligation to both justice and pleasure. The *Metaphysics* of Aristotle begins this way:

> All men by nature desire to know. An indication is the delight we take in our senses; for even apart from their usefulness they are loved for themselves; and above all others the sense of sight.

In the First Book of Aristotle's *Metaphysics,* there are many sentences that sustain the Aesthetic Realism view that seeing is the oneness of two opposites: obligation and joy, or what we must do and what we want to do. Everyone would agree that eating is something we must do, and that also it is something, often, we want to do very much. And most people would agree that the more we are compelled to eat or the more we must have food, the more we enjoy the eating when we get to it. The opposites, then, so important in liking the world—what we must see and what we want to see—are illustrated by the fact that we must eat and we also frequently enjoy eating.

I quote Aristotle because he is useful in having people see that when a baby first looks at her room and the people around her, the purpose is simultaneously one of getting information and of liking that world in which the information is to be found. A baby, as Aesthetic Realism sees the dear being, is already one who joins the arts and sciences; for the dear being is simultaneously asking: "What is this world I've come into, and how can I find meaning in it which will make me a greater dear little being than I am today?"

The fact that there is such a pother about or interest in the junction of the sciences and arts shows that the original purpose of seeing or knowing—getting the facts and seeing meaning in the facts—this purpose we all had when we were born, has been impressively renovated as the synthesis of the sciences and the arts. For are not science and art both present in ordinary seeing?

SOME CONSIDERATIONS

When we like something, it is well to see what we like. Aesthetic Realism says that whenever we like something, we approve of both ourselves and the world.

In the old and entrancing quatrain about Little Jack Horner, we have the problem of pleasure and self-respect; also the problem of what we owe to ourselves and what we owe elsewhere:

> Little Jack Horner sat in the corner
> Eating a Christmas pie;
> He put in his thumb, and pulled out a plum,
> And said, "What a good boy am I!"

The dramatic entrance of ethical considerations into a narrative of hedonistic activity is one of the notable situations in literature. When Jack Horner tells us that he is a good boy, even while he is conspicuously enjoying himself, he is blending the two great values of human existence, pleasure and self-respect. Perhaps Jack Horner's notion of the meaning of "good boy" is insufficient; yet it remains true that the time of our greatest pleasure should be the time of our least guilt, greatest respect of self.

EDUCATION SAYS TWO THINGS

I have written in TRO 12 that the purpose of education is to like the world. This, as I see it, will be true indefinitely. Yet liking the world should be seen as completed by the notion of being just to the world. Let us think of Dennis and Madeline. When Dennis loved Madeline, that much he was just to her. Love, when it is based well, is always a mode of justice. So, in liking the world, we may simply be just to it. And justice, as Aesthetic Realism sees it, is what the world, if it looks for anything, is looking for. Perhaps God is a means of justice to the world: the world's personal representative.

What I have just written is in accord with what was said years ago by a person who often is regarded as America's most important educator or writer on education, Horace Mann (1796–1859):

> Finally, education alone can conduct us to that enjoyment which is, at once, best in quality and infinite in quantity.

Horace Mann said this in the first of his lectures in *Lectures and Reports on Education* (1845).

Horace Mann, like Wordsworth, saw a child as related to the whole meaning of the world. Horace Mann saw every child in New England, every child in Boston or New York or Ohio, as related to the entire meaning of reality, however deep and comprehensive this meaning might be.

I believe that the mistake of Wordsworth and Horace Mann—and for that matter, of Immanuel Kant in his *Critique of Pure Reason*—was the failure to make a one of a child's being a representative of the universe in his own right—a miniature world of categories, intuitions, apperceptions—and the fact that evil was likely something of which the child was fond. Aesthetic Realism sees the ideal judgment of a child as true. But this judgment is also true of a child: In a fight between his ego's doing as it pleases and the happiness and beauty of the world, he may choose his ego's supremacy. Wordsworth, Mann, and Kant did not make enough of the self's amour with evil.

WHAT IS NEEDED

If, then, as Kant says, a child has within him the categories of Causality and Dependence—and who knows what else?—this should be related to the frequent selfishness, coldness, cunning of a child. It is then we shall have radiance and the abyss, luminosity and the weasel, together.

For every child has this debate: Shall I, with my categories and apperceptions, see the world as magnificently and as delicately as possible; or shall I see the world as the material for victories for just me? Most people would assent to Aristotle's statement that man has a natural desire to know; but most people, as yet, would not assent to the Aesthetic Realism statement that fully to know the world includes the hope to like it as much as one can. Knowing and liking in most people's minds are too disparate; too antagonistic, even. It is necessary, as I have said, if crime is to be unappealing, that persons like the world—and this is the same as being considerate of someone other than yourself.

These matters follow from the chapter on guilt in *Self and World*—written in 1942. Guilt is a result of insufficient liking of the world or a separation from it. How can we make separation from the world, insufficient like of it, less appealing? The only way is to give, in as lively a fashion as possible, all the evidence for the fact that liking the world is the greatest instinct man has; the finest and greatest possibility of his unconscious.

A way to begin is to show that any time we have a chance to like something and don't take it, we ourselves miss something; further, if we like something a bit, but can like it more, we miss something also.

So, wherever there has been a possibility of our liking something, and we did not implement this possibility, a loss for us has taken place.

It can reasonably be asked: Why, then, are people not so interested in knowing as much as they can, and in this way encourage themselves to like as much as they can? This reason is the fact that there are two pleasures. I do talk of "2-A pleasure" in *Self and World;* but I do not clearly enough show that this pleasure is the pleasure of contempt.

The existence, in everyone, as a daily possibility, of the pleasure of contempt, is the great opponent to the pleasure of knowing the world and, perhaps, liking it because one knows it.

In *Self and World,* the two pleasures in man are represented as being in a constant fight, with the body of man and his thought as the battlefield. It is this fight, as yet unsettled, which causes nervousness in man; and if it goes on exceptionally ill, insanity. For when the fight goes exceptionally ill, the constantly hovering pleasure of contempt has won. Contempt is not interested in knowledge as knowledge, only in knowledge making ego the one thing. The fight with contempt goes on.

Contempt must be defeated if man is to be kind. I said this in 1942; but I do believe, dear unknown friends, I can say it better now.

CONTEMPT HURTS MIND

I think as time goes on, the seeing by Aesthetic Realism of contempt as the cause of all mental disorder or disaster will be judged valid. I present some reasons for the belief that both nervousness and insanity are caused by the common human inclination for contempt.

That deep mental disorder is caused by contempt has been said indirectly fairly often. In a 1924 essay by Sigmund Freud, we find the Vienna practitioner saying that a going away from reality is the cause of psychosis. What the eminent doctor did not want to do—or at least failed to do—was to see that in a "flight" from reality, contempt is present. So let us look at a statement of the Vienna student of mind, implying that contempt is a cause frequently of inward disaster.

FREUD IS LOOKED AT

Here is what Freud writes in the essay I have mentioned, "The Loss of Reality in Neurosis and Psychosis" (*Collected Papers of Sigmund Freud,* Vol. II):

> Both neurosis and psychosis are thus the expression of a rebellion on the part of the id against the external world, of its unwillingness—or, if one prefers, its incapacity—to adapt itself to the exigencies of reality.

Freud was not interested in contempt. He does not see that the word *rebellion* could have in it the meaning of contempt. When a human being rebels against anything, there is anger in him; but he would like very much to change the anger into contempt. It is like a prizefighter summoning up his combative strength to defeat an opponent; but should he find the opponent lying on the floor with the referee counting over him, the prizefighter's purpose has been successful: he can now have the repose of contempt. All anger would like to become contempt. Anger has pain in it, but contempt is inward bliss; repose; some quietude.

It is contempt, dear unknown friends, which all journals and all hospitals will be studying. It is something that not only Freud has underestimated.

WAS THIS CONTEMPT?

Students of distressed mentality have, then, not seen the central role of contempt. It is well, after having regarded Dr. Freud a while, to go to his most eminent American colleague and representative, Dr. Abraham Arden Brill. In the early pages of Dr. Brill's edition of *The Basic Writings of Sigmund Freud* (New York: 1938), the New York psychoanalyst tells of his early esteem of psychoanalysis and of his using it to alleviate inward distress in Manhattan and nearby.

Dr. Brill tells, on page 22 of *Basic Writings,* about a patient of his who had succumbed to apathy. A question of ours is, Does all human apathy have some contempt in it? But to Dr. Brill's useful narrative:

> When an effort was made to arouse her interest, she usually reacted to it with some irritation. The patient evidently refused to be affected by impressions from the outer world, and also ignored or depreciated everything that she remembered from her past, namely, her inner world.

What the whole psychoanalytic profession has failed to ask concerning a human situation like the one Dr. Brill tells of is this: Is contempt for the world the chief, the crucial thing in this person's mind? Dear unknown friends, other words like flight, anesthesia, irresponsiveness, negativism, catatonia, anhedonia, dullness, aphephobia, are relevant; but there has not been asking about the place of contempt.

In the mental practitioner's vocabulary, there are many words ending in *phobia*. Aesthetic Realism asks whether every phobia or human fear has in it a desire for contempt. Aesthetic Realism believes that just as all anger would like pleasantly to convert itself into contempt, so every fear or phobia would also like to transform itself into contempt. How pleasing it is to say to something we once feared, "Pooh, I'm not afraid of you." Contempt, dear friends, is so much the repose that the tossed-about human mind is looking for.

A PSYCHOANALYTIC STATEMENT

Following the little narrative we have excerpted, Dr. Brill says (*Basic Writings,* page 23):

> The psychosis exhibits alone no compromise with reality, turns its back on reality, as it were.

Had Dr. Brill and Dr. Freud looked at the phrase, "turns its back on reality," they would have come into a treasure house of urgent perception. But as we said, psychoanalysis was not interested in studying the depth, the comprehensiveness and ubiquity of contempt.

So it is well at this point to present the general attitude of Aesthetic Realism.—We are looking for contempt at any moment of our lives. Contempt is our soothing revenge for a world not sufficiently interested, as we see it, in what we are hoping for. Contempt is not an incident; it is an unintermitting counteroffensive to an uncaring world.

There are two means, as Aesthetic Realism sees it, of bringing some satisfaction to ourselves. The first is, the seeing of something like a sunset, a poem, a concerto, which can stand for the world and which pleases us through what it is: its structure in mind, time, and space. This is the aesthetic victory, which is the most sensible of all victories. The other victory is our ability to depreciate anything that exists. To see the world itself as an impossible mess—and this is often not difficult at all—gives a certain triumph to the individual.

CHRISTOPHER MARLOWE

The way we get revenge on the messy, unsolicitous world is to make a comforting world of our own. To make a world of our own is related to magic. We have quoted Dr. Sigmund Freud and Dr. A. A. Brill; and now we quote another person of another time and somewhat of another outlook: Christopher Marlowe (1564–1593).

The renowned play of Christopher Marlowe, *The Tragical History of Doctor Faustus,* is about a person not pleased with the customary world nor the customary study of this world. Here Doctor Faustus is like a Manhattan patient of Dr. Brill, *circa* 1923. When, as Doctor Faustus does, we go for dismissing the wearisome world, we are saying hello to magic. Let us look at some lines of Marlowe, more famous even than the quoted little narrative of Dr. Brill:

> Philosophy is odious and obscure,
> Both law and physic are for petty wits;
> Divinity is basest of the three,
> Unpleasant, harsh, contemptible, and vile;
> 'Tis magic, magic, that hath ravished me.

One of these days some candidate for a doctorate in philosophy will write his thesis on this subject: Similarities in the Marlovian Concept of Magic with the Later Freudian Concept of the Id.

Marlowe uses the word *contemptible* in describing a most respected study, divinity. In Elizabethan times, the being able to despise contemporary restrictions of the adventurous mind was a relief. Marlowe, like poetry itself, had to make a one of restriction and abandon. He had to find a deep, authentic junction of the world as fetters and the world as happy material for the completion of self.

Doctor Faustus had contempt for the world as obstructive, niggardly, hostile. Surely, as we said, the world makes for anger and fear; but oh, how we should like to convert fear and anger into contempt!

Marlowe, like some other Elizabethan dramatists, is good at describing contempt latent, working, in every person. The tremendously attractive figure, about 1589, of Marlowe's Eastern potentate, Tamburlaine, again and again, makes resonant, powerful blank verse lines out of contempt. Perhaps the most famous depiction of contempt in early Elizabethan tragedy is Tamburlaine's changing various Eastern rulers into something like horses whom he drives. Here are remembered lines of sonorous contempt:

> *Tamburlaine.* Holla, ye pampered jades of Asia!
> What! can ye draw but twenty miles a day,
> And have so proud a chariot at your heels,
> And such a coachman as great Tamburlaine!

TAMBURLAINE AND OEDIPUS

Tamburlaine unquestionably and delightfully illustrates the possible and hoped-for victory of contempt in this world of ours. That Oedipus, in a murkier or dimmer fashion, represents contempt likewise is something that Dr. Freud did not see.

The famous Oedipus Complex of the Viennese investigator has faded. Very much alive, though, are the fear and contempt we have for the world, and the fear and contempt we have for our parents as representing the beginnings of the world and our beginnings. Dr. Freud found in Sophocles, that a child was a sexual rival of his father and had successfully the body of his mother.

Dr. Freud was essentially contemptuous of art: this can be discerned in a note about beauty in his *Basic Writings*, page 568. We quote the first sentence of the note:

> I have no doubt that the concept of "beauty" is rooted in the soil of sexual stimulation and signified originally that which is sexually exciting.

What presumption! What ignorance! What complacency! What contempt! What schlepperism!

But we need to consider Oedipus as Sophocles, centuries ago, saw him. We have said that Oedipus illustrates the contempt so attractive to human beings. Oedipus says this to Teiresias (Jebb's prose translation of *Oedipus the King*):

> What, basest of the base,—for thou wouldest anger a very stone,—wilt thou never speak out? Can nothing touch thee? Wilt thou never make an end?

Certainly, years and years after the displeasure of Oedipus, we can see a needless contempt in his words to Teiresias. It is true, Oedipus is fearful, for he feels some knowledge he does not wish to have is approaching him. This explains the contempt, hardly justifies it. Fear in ancient Greece, too, was looking for contempt as its dissolvent.

What Freud, in his immunity to certain aspects of literature and thought, could not see was that a person in Athens or Thebes had a feeling about the past as unknown; and also about his past in terms of the people he first saw. The past in which the cause of ourselves lies, is reality, too. We can be afraid of it or be awed by its unknownness and large meaning; and we can be disposed to dismiss it or lessen it.

If we could have prevailed upon Dr. Freud years ago, we should have had him meditate for some hours on this interchange between the blind seer of Thebes and Oedipus:

> *Teiresias.* Wouldst thou have me say more, that thou mayest be more wroth?
> *Oedipus.* What thou wilt; it will be said in vain.

How contempt is present in some turbulent Greek words which Richard Claverhouse Jebb changed into effective English! Teiresias is suspicious of Oedipus, for he has seen that the desire of Oedipus to know more is doubtful. We all of us at some time or other hesitate to understand something; and as we hesitate, we hope that what we don't want to understand is worthy of our contempt. Oedipus wanted to know; but in him also was a desire to make what he did not know unimportant.

Teiresias, having certain ancient advantages, sees that Oedipus has a greater desire to be angry than to ascertain what may be true. The dialogue of Teiresias and Oedipus is deeply equivalent to many a human situation. There is something we have to know and which we, too, are afraid to know. Sophocles felt that we were afraid to know who we were and what others meant to us.

Freud felt that in finding the Oedipus Complex in one of the noted Greek tragedies, he was more profound than earlier criticism. Freud was less profound, for the nature of man in its fulness is deeper than any detachable complex.

Teiresias has contempt, too. The difference between the contempt of Teiresias and that of Oedipus is that the contempt of the darkened seer is better based. Emotion is looking for its lovely fulness and exactness; and the Leader of the Chorus implies that even the emotion of Teiresias could be given more just expression.

We come then to a large question of Aesthetic Realism. This question was put once by the roaming Ophelia: "Lord, we know what we are, but know not what we may be."

Among the many, many things we can have contempt for, with sadness for, and mishap to, ourselves, is what Ophelia calls: "What we may be." The purpose of all education is to feel truly what we may be, without arrogance.

WHAT IS IN INSANITY?

I mean forthrightly to show that contempt causes insanity and, as I said, interferes with mind in a less disastrous way. Contempt is the great failure of man. This is the third sentence of a card published by the Terrain Gallery:

> There is a disposition in every person to think he will be for himself by making less of the outside world.

One definition of insanity is the leaving by an individual of the outside world as a means of safeguarding and asserting his separate individuality. The literature of the world tells us this. Letters, statements, essays, conversations tell us this.

JOHN CLARE

For instance, I care for the poet John Clare (1793–1864) a good deal. He was a true poet and saw musical meaning in a leaf, a field, a square of grass, a thrush. Wisely, Edmund Blunden reprinted some of Clare's poems in 1920. His most famous poem is still, perhaps, that which appeared in the *Oxford Book of English Verse*, 1900. Let us look at these lines of the last stanza of the poem, "Written in Northampton County Asylum":

> I long for scenes where man has never trod—
> For scenes where woman never smiled or wept.

It happens that many executives, after the day's work, go to some vast quiet desert under the stars: Arizona is often the place that is the means of getting away from the unsettling hurly-burly of recent hours. We all of us are fond of vacancy as a means of combating the humiliating bumps and confusions of the ordinary, unsolicitous world. We certainly have a right to find solace in quietude and solitude; but does contempt go along with our attainment of quietude and solitude?

This is not the place to give details for John Clare's anger with and contempt of his poetic patrons. He felt they praised poems, these patrons did, without fully seeing them. Clare's anger was like the later anger of Dylan Thomas, who also knew persons who lauded his poems without seeing them truly. There was, then, some ground for authentic contempt in the rural, Northamptonshire poet, John Clare.

It is where contempt doesn't serve justice, but is a means to our own superiority, that contempt is the handmaid or footman of insanity. Contempt that is accurate is always in behalf of beauty. Contempt that is inaccurate is in behalf of spurious superiority of self. Clare had both kinds. There is poetry in the lines we have quoted; but along with the poet, there is the person who had contempt not so musically, not so wisely.

DID DOSTOEVSKY HAVE CONTEMPT?

Dostoevsky is not seen chiefly as a humorist, as a satirist; hardly any Russian of the 19th century is. Yet Dostoevsky is one of the great humorists of this world, as, deeply, Ibsen is. There is, though, the humor of literature, on the side of beauty and sanity; and there also is the ridicule, the mocking, the sarcasm of the individual aiming to get revenge on a discomforting world. The large, remembered novels of Dostoevsky come from that in him which was kindly humorous. There was the Dostoevsky, too, whose mocking helped epilepsy.

As with Clare, what we can do now is to state something which we have seen as true, with documents the means. That Dostoevsky's epilepsy arose from a large fight between contempt and respect, between anger with the world and giving it meaning—this we hope to show as TRO goes on.

Meanwhile, it is well to present Dostoevsky as a humorist, with just a touch of that elegant contempt even a Russian can have. Early in *The Possessed,* Dostoevsky describes a vagueish liberal, thinking himself more of a terror to Czarism than he really is. Here is Stepan Trofimovitch Verhovensky at a card game:

> You should have seen him at our club when he sat down to cards. His whole figure seemed to exclaim "Cards! Me sit down to whist with you! Is it consistent? Who is responsible for it? Who has shattered my energies and turned them to whist? Ah, perish, Russia!" and he would majestically trump with a heart.

It can be said that the Russian novel in general is a laughable and tearful moving contradiction between contempt and reverence. All prose fiction, all poetry is concerned with how man can despise that which he wants to love. Perhaps, however, the Russian novel presents man as contemptuous and man as tearful and religious more sharply and deeply than other writing.

Dostoevsky was much affected by contempt for religion,

a satirical atheism; and a desire to think that the Christ and God loved in the fields of Russia were true. Belief and unbelief carry on a humorous and piercing fight in *The Brothers Karamazov*. There is a fight between mockery and love in *Notes from the Underground*.

The thing to see is that although Dostoevsky made literature from the incessant battle of belief and disbelief, of meaning and Nihilism, he, as a person, was not exempt from the consequences of this battle. I do not think that Dostoevsky ever made up his mind as to whether what rules the world was to be respected or mocked. This, dear unknown friends, I think is in the cause of his epilepsy.

BAUDELAIRE

Whatever writers are, they are persons. The greatest terrifying homage in verse to contempt is in some lines of Baudelaire in "Au Lecteur," or "To the Reader." I translated these lines in *Hail, American Development*—and the French should be looked at:

> There is one uglier, wickeder, more shameless!
> Although he makes no large gesture nor loud cries
> He willingly would make rubbish of the earth
> And with a yawn swallow the world;
> He is Ennui!—His eye filled with an unwished-for
>   tear,
> He dreams of scaffolds while puffing at his hookah.

Do these lines show complacent contempt? What does Baudelaire mean by Ennui? He implies that to be bored by the world is wearisome, but that it is a victory for the individual. We are in a fight between being bored and being aroused. Being bored is a victory for ubiquitous contempt. Interest is on the side of respect as one's bloodstream.

Baudelaire, like Dostoevsky, saw the tedious horrors of contempt; and, like Dostoevsky, never made up his mind. A large purpose of Aesthetic Realism is to have a person make up his mind as to the value for him of contempt and respect. Only through aesthetics as the oneness of opposites can he do this.

AESTHETIC REALISM ITSELF

Aesthetic Realism, in keeping with its name, sees all reality, including the reality that is oneself, as the aesthetic oneness of opposites. It is clear that reality is motion and rest at once, change and sameness at once. Are we ourselves change and sameness at once, motion and rest at once? If a person asks himself, is he in motion this morning at 11 o'clock, and also is he still as he was—the answer is: "Certainly, John Bell is moving and still is John Bell at 11 o'clock of an American morning."

It happens that music is felt always as a oneness of motion and rest, or of difference and sameness. A person, like music, is an aesthetic reality; for every moment of his life, he is at once rest and motion, sameness and change.

LIKING THE WORLD

Aesthetic Realism sees the largest purpose of every human being as the liking of the world on an honest basis.

If, as Aesthetic Realism believes, all the sciences, let alone all the arts, present reality as constituted or shaped aesthetically, reality or the world can that much be liked. Aesthetic Realism does not bid people to like reality; it does bid people to hope to like reality and to do all they can to like it. A seeing of the sciences in their relation and where they begin, is a means of seeing the world favorably; with order and surprise.

Aesthetic Realism is personally useful; it is all for personal development; but it is always a seeing of the whole world, and a hope not to miss anything which tells us what the world is. Aesthetic Realism, then, is unabashed philosophy, as it presents the moment as friendly to a person; as perhaps wider, deeper, more of oneself than was thought.

1

The Aesthetic Meaning
of Psychiatry

The Aesthetic Meaning of Psychiatry

A ESTHETIC REALISM has a relation to psychiatry, not so much in its current sense, but in its fullest meaning. The purpose of psychiatry is to make a self happily orderly, or "orderly" happy. This purpose, however, is too often obscured in particular methodologies, impressively complicated approaches, and unsure pedantries. If the word "psychiatry" is taken to mean an organized way of making a mind happier, it would then have that largeness, humanness of approach which, I think, would also make it more exact and efficient. Aesthetic Realism as it now is, and psychiatry as it now is, are different: the attitude to the human mind and the objective are different; and further, as I shall show in this book, the procedure, the beliefs, the viewpoint towards crucial facts, are different. With this caution, it is, however, well to see Aesthetic Realism and present day psychiatry as having an objective akin. In this chapter, I shall deal with similarities and differences between Aesthetic Realism and psychiatry.

Every person can be seen as having problems. A problem, in the Aesthetic Realism sense of the word, is any situation that can be made happier, more beautiful, more efficient. A problem isn't just a wish to jump over a bridge, or a desire to spit at one's mother-in-law, or a feeling at 4 A.M. that one is a gazelle, or a coupling of varicose veins with some incestuous attitude to a sister. These things, and things like them, are problems; but any person who is somewhere he doesn't want to be, or is doing something he doesn't want to do; or wants to be somewhere he isn't, or wants to do something he isn't doing, has a problem. This person can be pretty sensible, too. However, he wants to be happier than he is. So he has a problem. Aesthetic Realism sees this problem existing as definitely as hysteria or an obsession. The quantity and immediacy are different; just as two thousand dollars is different from twenty cents. Yet, just as twenty cents and two thousand dollars are both money, so the wish to be happier and hysteria are both problems.

Difficulties, Aesthetic Realism sees as "average" things. Every person, aware of himself, has noticed at times that his mind was refractory and displeasing. Everyone has been disturbed by the possession of feelings which did not seem right. No one has wished that his feelings be in disorder or that they be disappointing and grieving to him. Yet feelings not working as they should, feelings not in symmetry, thoughts that went ahead when they shouldn't and refused to act as seemed proper, have occurred with constancy not only in the crowded, mechanistic hurly-burly of New York, but, we may be sure, in Assyria, in Rome, in Elizabethan London, in 18th-century Paris, and in Canton or Calcutta. It seems that mind somewhat awry is a universal concomitant of life itself.

It is quite evident that mental therapy should, to be efficient, have a specialized meaning. One may feel that one cannot work with concepts as wide as the Pacific. However, in dealing with a specific problem it should not be forgot that any specific manifestation is an outgrowth of something general. Psychiatry may be defined (in words different from those used earlier), as a method, based on scientific data, of alleviating and annulling the disturbances or calamities of mind. The specialized approach is necessary. Yet the specialized approach becomes more efficient if it is understood that disturbances of mind are basic things; that there is a steady line of continuity between the feverish outburst of a harassed housewife on the way, perhaps, to a hospital, and the agonized contemplations of a Nietzsche, or the bitterly satiric thoughts of a Jonathan Swift. It should be seen that the disturbances of mind are of mind as a whole; and that these disturbances cannot be fully understood or dealt with unless a knowledge of mind itself is clearly and thoroughly possessed.

The idea of continuity between two contrary states of mind may be illustrated as follows: A person is $30,000 in debt. This person may be likened to the unquestioned neurotic. A man $30,000 in debt, we may suppose, gets some income-producing work or activity, which in time brings him out of debt and permits him to say truthfully: "I'm neither in debt nor have I any assets." In other words he is at "sea level" or "par." Yet if his income-producing activity continues in the same way as before, the man who was $30,000 in debt goes beyond "par" towards riches. The activity has not changed, but we have reached a point that is beyond the negative. This particular person may even become rich. We shall call the neurotic a debtor; and we shall call the intelligent, composed person a rich man; but it is obvious that there is a line of junction between the neurotic and the composed man, just as there is between the debtor and the affluent person.

A study of the vicissitudes, ailments, and catastrophes of mind will show that there is something in common in every situation of mind whatsoever; that the reality which, in a dim way, a denizen of a mental hospital is trying to reach (though in pathetic, self-interrupted fashion) is the reality of a Shakespeare, a Newton, or a Goethe. The personal problems and possible upsets of William Shakespeare in, say,

1610, were "disturbances of mind"; and there is a likeness between these and the disturbances of mind of a fidgety policeman or a problem child. Newton showed an apathy of mind which has a similarity to the apathy sometimes seen in an asylum. Goethe, it is said, complained he never had a full, happy day in his life; and this complaint, seen harshly, has a rather perilous likeness to that of a person who feels that the world is entirely against him.

Whenever there is unhappiness of mind, something is amiss. In the fullest sense, the purpose of psychiatry is the reaching of happiness through a procedure that is clear and orderly. In fact, the old term "happiness" is synonymous with the new term "adjustment." In adjustment there is the person adjusted and that to which one is adjusted. It is quite evident that adjustment cannot be fully understood without a knowledge of both the person and the world to which he is capable or incapable of adjusting.

It is regrettable, therefore, that the word "psychiatry" has taken on too much of a narrow, sick-room meaning. It isn't denied here it has that meaning. However, it has more. Psychiatry centrally means the bringing to a mind of any object making that mind more accurately at ease with what it has to meet. There is no limit to the field of psychiatry taken in this sense.

When, sixty years ago, a neurotic approached a physician, complaining about jumpy nerves, bad appetite, too great a readiness to be irritated, displeasure with his wife and children, and the like, this physician would recommend a journey to the seaside, the mountains, Italy perhaps, or even Morocco. We don't think these days that such a physician had a complete understanding of what was troubling his neurasthenic patient. We do not believe that ailments of the nervous, as they once were called, are to be remedied by journeys to new territory, by geographic alterations as such.

Yet, in the prescription of this physician there was something of good sense. He felt in a fashion that his patient wanted a different world. In saying that the practitioner of the past dealt with his patients superficially, we should not forget the proximity of something sound to an otherwise superficial approach.

Aesthetic Realism believes that the maladies of mind arise from the world as a whole, and that therefore the method of healing these maladies arises from the world as a whole. When a person is mentally sick, he is not interested adequately, rightly, in the world. We can say, if we wish, that this defect in interest is qualitative. Perhaps, that is, the individual simply sees the world too narrowly, too pettily, too personally, and too timidly. Perhaps he sees aspects of the world excessively: he gives emphasis where emphasis is not needed; he is disposed to find significance where it need not be; he sees tumult where tumult is not required: he adds a surplus of perception in a way that throws an object out of proportion. It seems, therefore, that what, in the long run, psychiatry should be after is to have an individual see the world in proportion, that is, truly, exactly. Now to see the world in proportion is to see it with knowledge. And just as the Greeks felt that happiness was related to knowledge, so it can be said today, that psychiatry is related to knowledge, not narrow knowledge—but knowledge of the world in its fulness and in its delicacy.

Were one to deduce from the foregoing that knowledge is therapy—it would be correct so to do. Psychiatrists have, in the past, tried to lead their patients to a love of the world, which they—the patients—think has dealt with them cruelly. The psychiatry of all times has had this as a final, if unarticulated, purpose. It can be said that a person, mentally sick, or insane, does not love the world.

Where the world is feared, it is because it is not loved and believed in. If a person does not like the world of reality, it does seem fairly clear that, somewhere, mentally he is a failure. To have people want to know and love the world— this is an enunciation, in the largest terms, of the basic goal of psychiatry.

Suppose we begin with the statement that the aim of mental therapy is to have men like reality. Doesn't that phrase "like reality" have an historical ring to it? Can it not be said that what Milton was after, and Beethoven, and Balzac, and Raphael, was the making one of reality and man? Was not their deepest purpose to bring about the liking of reality by man?

Still, one must deal with definite instances of insanity or neuroticism, that is, definite instances of dislike, hate, and evasion of reality. Let us see how the principle that insanity or neuroticism is a dislike and evasion of reality, manifests itself in the houses and hospitals of the actual world.—We shall take first a classical instance of the "older style" of insanity. Seventeenth- and 18th-century literature have many instances of persons who became insane in the pursuit of money. Why can these persons be justifiably termed insane? It certainly is not their like for money as such, because the 17th and 18th centuries, like our own, made it incumbent on everyone to be in possession of money.

Then where does an excessive love of money become a form of insanity? It is where a love of tangible wealth leads one to underestimate and neglect other forms of existence or other forms of reality; and therefore reality itself. Specialization is morbid when it is against wholeness of view. There is a demand within each person for wholeness of attitude. Certainly an excessive desire and regard for coin or bills is hardly fair to the world where it is not coin or bills. Were a miser of the 18th century, whom we may call Daniel

Parkinson, to be led to a perception that shining gold coins or attractive notes on the Bank of England were so much and no more—or for that matter no less—Mr. Parkinson would be relieved of his insanity or mania; for he would be seeing a world where birds, flowers, books, ants, coins, five pound notes, stocks, music, and food fell into some proportionate movement and relation. When Mr. Parkinson would be disposed proportionately to stretch forth a welcoming hand and proportionately to withhold a reluctant hand, he would be a sane man and a joyous man. Put otherwise, Mr. Parkinson would no longer be selling reality short.

There is Mrs. Letitia Wilkinson, a lady of Somerset County, England, enjoying fairly good health in the year 1842. She is outwardly a sensible person; has gone to finishing school; has read Addison, Johnson, Shakespeare—and even Thackeray in *Fraser's Magazine.* She is somewhat agreeable, and is inclined to be of use to her fellow-beings. However, she will visit no one and will invite no one to her house, unless she has first ascertained that the person in question has the proper family background, is of the Church of England, and has an income appropriately large. Were Mrs. Wilkinson to be called snobbish or unhealthily exclusive, she would object.—She once got into a fit because her daughter looked favorably on a dissenting young clergyman, the son of a boiler-maker near Birmingham. Her anger towards her daughter was extreme and brought Mrs. Wilkinson to a feverish and disabling sick bed.—Is there some relation between Mrs. Wilkinson's decidedly exclusive way of mind and the way of mind of that 18th-century extreme devotee of cash, Mr. Parkinson? There is. For the English lady of 1842 has, like her predecessor, taken part of the world and insisted that it was enough. This insistence caused her, when a critical situation arrived, to become ill. But she could have been termed ill all along: not furiously, unmistakably ill, but ill in the sense that her self was not complete, not a working integrity. In Mrs. Wilkinson's denial of the possibilities of existence, she followed a course akin to that which made Mr. Parkinson more obviously psychically sick.

In 1854, there is a working man of Glasgow who, in his life as a laborer on the docks, has often been out of work. He began to work when he was fourteen. Before then, he had had some difficult—if not frenzied—times with his teacher at the charity school to which his mother had sent him. He saw his mother and father quarrel, though they both regarded themselves as devout Presbyterians. When John McCrie got his first job, he quarreled with a boy doing the same work. Later—and justly—he felt he was under-paid. He read in a cheap newspaper that the whole world should be turned upside down and made just—though John never came to the reasons why. He became angry with his foreman once; the foreman struck him and discharged him. Many other things occurred.

Anyway, John McCrie, in 1854, is now lying on a dirty bed in a street of Glasgow. An hour before he had shouted: "They're after me! They're after me!" so loudly that the landlady came up in a rush to see what was doing. When she knocked on the door, John shouted: "I know you, you spying bitch. You've been sent by the King to keep me quiet, but I'll get you and all your masters." The landlady went off in a fright and called the nearest officer of the law. He is coming; and John McCrie will be taken off either to jail or an asylum.

This working man McCrie of 1854 feels that people are against him. He looks on human beings as his enemies. He feels that there is a conspiracy, participated in by the King and government of England, against his rights. He sees his rather gentle, though businesslike, landlady as part of this conspiracy (there he is definitely wrong). The belief that he is persecuted has been shared by thousands of people before this harassed Scotchman of 1854; and by thousands after. What is the chief thing amiss in the persecution-mania of the Glasgow laborer? Is there something in common between this mania and the cash mania of Mr. Parkinson? There is, of course. McCrie and Parkinson, for one reason or another, have come to see the world with a fierce narrowness; with unbending exclusiveness. They have made part, or a phase, of reality stand for all of it. It should be pointed out, though, that just as there is some justification for being interested in money, so there is some justification, in a world having competition as its economic basis, for feeling that the next man is against oneself.

Alice Stebbins is a New England lady of 1894. She has done well at school and at college. She wanted to do the right thing, as she put it, all the time. She was given, eagerly, to correcting herself, and to correcting others. At times she became a monitor of all the persons near her. She saw herself as an unintermittent, inflexible guide to perfection. She found herself at various times, however, disposed to see no one, not even her family. Afterwards, she chided herself for her aloofness and unsociality. But when she went out once more into the world, the desire to correct and admonish was irrepressible; and sometimes she got into social difficulties because her admonishing activities were not appreciated, and were even rebuffed. When these rebuffs were unusually severe, the sensitive Miss Stebbins was once more disposed to absent herself from the activities of New England and of the world in general.

Miss Stebbins now, at near forty, spends most of her time in her room reading—religious works chiefly—and sketching many objects she remembers from childhood. She is not disposed to talk to anyone. She is given to uttering extremely curt "yeses" and "noes" or "I don't knows," and sometimes not even these. Her relatives have decided that Miss Alice is sick and are wondering just what to do. They don't like the idea that one of their kin should be sent to an institution, but they are approaching the belief that this might be best.

Is there something in common between the hushed up malady of New England's Miss Stebbins and the not so obvious disturbance of Mrs. Letitia Wilkinson of Somersetshire, England? There is clearly a similarity in the careful snobbishness of Mrs. Wilkinson and the total aloofness of Miss Stebbins. However, there is a larger kinship of condition. Both Mrs. Wilkinson and Miss Stebbins have made a world of their choosing that has not the size of the world as it is; nor is it in accordance with the full demands of the world as it is. Mrs. Wilkinson's relatives never thought her insane. They thought, in fact, she was a very particular, determined lady who had a right to her exclusivenesses. Her illness they saw as something that might come to the best and noblest of God's creatures. The relatives of Miss Stebbins were minded at one time to look upon her as merely a too fastidious creature. It was only when she took a distressingly aloof and condemnatory attitude towards themselves that they began to see her as mentally ailing. Whatever else may be true, it is clear that the worlds of Mrs. Wilkinson and Miss Stebbins were not sufficient.

In the year 1812 a male child was born to Lord and Lady Strathspey, peer and peeress of the British Isles. Much was hoped for from this new arrival among the titled and noble of the United Kingdom. Lord and Lady Strathspey much desired an heir who would administer with wisdom and prudence—perhaps even brilliance—the possessions which had been their family's for centuries.

But when the child Donald reached the age of twelve months, fear came upon the hearts of the lord and lady; for they felt that at this age, a child, noble or otherwise, should be showing a kind of infantile alertness, and perhaps be even mumbling the immemorial monosyllables. The parents of the mute Donald bided their time and thought their child would talk later. But he reached eighteen months and two years, and he was still a sluggish infant. Nothing more than a grunt, or something resembling an assertive slobber, came from his lips. He did not laugh, he did not cry much, he was not eager for new objects. He walked, but only when urged. Age three came: with some reluctance he was uttering a few syllables. He was, though, likely to be forgetful for days at a time that he could talk. He slept more than a child should. He was inclined to be too fat. He did not respond when his noble relatives chucked him under the chin or gave him presents; soon these relatives discreetly did not try to bring elation to his heart. He was given a tutor at the age of six and learned to read; but he read no more than what the tutor, in his discreet way, forced upon him. Donald talked little at the age of eight. At the age of ten, he showed an interest chiefly in horses, cows, geese, pigs, and insects—including vile ones.

Lord and Lady Strathspey have been unwilling to say that Donald should not be the active and legal heir of the Strathspey possessions; for one thing, there was no other child. But now, though their hearts are sick, they are disposed to seek for a special enactment whereby the Strathspey estate would be legally inherited by the brother of Lord Strathspey (whom Lady Strathspey does not care for at all). Lord Strathspey has heard whispers that Donald does not have all his wits; that the child has been denied a complete mind by the God who creates both nobles and dogs. Some persons in the family, or near it, have even entertained the idea of isolating Donald from his kin and the world in general. This has not as yet been done.

One can see the noble child pursuing geese, and lying on the ground watching a horse for hours; and, if not stopped, suddenly darting for a household insect. It is true that geese, horses, and pigs are realities and worthy objects of science; but Donald, in his preponderant consideration for these living things, has shown a state of mind akin to that of the too acquisitive business man, Mr. Parkinson. Donald is so exclusive in his attitude towards the objects of the world that he is a subject for commiseration and whispers. His insanity, however it may have come, consists, like other insanities, of the fixation on a partial, limited, unrepresentative world of his own, as against the great world in its completeness.

I could deal with many other examples of inadequate, or alienated, or disturbed, or wounded mind. The important thing to see is that a curtailment of the world in its completeness is present in every instance of insanity, in whatever period of history it may take place. More: there is a likeness between an instance of insanity and incomplete or disproportionate perception of a "normal" or "sane" kind. One may have insane traits and yet not be "insane." For example, a man need not go as far as did 18th-century Mr. Parkinson to have a disproportionate attitude towards 20th-century stocks and bonds; one need not fall ill, as the Mrs. Wilkinson of 1842 did, to have an unfortunate mental position towards Poles or Negroes or Jews; a human being need not shriek in persecution-mania, as did the Glasgow laborer John McCrie, to be improperly suspicious of a person he may meet or know. A woman need not shut herself up in a room, as did New England Miss Stebbins, to be unhealthily aloof from people; and a person, young or old, need not forget everything but cows, horses, geese, pigs, and insects to have an insufficient awareness of the objects to be known and felt in a wide and various world. This amounts to saying that where there is inadequate perception of any kind, a something resembling (however faintly) insanity is already present. The difference between insanity and unjust perception is, it is true, qualitative, but from another point of view it is also quantitative—that is, a certain *amount* of unjust perception will make for the new situation which is insanity. In the same way, a man in the midst of life is qualitatively different from a new-born infant, to whom the world is a blur yet to be pierced and arranged; on the other hand, there is only a difference of "quantity" between the baby and the man: that is, the forty years, say, separating them.

If there is a likeness in all instances of insanity, is there a likeness in the methods that have been used at various times to alleviate it and cure it? I believe there is.

Methods in mental therapy have, from the beginning, attempted to change conditions of mind which may be called too little, too much, or upset; put in more formal language: insufficiency of mental approach, excessiveness of approach, or confusion of approach. Psychotherapeutic processes all through history have tried to alter one, or two, or all three of these conditions. Even in methods that are now decried and avoided, or looked upon as silly or unjustified, we may find something akin to a sensible procedure.

An approach common in the history of psychiatry is one of punishment. Persons mentally ailing have been whipped, put in chains, denied food, or isolated. We don't put the mentally sick any longer in chains or whip them; though at times, there is a rigidity of diet and isolation. However, the principle on which the older methods went is—seen coolly and comprehensively—one followed today. We may not feel that a psychopathic person is possessed of the devil, or that he has sinned; but we do think that he has done wrong, and that in one way or another he is guilty of something. Sometimes we try to change his personality by shocking him. Whether this shock is of the electrical kind, the metrazol kind, or the insulin kind, considered closely, it has a likeness to old fashioned whipping aimed at getting the evil out of the patient's personality. It was felt in a dim fashion by a practitioner in mental healing of the 17th century, that certain ways were to be driven out of the sick person, that the constituents of his personality were to be rearranged. The belief that a sudden and shocking rearrangement of fundamental human attitudes could dispose a sick person to accept new, more accurate, and healthful attitudes, makes for a similarity between, say, whipping and metrazol.

A psychiatrist quite often is in a quandary as to just how severe he should be with a neurotic patient; every mental therapist may be in such a quandary. Gentle exposition and friendly comprehension are useful; but it is quite clear that if the patient is to change himself, he must be jolted deeply; must be told things he doesn't like hearing; must be dealt with severely, in other words, must be punished—as the unfortunate 17th-century patient was punished. For as soon as we say that a personality has succumbed to a dependence on his own unjustified attitude to himself, regardless of the rights of other persons and of reality,—whether we like it or not, we are saying that this person has "sinned." In order to do away with the imperfection, we must make the person lucidly, completely ashamed of that imperfection; and that is not done without a kind of punishment. We still use and should use some *principle* of punishment. Psychiatry in all its forms has, despite the many assertions to the contrary, an ethical basis.

Along with the severe method of dealing with the mentally ill, there has been the ingratiating, humoring, "kind" method. Those in charge of the mentally sick in the past could be "kind," too: particularly with more well-to-do patients. A patient, it is true, may run on a rampage with notions of what is coming to him, and how much more important he is than other people; but the same patient may have a quite insufficient notion of what he deserves. Arrogance and humility have been constant, recurrent phases of a mind in distress. The arrogance needed jolts, reprimands, intolerance; the humility needed gentleness, friendliness, caresses, so that confidence might arise. Looking upon a patient as an unfortunate being was, in the past, not so uncommon as is supposed (particularly this attitude was frequent in private asylums).

This may be surprising at first view, but there is a likeness among the drug, rest, and electric shock methods of therapy. They are different; but the purpose in all three instances is to have a patient say: "Reality is my friend and not my enemy." When a doctor advised rest in the 19th century or prescribed drugs in the same century, he was after, in his particular way, the objective sought for by a physician prescribing electric shock. For *any means* which will bring about a feeling—however inarticulate or articulate—that the world and one's self make a team, and that the world need not be hated, is justified in some degree. To take an ordinary situation: If a person is sulky or peevish, perhaps a few words may work against that sulkiness or peevishness; perhaps a good meal will do the same thing; perhaps a drug of some kind will; perhaps even a slap in the face will. Words, food, drug, and slap have the same objective; each may be justified.

In saying that methods of therapy used at various times in history have some use, I am not saying, of course, that these methods are to be given complete approval or that they are interchangeable. In dealing with any personality we must think of the *whole* personality at all times. The chief thing amiss with methods of mental therapy is their narrowness; their lack of thoroughness and comprehensiveness.

Every personality in a certain sense is encyclopedic; every personality is unique, and yet has something in common with every other personality and with every other object. Furthermore, each personality is looking to be entirely itself; while it is not, it will be dissatisfied. A personality, deep down, wishes at times to be jolted, shocked, punished; it wishes at times to be cheered and befriended; it wishes to be alone and it wishes to be in the midst of the manyness of life.

This means that though electric shock up to a point is useful, salutary, even revolutionary for a human being, since it may bring about a sudden readjustment of attitude—if this shock is not followed through and completed with the diverse means by which a personality can see itself and the world about it, the shock will hardly be of much avail from a long term point of view. I should say that some of the methods preferred by many psychiatrists have in them, despite their modernity, the same critical defect observable in methods of the past. They are insufficient for a human being in a rich and puzzling world, with which he has an inescapable and many-sided relation.

I have stated that any means by which a self may come to an understanding of what it is, and a like for what it is; and to an understanding of the reality about this self, and a like for this reality—is of use. I have considered these means as fairly as I can: I have tried to maintain a perspective on the problem of the ailing mind and the world by which it is encompassed. This consideration has led me to think that within every method, in so far as it is useful, there is a something which puts together in a happier and more effective way that object which is a single self and personal, and that object which is the world and impersonal. It is my belief that when personality is also impersonal there is the *aesthetic situation.* There is no other word I can use sincerely than "aesthetic." I know that the word has many unnecessary, inexact, and undesirable connotations about it: this is unfortunate. Nevertheless, if the word "aesthetic" is looked at carefully, used soberly and truly, it will have a precision and a comprehensiveness making it equal to the word "real." It is my purpose to present evidence justifying the foregoing sentences. In doing so, the method of Aesthetic Realism will be presented and sustained.

2

The World, Guilt and Self-Conflict

Introduction

The Guilt Chapter as it is now presented was first written in December, 1942. It arose from the increasing feeling that what bothered people was their inability to like the world of the outside sufficiently.

Furthermore, this inability to like what was not themselves was the essential cause of guilt—a word more in use in psychiatric circles than it is now. The word now is, often, alienation.

If persons felt guilty because they were not enough of the world, it would follow that they would be pleased, not guilty, happy, if they were *of* the world. Therefore, the question was, what does it mean to be of the world?—to an individual?

It is said in the Guilt Chapter that good sense in life is the same as aesthetics; that ethics in life is also aesthetics. This, however, was not made as much of as could be.

What wasn't said is that the only way to be of the world is through the aesthetic sight of objects. In ordinary life, people grab too much and they also are aloof. The grabbing and the aloofness are both causes of the alienation of 1966 and the guilt of 1942.

In aesthetics, we are simultaneously of an object while the object is of us. The object grabs us as much as we grab it. If the object does not seize us or grab us, the aesthetic response is not great enough.

Can the world as such be seen as an object capable of making for an aesthetic response? Aesthetic Realism says, Yes: and moreover, that to see the world as an aesthetic object is the only sensible way to see it. However possible this may be, it is necessary at the beginning to ask whether in having an aesthetic response to any object, some kind of an aesthetic response is present for the world itself.

Can we listen to something musical, like it, and not have some response to the world itself? Can a painting—still after much debate, color and line—affect us without our having some notion of the world itself? Is some idea of the world present in every poem? Is it present in an instance of pottery? Is the world present in a play, whether of Barrie or Sophocles or Ionesco? Is it the world that, along with the dancer, is moving? Is the world present in a jest that has substance—that is, is it at the very beginning of humor? Is it present in a sentence like, "I like my friends, but I'd rather have leaves on the windowsill"? Is the world present in a well made cabin, a Greek temple, or a Minneapolis grain elevator—as architecture? The world is present wherever a thing is, and everyone knows that it's hard for a thing to be absent when we are present.

Liking the world, then, can be made akin to loving God as, say, the Jews have it. A statement like, "Thou shalt love thy God with all thy heart," is equivalent to, "You shall like the world as much as you can, by using the things you meet in the world." God can be seen as the cause of the world when that cause is given personality in some sense. God is the cause of the world, the process of the world, the purpose of the world and the things of this world—if these are seen as having personality with them.

When we like the world, we have to like it as cause, as purpose, and as structure; and particularly if we see the

world as having a purpose, do we see personality in it, or
something like it. In the long run, personality is the possibility a thing has of being pleased or displeased; and the Jews
gave the God of Exodus a great power of being pleased or
displeased. When we think of reality punishing us or being
for us, being against us or with us, we endow reality with
something of the beginnings of personality. It is true this is
what Roderick Usher did when he gave the territory around
the House of Usher some kind of feeling. Roderick Usher,
yes or no, it is well to ask what is the relation of reality to
feeling: where are reality and feeling the same?

When we are unfair to the world, it can be shown that
something in us which is the world itself, doesn't like it.
There are two worlds in us: the world that inclines to be just
for ourselves, and the world that is interested in being for
everything as much as it deserves. It is the world-that-is-for-
everything-and-self which makes us triumphantly be within
music; see something stirring in a painting; find something
giving us strength and meaning in a New England object;
find something persistently grand in this line and a half of
Wordsworth:

> Dust as we are, the immortal spirit grows
> Like harmony in music;

find something changing us deeply and pointedly in a play
by Hochhuth; meet something that is strange and familiar
in a passage from a novel by Scott.

We are making up our minds about the world every
moment. The world can be defined as everything that we
can meet, that we can think of, that can affect us, and which
we can honestly see at that time as not ourselves. The relation of the world is a relation of sameness and difference; and

sameness and difference is a beginning thing in drama and in all art.

As we look at something sincerely, we think that something is ourselves and ourselves are it. The remembrance of a round growing thing in red, is now it and also ourselves. The round growing thing, popularly called a cherry perhaps, is now what it is or once was, and is also ourselves— because we can now look at it and see it as ourselves in a way that makes a knuckle of ours seem ourselves.

To have pleasure from the world in such a way that we were seen as it and the world was seen as ourselves, was described as 1-A pleasure in the first form of the Guilt Chapter. The two evils, distresses, and drearinesses of ego are, as was said, to acquire an object without respecting it —or to grab it—and to put it aside, be aloof from it, not care for its existence. Ego has two awful tricks, grabbing and hiding. The combination of these may make for sinuosity, swerving, evasion. To see the world in such a way that one gets pleasure from being superior to it through how one manages it or gets away from it, is to have 2-A pleasure. It is the pleasure of vanity, greed, and essential coldness. To have pleasure from something and through being pleased by it, respect it more, is to have 1-A pleasure. This is on the side of aesthetics; and in so far as the pleasure is neat and whole, is aesthetics.

It was implied in the Guilt Chapter of 1942 that the way to have a person better off in a city or with himself, is to strengthen in him the seeing of life as having an aesthetic process and objective. In terms of ethics, this would mean that every situation was one in which you had to be completely fair to something outside of yourself and yourself too. This simultaneous fairness in inextricable duality is ethics as aesthetics.

But the need for being just to oneself and not oneself at

any one moment is a making one of two opposites, self and not self, in a manner that needed the accompaniment, the illustration and the sustenance of the making one of any two opposites.

This means that if a person were angry with something outside of himself, and self-critical or possibly angry with himself too, he would be that much making the world and self, or not-self and self, one. All ethics is an attempt to make the world and self an aesthetic one.

However, the opposites, being reality, are as diverse as it and as continuous as it. When we are critical of ourselves, truly critical, we see ourselves as an object like the world: the self has then lost its sacred and segregated subjectivity. So we ask ourselves, how can we be serene and active, reposeful and energetic at once? We have been aware—most of us have been—that we have gone too much towards being constantly busy or too much towards sluggishness. The only way we can be pleased with the world in ourselves is to see that the problem of how to avoid being either too much of a busybody or too bucolic, can be beautifully dealt with. What is being said is that we cannot like the job the world has done with us unless we see the glaring opposites in us as somehow making sense.

We find that we are too wrathful with a person, and then we find that we think we have been too unkind to that person, or unjust or mean. How can we make a one of our feeling that others are too harsh with us and also that we have been too harsh with them? Harshness and softness or rigor and sweetness are one in art. They are so in Bach, in Haydn, in Stravinsky here and there.

Every time we make the contraries or opposites in us more friendly, more one, we are bringing ourselves closer to the world as having the same opposites. This is a way of liking the world—to see that the opposites in ourselves are one like the opposites in the world itself: and, too, that the opposites both in the world and in oneself can be honestly felt to be one.

I didn't say this in the first form of the Guilt Chapter, so I say it now. Not to honor the aesthetics in the world, not to honor the aesthetics in oneself, is to feel guilty. I certainly didn't say anything in the 1942 Guilt Chapter which is against this, but I did not follow through with implications as much as I might have. The years were necessary for me to see this.

In 1942, it was a Freudian world predominantly—and it is still somewhat Freudian. Since 1942, the tendency has been to see sex as a manifestation of self, and, for that matter, to see the death instinct too as a manifestation of self. Self has a body, and through the use of another body, it can for a while feel that the world exists ecstatically for that self.

What has been felt more and more is that while the self functioning as body may sincerely, unquestionably get to a state of lightness, ecstasy, indescribable ease in reality, this organic, explosive propulsion to indescribable ease (the chief thing in sex for a long time) could be accompanied by a general self, a self busy with what it is and nothing else, that might not go along. It happens that the self even in sex does not want to be as much pleased with another thing as with what it is.

This is why there has come to be what has been called the self psychology. The self psychology is related to existential psychoanalysis. Sex is seen as something the self does, related to the self's feeling of externality as such, of evil, of change, of humility and pride, and such large matters.

Existential psychoanalysis has felt that the self can feel abased through sex, with all its release, just as it can feel abased by the indifference of an infinite world, sometimes called nature. Existentialism, then, being first an assertion of the definite existence of the individual or self as such, despite the indifference of external vastness, could see sex as a force it must be in proud and accurate relation to. However, existential psychoanalysis does not see the problem of pride and humility as essentially aesthetic, aesthetic in a way that includes all the arts and all their problems.

If, then, one gets the feeling that this introduction is saying that the world has gone more with Aesthetic Realism than it did in 1942, the feeling is correct. Fromm and Sartre go towards having Aesthetic Realism seem valid. Existentialism itself is the needed assertion of self as existence before this assertion is seen as a great love for, junction with everything else: insects, mountains, time.

People are guilty these days. They are guilty because they don't like the world enough. Aesthetic Realism is still interested in doing something about it.

ELI SIEGEL

November 6, 1966

The World, Guilt and Self-Conflict

THE BASIS of the Aesthetic Realism method is that every human being is a self whose fundamental and constant purpose is to be at one with reality. It is impossible for that self to evade this purpose, although he can curtail it, obscure it, limit it.

Sex is an essential situation in the effort of a self to be at one with reality, but is not, as such, the ultimate or the fundamental situation.

There is no situation whatsoever in the life of any human being, at any time, which cannot be described as one of self-and-reality. In sex, for instance, though the procedures and objects involved are different from those involved in a person's meeting a stranger, looking at a crowd, or wanting to make more money, there is nonetheless a human being trying to do something about reality. I insist on this point because it seems to me an inescapable constant that no matter what the happening, a human being is trying to please himself by getting into a relation of some kind of oneness with something seen as external. When a person is in a "tussle" with himself, it is because the external reality, as seen, is within himself—not because there is no external reality.

Another fundamental concept in Aesthetic Realism is that the chief or ultimate purpose of every human being is to like himself or herself and at the same time like the reality that exists along with himself or herself. I state this also as a constant. It is apparent that everyone is trying to please himself, but it is also true that everyone is wishing to find as large a basis as possible justifying his being pleased with himself; in fact, that basis with every person is, as much as possible, the whole of reality.

A great deal has been written on the "guilt feeling." It is fairly clear that every person has this guilt feeling in one way or another. Attempts have been made to identify this guilt feeling with some sexual situation in the life of the person; usually, the very early life. However, in keeping with the statement already made, sex is an incident in that guilt feeling, not the staple.

In every instance of a guilt feeling, there is evidence pointing to the fact that the cause is *a feeling of separation of oneself from reality as a whole.* The greatest biological fact in human history is this: that the whole world went to the making of every individual; in other words, that it was the universe, or existence, or reality, which gave us birth. Therefore, to associate guilt only with parents is superficial. I suppose this statement sounds philosophical or metaphysical. Statements that are metaphysical can hardly be avoided in dealing with the self. Otherwise we are not really dealing with the self. There has been much silly, ignorant misuse and denigration of metaphysics. There is no reason to be appalled by the very frequent outcry against the "dangers and pitfalls" of metaphysics. I wish to make it clear at this point that I look on metaphysics, in its best meaning, as good sense concerning the world as a whole, not as some sort of religious, terminological running away from fact, as many have unwisely seen it to be.

It is quite clear that if a person is born of the world as a whole—however large and massive the notion may be—he, willy-nilly, is in some relation to the world as a whole; and that again, willy-nilly, he feels he has some duties towards it. In fact, it is true that a good deal of the intense and ramified feeling which a person has towards his mother and father comes from the fact that they are symbols of reality as a whole, not because they are simply his parents.

I have mentioned duties to reality as a whole. What is the chief of these duties? The unconscious, as judge, has said: "Do not separate yourself from reality. If you do, you are not being yourself entirely, and one side of you will punish the other." When I use the phrase "unconscious as judge," I mean the something deep in us, definitely existing, which looks on us and what we do all the time. We are *always* criticizing ourselves. The criticism exists, even if we do not articulate it, or cannot. This criticism is made up of feelings we often do not know and often do not wish to know. We are a judge of ourselves. Where we have judged ourselves and where the decisions or feelings arising from our judging ourselves are considered as part of us, part in fact of our bodies in action—this aspect of ourselves can, I think, with propriety be regarded as the "unconscious as judge." I don't see the necessity for calling it the "superego," either. I mean something else.

In keeping with notions that have been present all through history, the human being does have two sides, just as he has a profile and a full face. These two sides, it is true, make up a one; yet in the same way as you get a different impression from the side view of face from that got from a full view, so, though these two sides of self make up a one, they can have different effects.

Whether one side of self or the other is in play, the purpose is, in a sense, the same. A person is trying to please himself. But one side of a person wishes to please himself by thinking of himself as apart from reality as a whole; the other side wishes to see the person as related to, and part of all reality.

The side of a person which wishes that a self get its importance from how much it can be aloof from the world, or not-self; how much it can despise the world, or reality; how much it can manipulate it, distort it, or destroy it—that side in Aesthetic Realism procedure is termed 2-A. The side of a person (like the other, it is in everyone) which wishes that the self get its importance or pleasure from seeing the world, or objects, or the not-self as it is or they are, in Aesthetic Realism procedure is termed 1-A. This side finds its individuality, or glory, or happiness in the constant becoming one with other things and the constant wanting to know these things and to love them through knowing them, not by despising or by possessing them.

When 1-A is in action in the self, there may be a feeling that the individuality in its snugness and kingliness is interfered with: then may arise a pain or confusion which I have termed 1-B. On the other hand, if 2-A or the false monarchical, and at its worst, schizophrenic element in the self is ruling, there arises the pain of guilt or separation which I have termed 2-B. In other words, 1-A is pleasure from reality; 2-A is false pleasure from being unfair to reality; 1-B is false pain coming from our giving ourselves more to reality than the weak side of ourselves can accept; and 2-B is a true pain, a pain of guilt coming from our having made ourselves important by being unfair to other things. A maxim of Aesthetic Realism is: If you like yourself for the wrong reason, you will dislike yourself for the right reason.

That which Aesthetic Realism calls 2-A can likewise be described as the "vanity feeling." 1-A can be described as the "pride feeling." Vanity, in other words, is the desire to please oneself though it may mean the excluding of reality. Pride is the desire to please oneself through the seeing and including of reality. When our vanity has been successful, the matter does not end there. The other side, the pride side, feels itself neglected and affronted; and demands what is coming to it. The demand constitutes the guilt feeling.

The following story illustrates what I have just said:

A painter of the Middle Ages was going to be put out of his lodgings by his landlady for not paying rent. The night before the eviction the devil comes to him and says: "My friend, between you and me, I know you're in a tough spot. Now I've a good idea. I know you're a good painter, I know that all right. But nobody knows you're a good painter; and maybe nobody will. My idea is this: I can make you the best known painter in this town, province, maybe in all Germany. But you're going to be a bad painter. However, no one will know about it in your lifetime, so you don't have to worry about that. Now what do you say?—Do you want to be a good painter and have no one know about it or do you want to be the best known painter in Germany?—Oh, I know all right, there's something about this you don't like. Anyway, think about it and any time you make up your mind I'll be around again."

The painter had a hard time making up his mind. The next morning the landlady's child saw the paintings of the to-be-evicted artist and said: "Ooh, I like that." So the artist was encouraged not to take the devil's offer.

The story illustrates the fight that goes on in everyone. We want to be praised, to have power, but we also want to deserve this. There is such a thing as the ethical unconscious. Well, if we praise ourselves and we know we have been unfair to outside reality in doing so, there is a nervous conflict in us. This conflict shows itself *in* sex: as it does in other things. We can't really think another person loves us unless *we* really *like ourselves* with the facts present, that is, have the 1-A feeling. To love ourselves really we have to love and want to know outside reality; that is, the outside form of ourselves, or the world.

Guilt, as I have said, is, therefore, the feeling that one, in one's efforts to please oneself, has excluded the reality belonging to the other side of oneself. Guilt is a feeling of incompleteness; it is a feeling of separation.

Guilt is pain. Pain essentially is a feeling that the self is not at one with an object meeting it, or related to it. (This is true both of what is called "physical" and of what is called "mental" pain.) The pain of guilt is obviously not desired by a person, but neither is the doing away with its cause desired. Therefore, the self is up against a common and severe dilemma. It is uncomfortable in its guilt, but cannot see its way clear to do away with the cause of it. In guilt we have pain, with ourselves looked on as that which brought it about.

Since this attitude is unbearable, and since, as I have said, we cannot do away with its cause, we may change the sense that the cause of the pain is in ourselves to the sense that it is caused by an external object or external objects. When we feel that our pain is caused by something external to us, and we wish to destroy the pain by destroying its cause, we are angry. This anger should be seen as a transformation of guilt. It is not based on accurate, honest seeing of an object. There is another kind of anger which is an honest, accurate, or 1-A anger. When we have anger which comes from an awareness of ugliness, injustice, this anger we are proud of. It integrates us. We can look at it clearly, boldly, and like it. It is a beautiful anger; for the honest desire to destroy ugliness, to give pain to him who makes or supports ugliness, so that the making or supporting ugliness is associated with discomfort—this anger can be commended. The text of this writing is not chiefly concerned with honest anger.

There is a kind which, in ordinary life, takes form often as hectic peevishness, a smug sulkiness, an ugly outburst, a covert sarcasm, and sometimes a sudden or brutal violence: this kind of anger is not based on seeing a thing honestly, but is a changing of displeasure with oneself, or guilt, into displeasure with what is not oneself.

Guilt also makes for fear. We cannot bear or see our guilt, and therefore, as I have said, change it into guilt-anger. That means that we have been unjust to reality, for where we should be against something in ourselves, we have chosen to be against what is not ourselves. We have chosen to oppose it, to hate it. We have come to feel that this great "not-ourselves" can give us pain. We are angry with it. Once, however, we see the world as giving us pain, we can see it as giving us pain in the future, too, and in ways we do not see. We feel also we deserve this pain; we must, in a sense, feel that this pain is continually given to us in order to sustain our anger, which in turn is the one way we have of blurring or concealing our guilt. All this has to do with the existence of a pervasive, vague, and constant fear; a fear whose vagueness in no way is against its existence as such.

Fear, like anger, can be of an object, or can be another aspect of guilt. The fear that one can have of being hit by a brick, or shot at, or losing one's step in the dark and on the ice, or the fear of not knowing something—this kind of fear is useful. It is critical. It has good sense and even a kind of honesty to it. We should fear that which can make our selves less, or cripple us, or hurt us.

The fear arising from guilt is a fear which can hide the guilt. The fear of a neurotic is a fear which he has come to have because he does not wish to see or cannot see what he does not like in himself; for if he did, he would have to give up a deep importance based on vanity and unconscious pleasure attached to this importance.

In summation, shame or guilt, anger, and fear, are a trio consisting of guilt and its two fundamental transformations.

Every person, good or bad, wishes neither guilt, nor anger, nor fear. Every person, deeply, wishes to like himself with reality present: not with reality excluded. However, it is difficult to put the very depths of personality into everyday action. A general maxim emerges. The purpose of all psychotherapy is to have a person like himself with the facts present.

Aesthetics is the one fundamental means a person has of liking himself. It is important that the meaning of aesthetics not be lessened. It is necessary to state that the usual psychiatric or psychoanalytical approach to aesthetics is hardly adequate. We see various psychiatrists or psychoanalysts complain of how human beings evade reality, and yet we see those same professional people in the field of mental therapeutics likewise evade an exact approach to such a major interest of the human mind, at all times, as is aesthetics.

A major purpose of psychiatry is the resolution of conflict; and in essence the basic activity of aesthetics is just that. Why, then, have psychiatrists generally looked askance at, disparaged, not cared thoroughly to understand the meaning of aesthetics? What really has occurred is that students of mind have fallen for the superficial notions of aesthetics. They have confused a strict, sound, exact mental procedure with the weaknesses, vagaries, and failures of persons who have announced themselves as devoted to this procedure; or in any way have been connected with it. This is just as bad as would be the denunciation of the escape quality of engineering or meteorology just because engineers have become drunk and meteorologists have beaten their wives. I have to insist that an insufficient knowledge of aesthetics is a great drawback in the equipment of anyone whose purpose it is to understand mind.

It would not be denied by anyone that where aesthetics really exists (that is, has been successful), things like harmony, proportion, unity, beauty also exist. These are akin to the objectives of any worker in the field of mental therapy. The question, therefore, arises: Can there be the effect of harmony, proportion, unity, beauty, from a cause which is disharmonious, disproportionate, ununified, and not beautiful? To say that an attempt to present reality with both personal and impersonal feeling involved—and that is the attempt implicit in aesthetics—means "sublimation" in the bad sense, or "substitute for frustration," is superficial and ignorant and unscientific.

Emphasis is proper here. Aesthetic Realism believes that the aesthetic, in essence, is the only way by which the fundamental conflict or conflicts in a human being can be resolved. For the human being is trying, whether he knows it or not, to be both personal and impersonal. Wherever a human is both personal and impersonal, he has in one form or another followed the aesthetic process. The seed of a tree does not have to know that it is showing form when it develops into a tree with symmetry, unity, and organization. The aesthetic impulse or desire is our very deepest. Being the deepest, it can be interfered with by more superficial, or narrow, or 2-A tendencies. Still it is there; for the aesthetic impulse or desire is also the reality impulse or desire.

What must the self do to be successful in its fundamental motive which, as has been pointed out, is the desire to look at what it is with pleasure? If in fulfilling this motive, he uses data that are only "personal," he is not satisfied, for the judge that is his unconscious, aware of a relation with the world as a whole, says: "This won't do. You can't be at ease with yourself, or complete, just by being 'personal.' You must include what isn't yourself." A fear arises. How can the self maintain its oneness, its uniqueness, its warm being, by risking its own submergence, its own decrease, welcoming a vast territory seemingly alien to it?

Aesthetic Realism believes in the uniqueness of a self equally with its being related to all things. In aesthetics the personal side of a human being is not interfered with by its being given to an object representing the universe. The personal becomes the impersonal, for the artistic seeing of something does not mean the engulfing of a single human vision, but the completion of a human vision by something else. In aesthetics the world intensifies uniqueness. It shows that relation individualizes, does not deaden. But without aesthetic perception or procedure, we can be frightened. We want to save ourselves. And we often think we save ourselves by contracting. All this means that we are always seeking an equilibrium between, and including, the satisfaction of the personal self and impersonal reality.

Mental therapists have used the terms "adjustment" and "the accordance of the ego with reality" to represent the object sought for in the healing process. It will be found that this "adjustment" and this "accordance" are equivalent to the aesthetic state made up of both personal and impersonal perception. This means that the ideal, the sound objective of therapy of the mind, is equivalent to aesthetic success. Later, in the instances that I will give of Aesthetic Realism lessons, the practical import of the foregoing statements will, I believe, be made clear.

Another general matter to be taken up is the question of the data and definitions of psychology itself. I have found that the words "desire," "will," "instinct," "reason," "conscious," and even "unconscious" have been given a narrow, temporary, inadequate meaning. After all, in the field of mental therapy we are not in a hothouse of recent terminology. A "patient" still takes subways, uses slang, admires the green of a field, and likes a photograph of an efficient machine. The sickest person in this world is still living in the entire world: the world of objects and endless, delightful, astonishing, and familiar forms.

To understand sickness of mind, it is necessary to understand wholeness or felicity of mind. It is true that the abnormal explains the everyday or expected or praiseworthy, but it is also true that the everyday can be used to explain the abnormal.

The terminology, or to use a more condemnatory word, jargon, of many mental therapists is still a hindrance; in fact is often a concealment of lack of perception and understanding. We can't afford to give meanings to certain terms that separate these meanings from those that the objects in question have in a larger sense.

The psychology of most mental therapy of today is too exclusive, too fearsome in its pretensions, to be of unquestioned value. It lacks a clearness, an immediacy, a certain combination of sharpness and comprehensiveness, which are needed for that definite and deep stirring of the conscious, large enough to affect the whole being of a person.

And there is, as I have mentioned, this contempt and fear of metaphysics or philosophy. This is somewhat contrary to the therapists' advocacy of reality. On the one hand, a patient is instructed to be in touch with reality and adjust himself to it. On the other hand, any asking of the question, "What is this reality?"—to which the patient is to adjust himself and with which he is to be in accord—is looked on as unnecessary and even silly.

It must be pointed out here that reality is not just one's mother, father, sister, brother, uncle, job, friends, food, and so on. It is the whole world, past and present, with which a person has relation. Reality, it is pretty clear, is much wider and deeper than the "reality" of the most-often-to-be-met-with psychiatrist. It *is* important to ask, "What is reality?"—because without a clear notion of what it is, one can hardly expect a person to adjust himself to it.

Well, "What is reality?" is the chief question of metaphysics. Should certain people called metaphysicians do some fancy spinning around in answering this question, or get themselves into useless labyrinths, or generally evade concreteness and tough-mindedness, that no more invalidates the subject than do the quackeries of many persons calling themselves doctors invalidate the study of medicine. To-morrow a certain practitioner of medicine in good standing may—it is quite possible—pretend to knowledge that he doesn't have, or be unclear, or not examine a situation thoroughly; yet medicine, as such, is a good thing, a great aspect of man's mind. The same justice can be asked for metaphysics as a *thing*, not as a study confused with the deficiencies of some persons. What science or study, after all, answers the question of "What is reality?" *as such?* If any science other than metaphysics claims to do so, that science by the very claim—despite terminological protests—is that much metaphysical. Let us not be dismayed by the portentous, or unliked, or difficult associations of a word.

The method of Aesthetic Realism has within it, therefore, an approach to aesthetics, psychology, and metaphysics different from that which is customary.

Guilt is essentially a philosophic idea. It is organic or unconscious self-disapproval. It is not something in itself morbid or melodramatic. In this sense of guilt, it is apparent to me that every person has guilt feelings in one way or another. In fact, it can be said with essential truth that to be unhappy is to have guilt feelings; for everyone has, in some fashion, what Aesthetic Realism calls 2-A. However, it is well to present a specific and salient instance of this universal trait of guilt.

Hazel Dean hated members of the family without being able to acknowledge that hate. She married without fully loving her husband. Hazel wanted to get away from the family she hated. Her attitude towards her husband, John, was not something she could face with equanimity. She saw, however, no means for a divorce, nor in fact did she want one particularly. Yet she knew that she was somewhere acting falsely to the immediate realities involved in her life. Previously, in finding interferences to her wishes from her family and others, Hazel had unconsciously decided that outside things were against her and didn't make sense. The one way to get away from these interfering and hateful external things, was to make a substitute Hazel-personal world for herself. The guilt feelings arising from having separated herself from outside realities did not come to any overt, tormenting state until after she had married. She knew that she did not love her husband, and yet day after day she was compelled to act as if she did. This made more of a cleavage than ever between her outward activity and the life in that inner world where she had supremacy. But in proportion as she was driven to this inner world where Hazel ruled, the separation between that world and the general outside world was made sharper and more evident. In proportion as it was made sharper, her guilt feelings grew more acute. Hazel found more of a necessity for living in the interior world where she was queen: but simultaneously, there was more pain arising from the separation.

There are supplementary facts that I could present. I shall be selective here. Hazel told me that whenever she mislaid for a moment a dish, or a towel, or some other thing around the house, she would have agonies of torment. She knew that the domestic article was in the room somewhere but that she could not put her hands on it.

I am quite aware that the likelihood this woman had of

misplacing a domestic object and her having sharp torments when it was misplaced, would be given by many a sexual interpretation. In fact, as she told me, one psychoanalytic practitioner had told her, among other things, that her trouble was that she wanted to compete with her husband by having a penis likewise.

I do not wish to deny (though in sincerity I look on the psychoanalyst's explanation as hardly adequate to the facts) a presence of a sexual attitude in the general way of mind possessed by this woman, because after all, sex is connected with every form of behavior and every kind of perception. That is different from saying that the cause of a particular morbid activity is definitely sexual in nature. In this instance it was not. What I found was, that Hazel Dean had so separated the world within herself from outside things that by this time any strong appearance of the two worlds' being immediately together, was painful.

Hazel could participate in the life of her neighbors and seem a contented, happy wife to them. She could visit friends and relatives and seem likable. She put on what can be called a natural act of sweetness. However, this world of friends, neighbors, husband, was apart, whenever she chose, from that world in herself which she ruled. Yet the judge behind the guilt feeling condemned her seeing these two worlds as opposed to each other. Hazel could not do away with the cause of that guilt feeling, yet she wanted to punish herself. It appears that she mislaid objects so that the symbolism of an object that she could not put her hands on—that is, outside of herself—should be seen at the same time as an object within a room—that is, something identified with herself.

What one side of Hazel wanted was to have the two worlds separate; the other side would not stand for it; and when she found, through the symbolism of an object lost within her own home, that there was an inescapable connection between something inside and outside, she was reminded consciously of the guilt feeling which she had. For the equivalent, on a large scale, had been assented to by herself. That is, Hazel had separated something inside her from that which was outside. The conscious apprehension brought the guilt feeling to a head, making for the situation approximating panic.

When I told Hazel Dean that this was the symbolism involved, and it became clear to her, this particular situation lost its fears and its pains.

The same symbolism was present when, having already ordered an article in a grocery store, Hazel was compelled to wait for it. The object was hers, that is, of her, and yet not hers. This again, in outline, was like the situation which she had been trying to avoid in separating herself from things outside herself. This situation also was remedied when she was told of the symbolism represented, and when she accepted the meaning given.

Certainly guilt has to do with sex or love. The general source of guilt, however, persists when guilt concerns the erotic. This is because everything which is loved is a symbol of reality as a whole. What goes on in the mind of every person who is loving someone or something is: "I like this thing; therefore, in so far as this thing stands for existence, I like existence. If this thing likes me, then because it stands for existence, existence approves of me." Love is essentially a way of liking oneself, for in liking an object one feels somewhere a kind of success; and in having an object like one, a person feels justified. But the same pattern that exists between self and reality as a whole, takes form in a relation between one human being and another human being.

To love another human being simply as an outside object

is decidedly hard for nearly everybody. If this were done it would mean that something external has been permitted—so it seems—to affect the autonomy of a self; and there is a disposition fiercely, constantly, deeply, ramifiedly to maintain that autonomy. Therefore, when we have decided to permit an outside human being, whether in the family or not, to affect deeply what we are, we first must come to see that outside human being as belonging to us. This means that our self has taken a new self in. We look upon the human being we have made ours as an addition to what we have been. Consequently, when this human being acts not as if he or she were ourselves but as a human being in his or her own right, we become excessively displeased. For we have done the inestimable favor—so we deeply regard it—of making something else part of ourselves, and that something else shows the temerity and injustice of not appreciating it. That is why such great resentment has been shown and is shown to one close to us who, however, acts sometimes as if he weren't.

What I have just described is what most often occurs. To many persons it unconsciously seems much the easiest way. All of us have an inclination to love by owning a person, in the depths of our minds. The very point of Aesthetic Realism is that though the situation described is frequent, it need not occur. The whole self and the truly free self wants something else, something larger.

I have said that we use another person to like ourselves. In the first place, a person whom we like very much has praised us; in some way justified our existence; in some way given us the warm feeling that we were approved by the forces about us. The person, then, who has said pleasing words of us has done or helped to do that which we are always trying to accomplish. A woman when listening to the words "I love you" hears somewhere this statement:

"The universe talking through a chosen representative is saying, 'I love you'; therefore your desires had by you since birth are corroborated and affirmed, for it is not only you who think you should be loved, but more than you, a chosen aspect of the universe itself." Most women, or for that matter, most men in a situation like this will not ask whether the person approving of one's ego truly represents the world as a whole; whether the laudatory statements and actions of the admiring person are sufficient evidence for a deep, accurate like of oneself.

There is satisfaction for a while. But the insistent question, "Can you really like yourself with the facts present?" is repeated. Somewhere there appears to the distressed unconscious and even to the conscious of the seemingly loved person, a feeling that one has simply repeated one's own evidence; that what has happened is really a repetition, without confirmation, of self-love. In proportion as the person is sensitive there is difficulty and tension. A woman may be able to have her husband say, "I love you," morning, noon, and night, but the evidence still does not seem complete.

However, the woman still chooses to look on her lover as an adequate representative of the universe as a whole. For a while, the more she is uncertain of the value of the evidence pointing towards her own self-approval, the more she wishes to shut the universe out. The greater her doubts, the greater her irritation. She begins to find fault with the person she has chosen as a symbol. Perhaps at this time she will go deeper into herself than ever before, for she has all the while not really looked on her husband as a being in his own right. And her feeling of guilt is telling her—and has been telling her: "It is not you or someone you see as belonging to you that will enable you to like yourself. Something apart from you, independent of you, outside of you must say this. And it is only when you are able to love something not as possessed by you, but as what it is in its own right, that you will think the facts in you are working together in approving of you."

The tendency to have persons belong to one, and as such be loved, has been a prolific cause of disturbance, tension, misery.

Rachel Long, ethical and somewhat religious, was surprised at how much her brother was on her mind. (The facts of the relation between Rachel and her brother, taken as a whole, make it clear despite the possible inferences of zealous psychoanalysts, that no important or decisive incestuous feeling existed.) She told me that sometimes at four o'clock in the morning she had to get up and call him on the telephone to see how he was. At other times Rachel felt like killing him.

The causes were the following: There was a time, as a child, when Rachel took care of her brother. The brother needed her. In his need he said to the girl, "You are important, I need you. Therefore, the universe needs you." Rachel endured a great deal from people about her: from grandmother, from father, from other relatives. Because the world seemed cruel she created within herself her own world to take its place. Even at this time, she felt somewhere that this was wrong, but the fact that her brother needed her seemed somewhat to justify this interior isolation. Therefore, she saw her brother as indispensable for the approval of the inner structure where she had supremacy.

As she grew older, and she saw more and more what objects required her consideration and care, she hung on to her brother. But at times the sense that her brother was justifying something evil in itself was used as a weapon against him. Rachel became angry with herself and therefore angry with her brother because he now had become an equivalent of suffering. She wished to maintain the separate existence in her self that had given her an apparent gratification. Her guilt feelings assailed her, however. These guilt feelings changed to anger. Sometimes her brother acted not as belonging to her but as an independent being. This would infuriate her. When he married, her fury came to a high pitch. Through it all her brother remained as a symbol of her "conquest of reality," for wasn't his need of her an atonement for guilt? She sent him money and did other things for him while he was growing up, became a young man, and even while he was married. The money affirmed the fact that he lived because she lived.

I had a strenuous time pointing out to Rachel Long that what seemed great kindness to her brother was really based on a possessive love attitude. I also had a difficult time making it clear that her anger with him arose from his daring to act as an independent being. It was, however, shown to her that her attitude to her brother, being an evasion of her relations to reality as a whole, had outraged her guilt feelings and had upset her. As she accepted this explanation of her attitude to her brother, she grew calmer about him. The understanding of a bad attitude takes away the force of that attitude: I mean of course whole understanding, that which implies the *clear* externalization of a feeling.

This substitution of a possessive feeling for an attitude of accurate love occurs frequently within families. Any member may be in this possessive relationship towards any other member: mother towards child, child towards mother, sister towards brother, brother towards sister. The same, in essence, occurs with people outside the family group.

Ann Devree told me of a dream which had disturbed her. She had provided a hammer to someone who had used it to kill a man with whom she had lived. Ann was going to be tried in court for having taken part in the murder; and in the dream was very fearful of what the outcome of the trial would be.

The young man, it seems, was "dependent on her." He had told Ann Devree that he needed her. Ann had seen him as weak, but there was a great gratification in seeing that his existence depended on hers; for in having another person depend on us, our justification is asserted. She had had misgivings about the source of this love, and had finally separated from him. But she was a "strong-willed" woman, and something like the same relationship was sought again by her. Now, when one is dependent on another, the person dominating looks on the other as not independent. This attitude is taken by the unconscious as amounting to the dominating person's having killed the person dominated. For when a self is annexed to another, the first is no longer fully alive. Ann Devree had had likewise a definite sense of power in using a hammer. The dream therefore was her own guilt feeling saying that her having consented to the dependence of another and having got satisfaction from that dependence was a way of murdering that person.

Our unconscious does not wish us to love by possessing or smothering. I have met this dream of the dying or killing of a loved person in other connections; and here I wish to deny the common interpretation of dreams dealing with the death of mothers, brothers, wives, husbands, and the like. It does not mean that the person dreaming actually wishes to kill the person seen as dead or murdered in the dream. This, to me, is part of that melodramatic excessiveness, that inaccurate evaluation of the unconscious too often found in psychoanalysis.

For instance: Dora Hill disliked her father exceedingly. He seemed to her weak and selfish, and apparently this belief was somewhat justified. But she had used her father as a means of justifying her separation from reality. I told her that no matter what faults her father may have had, that would not have caused the guilt feeling which was plaguing her; for the feeling of guilt does not arise from the misdeeds and deficiencies of others, no matter how great, but from what we ourselves have done or failed to do. She insisted that her father was the main cause of her dislike and fear of the world. Dora had had dreams before of his dying. There were also frequent dreams of the dying of her mother. While I was trying to explain to her that her father was not what her unconscious saw as the culprit in her own self-separation, she dreamed the following: Her father was dead in a small box (he is a small man and she has always disliked his smallness). But while he was lying dead, Dora heard him shout—"holler," as she put it—and at the same time she saw the cover of the box-coffin wriggle.

This dream, it seems to me, makes it clear that despite Dora's asseverations, the guilt feeling in her unconscious had been affected by my statements, for previously she had "killed" her father by denying to him an existence outside of herself. Therefore, she had denied him existence as an independent object; but when she heard him in her dream shout, and at the same time saw the cover on the coffin move, she was saying that he was not only dead but alive. That is, he was beginning to take on qualities of something else than an extension of her own personality.

The dreams Dora had of her mother came from the same source. She felt guilty about her mother because she had seen her only as a possession, not as a human being in her own right.

Sex, then, does not "run" reality; it is included *within* reality: reality is quite clearly big enough to include all erotic phenomena. It is interesting that at the present time there is a growing departure from the narrow psychological idea that sexual disturbances have their basis in infantile experience relating to the "libido."

The Freudian "deviationists," such as Dr. Karen Horney, are opposed to regarding the neurotic state as a result of sexual distortions in early life. Nevertheless, there is still an indisposition to see sexual disturbances as proceeding from some disproportion between the self and reality as a whole. Even Dr. Horney's attitude has the cause too closely bound with "environment," "social relations," and "family life" in a narrow sense.

I must insist again that sex is not to be separated from reality—a reality that goes beyond the sociological from a confined point of view; or even the biological from a confined point of view. It may be a hazardous statement, but the sexual life of an individual is related to such things as inorganic chemistry, physics, and even mathematics and logic—let alone the much insulted and misused metaphysics. Sex has certainly to do with these studies; but they can also be used to *explain* the deepest, most compulsive, and most practical meaning of sex. For is not the reality of human life—which takes in the sexual—connected with the studies I have mentioned?

But to get closer to matters at hand.

Is it to be expected that an individual having difficulty accepting existence as such, will not find difficulty in accepting the particular representative of existence that is another human being? For it is true, sexually and logically, that we cannot accept an instance completely if we are not willing to accept that of which a thing is an instance. We cannot accept a symbol if we are not willing to accept completely the *thing symbolized.*

The shame of masturbation, for example, does not arise from the act itself and its somatic content. This shame arises from the fact that in masturbation, one may separate oneself from all people, despise people, look upon them as the shadowy servants of an ego alone. If masturbation did not take with it *a hurtful glorification of oneself based on an ugly contempt for what is outside oneself,* its effect would not be as bad as it most often is. It can hardly be expected, however, that as this world is now, masturbation can occur with the person doing it having a full respect for outside reality. For is a person ashamed of cooking a meal for oneself, building a house for oneself, or making clothes for oneself? If a person is not ashamed of an act which can be done with another, why should a person be ashamed of that thing if done by oneself? It appears then that the phrase "done by oneself" is central. For sex is an expression of a deep relation to reality and where that expression is not complete in terms of its *relation,* there is a feeling of shame or guilt. Sex is a means, despite all its physical opulence of detail, of affirming that there is a oneness between one's body or one's self and something outside of one's body or one's self.

It should be remembered that a person, without needing to be learned or a master of logic, unconsciously goes after a sense of the whole in accomplishing a detail. In eating an article of food, we are affirming an attitude towards food in general, though we don't use the word "affirm" and we don't use the word "general." In wearing clothes, we are affirming an attitude towards clothes in general. In sex a *general attitude* despite our conscious selves, is somewhere within us. We may never express this attitude, but it is working within us, anyway. If we feel that we have separated a detail from what it should stand for, we naturally miss something.

Should a child come to a feeling of uneasiness as to what is called "self-pollution," there is a mighty principle involved. For the human being is going after, all the time, what sex stands for, that is, meaning. If the meaning is gone the thing itself seems to be crippled, not entirely there; and that means that something is missing in ourselves. That something missing makes for the sense of guilt.

This feeling of something missing is also the essential factor in frigidity and impotence. By now the physiological aspects of masturbation, frigidity, and impotence have been muted, the psychic aspects heightened. One doesn't hear so much of the terrifying consequences attending masturbation. There isn't the strong belief any longer in there being a simple physiological cause for impotence and frigidity. Yet there is a feeling that something amiss attends masturbation and something "not just right" attends frigidity and impotence. It is not just the "physical" facts.

Helga Davenport told me she had fallen in love with a man because he was at once an enterprising, somewhat dashing business man and a eulogizer of her own qualities. Helga was exalted by the fact that this business man preferred her to his wife. This made her feel distinguished. There was no deep feeling for the value of this particular business man as a human being in himself. There was in Helga's mind a sense of exaltation, thrill, adventure. But it all came from the fact that this man belonged to her. Helga was pretty timid on her own account and here was somebody who said she "belonged"; she was "all right." In loving this man she did not come to love the world of which she was afraid and from which she had secluded herself. Helga could not, therefore, give herself to him in the deepest sense of the word. Despite herself she was frigid.

Helga told me that people in general and other things were disliked by her. Her guilt feeling told her that she should not dislike them. Helga tried to annul this guilt feeling by clandestinely and isolatedly being with a man who most decidedly approved of her. But it wouldn't do. Helga's sensitivity could be obscured, but it could not be annulled. Her guilt feeling told her that she did not really love the man who was praising her. Her doubt, her shame, her fear took the form of frigidity.

Another instance in my experience is that of a painter, David Hanson, who became impotent with a woman he had been living with. There had been a cleavage between his aesthetic life and his personal life for some time.

The aesthetic attitude, as I will show more at length in another place, is that which demands of a person that he express himself, that is, give himself an outside form. It also means that objects be so fully seen, have the eye of the person perceiving so much in them, that the person *becomes* the thing seen. This aesthetic drive on the part of David Hanson was not at one with his personal drive to have someone "possessed" by him without his really having seen that person or truly approving of her.

Conflicts having an intense manifestation had occurred before the onset of impotence. There were feelings of excessive humility followed by feelings of excessive rage. There had also been desires on the part of David Hanson to leave the woman and to forget sex, for the sexual attitudes were felt to be rivals of the aesthetic procedure. There had also been inclinations to give up painting. The artist was on the one hand trying to give himself entirely, and on the other trying to withhold himself. Arrogance was followed by slavishness. The culmination was an unconscious compromise— impotence.

It needs to be noted that along with the instinct to act there is also the instinct to abstain. These are together. There is no such thing as a choice of an action without the exclusion of some other action. And exclusion here, in the biggest meaning, is the same as abstinence. The sexual instinct, as it is called, is not simply torrential, raging; it is also, in its way, logical and selective. It is in an inseparable togetherness with every perception had by a human being—including the perception of order, logic, completeness.

A good deal has been written on the influence of sex on aesthetics. Less has been written of something like an aesthetic causality of sex itself.

All human minds seek joy. But joy is not opposed to ideas of accuracy, order, and ethics. When a human mind feels that it is in pain because it isn't doing what it sees as its duty, does it not mean that if its duty were fully done, it would have joy? Does it not mean that duty has even a relation to ecstasy? Is the guilt feeling that I have written about simply negative? Does it not mean that were the demands of guilt fully to be satisfied, joy would ensue? I state that somewhere the unconscious regards things in this manner. The ethical unconscious is, after all, interested in our joy. What we want to do, in the long run, is what we have to do.

For the understanding of self and its deep and outward battles, it is necessary that persons be less afraid of the word "unconscious." Many have been intimidated into believing that the unconscious is an unknown, subtle, shadowy, but omnipresent, and terrifying beast, whose purpose is to upset the methodical, cheerful arrangements of mankind. The unconscious can be terrible, but however unknown it is, it cannot be separated from the conscious. Heavy accent has been given to how the unconscious, burrowing far, far beneath the conscious, influences it, twists it, and defeats it. Yet it is also true that the conscious is, every moment of one's life, influencing the unconscious. The fact that an object observed by the conscious eight hours before, may be in a dream that night, points to a quick transferability of something conscious into the unconscious. Cannot this transferability of conscious influence or drive into the unconscious be planned? This may be difficult, but it can be accomplished.

However unknown the unconscious is, it after all exists. The mysterious, as such, exists no more fully than the everyday and known. The most elusive subterranean pulsation of the unconscious is no *less* a reality than a humdrum perception of a dull afternoon; but that subterranean bit of the unconscious is no *more* a reality, either. Let us not make a misty, swift, cavelike terror of the unknown and a meek thing of the known. The known has just as many terrors and subterraneities as the unknown, for the known is not completely known either: all reality is mysterious.

Freud and his successors have dealt with the unconscious too melodramatically and yet too scantily, even though they may not have wished to do so. Just as in chemistry there is no reason to exalt the unknown chemical elements over the known, so there is no reason to exalt impulses that we do not know over the things that we do know. The unknown, when found, will make the known more important.

Were the unconscious and the conscious acting as one, even if the unconscious were not fully known, the human mind would be in a state of dynamic tranquillity. (The Aesthetic Realism definition of happiness is: A state of dynamic tranquillity in the self.) We may not know the names or appearance of a thousand inhabitants of a Vermont town, and yet we may not fear those inhabitants. It is only if we are against knowing the unknown, the far away, the mysterious, that these continue to be frightening of themselves.

The method of Aesthetic Realism is, then, based on the possibility and necessity of making the conscious and the unconscious work as one. Where there are any hidden fears, obsessions, aversions, disproportions, these attitudes of mind are brought into juxtaposition with more everyday things.

There is a tendency on the part of many to separate "romantic" from factual things, family concerns from exotic concerns, everyday matters from matters that have strangeness. Wherever such a separation occurs there is also some hurtful sign of separation in self.

For example, a person may have put her mother into some isolated field of attention. She regards her mother as belonging to her, and she has towards her mother some of that lack of esteem which one associates with taken-for-granted familiarity. It is important, therefore, to place the idea of mother along with some idea of aloofness, strangeness, remoteness. For instance, in one Aesthetic Realism lesson a girl rebelled at the notion of putting a fat mother and the Renaissance period of Italy in the same sentence. The Renaissance stood in the girl's mind for a leaving of family and old associations, a cessation of being caressed excessively and tyrannized over. The Renaissance represented in her mind a later life of freedom and change. Yet when she realized the fact that there was a relation of mother and Renaissance, she was ready to accept other relations—perhaps even more unwelcome.

For us to like the world, the world must make sense. Furthermore, it must make sense without any of it blurred, disregarded, rejected. Once we have decided that a separate portion of the world only is fit for our attention, we naturally shall have fears if other aspects of reality suddenly meet us. A first requirement, therefore, in dealing with mental disturbance, is to present a notion of both the unity and diversity of reality; to present the unity of the strangeness of reality and humdrumness, of its farawayness with its intimacy, of its immediacy with its abstractness. If reality is not seen as unified and diverse, there will be a tendency to approach it lopsidedly. A lopsided approach to the world makes for pain, and with pain there is a likelihood of a mind's going back to a world within self as a rival to the unsatisfactory external universe. It is apparent that unless a person is consciously ready to accept reality as such and unless the unconscious also accepts that reality, all the admonitions to adjust one's self will be given in a language that can only be faintly heard.

A mind that looks on the world of objects as a rival to its own comfort will go after patterns making for complacency. These patterns will be safeguarded when had. But for a self to be truly at ease, it must welcome new arrangements, see surprise as an ingredient in everyday life, look upon new combinations as friendly things not hostile to its notions of comfort. In order to do this a person must consciously see that ideas which have been put in separate portions of one's mind can be aesthetically placed together, and that the result is sensible, necessary, and pleasing.

3

The Aesthetic Method in Self-Conflict

Note to Second Edition

The Aesthetic Method in Self-Conflict, originally published in the spring of 1946 and reprinted later the same year, has historical importance as the first publication embodying the philosophy of Aesthetic Realism, founded by Eli Siegel in the early 1940's. It is perhaps the most compact and comprehensive introduction to an understanding of Siegel's central idea: "The world, art, and self explain each other: each is the aesthetic oneness of opposites."

An earlier phrasing of this idea—a phrasing which dates from 1941—was printed on the back cover of the first edition of *The Aesthetic Method:* "The resolution of conflict in self is like the making one of opposites in art."

The present edition is a photographic reproduction of the original, with one editorial change. The term, Aesthetic Analysis, was found to carry too narrow a connotation, and in 1948, Aesthetic Realism was adopted as more exactly descriptive of the philosophy. The author's preface, in which some of the difficulties of nomenclature are discussed, is as it was written in 1946; but in the text itself, Aesthetic Analysis has been changed to Aesthetic Realism.

MARTHA BAIRD, *for*
Definition Press

1965

Preface

This is the first publication of Aesthetic Analysis. Aesthetic Analysis looks on mind as an object like any other object. We believe that what makes for organization of mind is like what makes for organization of a city, a book, a symphony, a store.

The word "self-conflict" is used in the title. It has been found useful to avoid terms of too narrow a medical connotation. Aesthetic Analysis is not medicine or psychiatry in the current sense. Still, it is well to regard self-conflict as meaning "neurosis," when that word is given scope enough and precision enough.

Aesthetic Analysis is practical, for the problem of the integration of self is most unquestionably "practical." It is the "practical problem" beneath all decisions of everyday life. And the first thing necessary in dealing with a practical problem is to see it rightly. There must be seeing before there is remedy.

In our method, the problem of problems, the major, constant, underlying, inevitable thing to organize, deal with sensibly, is: Self and World. However philosophical this phrase may sound, it concerns everyone in the U.S. census or any other census or possible census. Everyone is confronted with, has, the job of: I and All That. Others might call it "one's self and one's environment" or "the individual and society."

Where self-conflict exists or nervousness does, it arises from some inefficient or incomplete or ugly dealing with this problem beneath problems: I and All That; or I and Things; or I and All They. (This is the problem one's talking about when one asks: "How's the world treating you?") To see the question meeting everyone as anything smaller, is unwise.

In Aesthetic Analysis, inward sexual hindrances and "anxiety" and "inferiority" and an untoward "death instinct" are phases or manifestations of the larger problem. If a person's relation with everything which is not himself is sensible, so far will the way he sees sex be sensible. One universe preceded one woman or one man.

In this publication of Aesthetic Analysis, aesthetics itself is the chief matter. In other, coming publications, the general subject will be dealt with otherwise. For example, for a self to separate from the outside world means guilt. The separation can also make for symptoms of a physiological kind: in Aesthetic Analysis the separation is dealt with directly, not the symptoms as such. However, where a self is not at one with the world, is separated from it, the situation is also ugly, against aesthetics in that deep, sober meaning which aesthetics has. And Aesthetic Analysis combats the acquisition in economics which, being a manifestation of self against world or others, makes for disintegration and weakening of personality.

I have elsewhere shown how the unconscious disjunction of a person from the world about him makes for guilt, anger, fear. I have also dealt with how separation from the world has to do with stuttering, insomnia; digestive, menstrual, and other difficulties. Further, the attitude of a person to what is not himself affects what he does in sex; and this matter has also been a subject of Aesthetic Analysis examination. It should be remarked here that Aesthetic Analysis is not merely abstract. Documents exist showing how very precise and earthy it can be. Certain of these documents will be published.

For a fair consideration of this publication, a person must put aside probable previous associations with "aesthetics." Were there a word as exact as aesthetics for the purpose, we would have been glad to use it. The nearest word, other than aesthetics, is dialectics. Dialectics, however, would not express as much as aesthetics does. Terms like Ethical Analysis, Philosophical Analysis, Reality Analysis, we have likewise seen as deficient in one way or another.

It is hoped that Aesthetic Analysis will be seen for what it is: nothing less and nothing more. The method does things to people of a most discernible kind. It has helped to organize lives. It is hoped that before some phrase like "abstract," "impractical," or "I know all that," is used, there will be more seeing—plain seeing. The present pamphlet we hope may serve as a beginning of that seeing.

ELI SIEGEL

P.S.—We have included "Author of *Hot Afternoons Have Been in Montana*" on the title page. The reason is that this poem, which won the *Nation* Poetry Prize of 1925, is, as we see it, a precursor, in fact, a "first publication" of the Aesthetic Analysis of now. For example:

There are millions of men in the world, and each is
    one man;
Each is one man by himself, taking care of himself all
    the time, and changing other men and being
    changed by them;
The quiet of this afternoon is strange, haunting,
    awful. . . .

E.S.

The names of the persons in this work are imaginary. The persons are real.

The Aesthetic Method in Self-Conflict

Tom, dick, and Harry; Brown, Jones, and Robinson; Hilda, Hulda, and Matilda; little Johnny, tiny Eva and wee Dickie; and the man or girl you know—all have problems by being alive. Aesthetic Realism says that in all of them, and in all persons, tough and genteel, hard-boiled and dreamy, vulgar and elegant, the beginning, large problem is aesthetic: just that.

There is a deep and "dialectic" duality facing every human being, which can be put this way: How is he to be entirely himself, and yet be fair to that world which he does not see as himself? The definition of aesthetics is to be found in a proper appreciation of this duality.

We all of us start with a *here,* ever so snug and ever so immediate. And this *here* is surrounded strangely, endlessly, by a *there.* We are always meeting this *there:* in other words, we are always meeting what is not ourselves, and we have to do something about it. We have to be ourselves, and give to this great and diversified *there,* which is not ourselves, what it deserves. This means we have to be personal and impersonal, snug and exterior. If we do this successfully, whether we know it or not, we have arrived at a beauty which is efficient; at aesthetic good sense. Psychiatrists, should they go about their business completely, boldly, clearly, would be trying to attain this aesthetic propriety and wonder of human behavior.

For psychiatrists do tell persons to be "objective." These psychiatrists certainly would also tell their patients to be "themselves," to have their own opinions, to have lives of their own. What this psychiatric advice really comes to is that people want to be "subjective," too. Therefore, people have to be "objective" and "subjective." Should they be objective one hour and subjective the next hour? Should they be objective about *this* and subjective about *that?* It is not good, it appears, to be shuttling from the factual point of view to the personal point of view. What is left from all this? The following: That a person should, for his mind's health and his deep contentment and his profound efficiency, be objective and subjective at the same time. If he is, he will be aesthetic—for aesthetic means, having an adequate, alive, "personal" perception, while giving oneself truly to the fact outside, the specific reality, the *that.*

There is conflict in most minds as to "personal" and "impersonal," "subjective" and "objective," *here* and *there.*

The idea of conflict is essential in any concept of an ailing mind or an ailing self. Were mind or self to be one, it would be sane; where it is not one there is lack of saneness or wholeness; that is, conflict. Conflict as such, in every instance, has two phases to it: there is separateness and there is togetherness. If things in conflict were separate only, they would be too remote to disturb each other; therefore, all would be well. On the other hand, if things in conflict were together only, they would be one; and again all would be well.

To make concrete the rather abstract language of the last paragraph: A girl, Edith, has a sick father whom she does not care for too much but whom, after all, she sees as a father. She thinks of leaving him and she also sees it as her duty to take care of him. These two thoughts are, of course, in conflict; they make up a typical mental field of war. When we look at these thoughts we see that they are together. When Edith thinks of one she may, the next moment, think of the other; she finds reasons for the justice of both. They are like a team of horses which insist on biting and interfering with each other. But a team of unruly horses are definitely together. Yet if they were together in the full sense they would be an orderly team; therefore there is something else than togetherness; there is separateness or opposition.

What emerges, then, is a simultaneity of conspicuous togetherness and conspicuous separateness or opposition. A situation of mind in which there is unavoidable togetherness and unavoidable separateness or opposition, is a conflict.

The basic conflict in the human mind—present, I believe, in all particular conflicts—is that between a person warmly existing to his finger tips, and that person as related to indefinite outsideness: this is the subject and object conflict, the personal and impersonal conflict, the Self and World conflict. In every person there is a drive towards the caring for and pleasing of self; in every person there is a drive towards other things, a desire to meet and know these. Often this drive towards self as an exclusive thing collides painfully with the drive to widen the self. The drives co-exist, that is, they are together; the drives also can be seen as apart, that is, they are separate.

These two drives have their likenesses in art; for at a time of aesthetic activity, a person wants to show his own feelings in a painting, novel, or poem, even if it means lessening objects just as they are; and he also wants to see these objects without imposing narrow desires of self making for its comfort or premature complacency. When an artist is successful, he does not deny either one of these drives, for each is essential; each has its necessity; even its inevitability. But he is not lopsided; he does not accent one, and muffle or curtail the other. The perfect work of art is that where the artist, while entirely himself, while a unique individual, also sees an object in its completeness and precision. If it is possible; if, in fact, it is the great purpose of art to be one's self and yet give everything to the object—can we not find here the just purpose in life itself?

I have observed that in every conflict there is no side which is to be suppressed. The person suffering with a conflict, trying to come to peace, has a tendency to say of a Tuesday: "To hell with *this*"; and on the next day, or for that matter, in the next hour, to say: "To hell with *that.*" A neurotic, somewhat jocosely, yet with precision, can be described as a person who makes a loud outcry over losing something which he does not wish to find. He rings doorbells hoping no one is at home.

The neurotic does not wish to destroy either opposing side of his conflict. Still he knows that one side of himself stops him from being at peace with the other; therefore he curses now one, now the other. But even while he outwardly curses something, deeply he hangs on to it. What he needs to do is to see that in having one essential aspect of himself, he need not get rid of the other.

Well, just that thing: having one attitude and also its opposite, is to be seen in art. If an artist felt that in presenting his feelings intensely, he had to be against seeing an object as it was; if in being excited, he had to neglect calm form— or, put more generally, if he felt that to be his individual self, he had to keep from seeing the outside universe—then the artist would be neurotic, too. Some artists are, but this is not because they're artists, but because they're incomplete artists.

Aesthetics is related to every particular conflict; to everyday conflict. Aesthetics is related to the problems of the ordinary man, the tough guy, the people we meet in our homes, in theatres, in streets, in stores.

For example, there is Harold Jamison of Wilkes-Barre, Pa. Jamison is undergoing a basic, run-of-the-mill conflict. However, what is in his mind, and the possibility of making serene good sense out of it, are of the very heart of psychiatric method. And the only way of making serene good sense out of what's on Jamison's mind, is to make aesthetics out of it. He most likely has had very little to do with the word, maybe he hasn't heard of it; but if Jamison is to walk confidently and sleep well, aesthetics will come to his incompletely articulate mind.

Look at Jamison. He is shy and he is arrogant; in fact, he is like most people. Sometimes, Jamison looks at himself and finds a person who is timid, wants to evade people, thinks people don't like him; is unassertive and inferior. At other times, Jamison is raring to go, feels like an excited regiment, and like a dozen energetic lions up to something. In other words, Jamison of Wilkes-Barre feels both inferior and superior; and when he feels superior, it's hard for him to realize he ever felt inferior. (This also is common.) So the inferiority and superiority feelings of Harold Jamison are in conflict. If he were to visit a mental practitioner in a mood which made him despise wife, children, relatives, and fellow office-workers, of course the practitioner would advise his visitor to get rid of something like narcissism, megalomania, autistic thinking, or the lack of an objective attitude to people.

If, however, Harold Jamison, of a Thursday, feeling de-

pressed, shy, ashamed, and timorous, were to visit a practitioner, he would be told to get more confidence in himself;
to be abased no longer; to walk about proudly and confidently. It might not happen just this way; but I have noticed
that mental counselors have told persons to be both less
narcissistic and more confident. This may be done subtly,
quietly; but it is confusing. How, after all, is one to be full
of confidence in himself, and yet not the least bit "narcissistic"? How is one to be deferential, obliging, at times yielding
to other people, without being the least bit "dependent" or
inferior? This question has to be answered straight; without
terminological curlicues or erudite evasiveness. Mr. Jamison, it is clear, has to be both modest and proud—and at the
same time, too. He can't be submissive at 4 P.M. and tyrannical at 5 P.M. Well, if the Mr. Jamisons of Wilkes-Barre and
the rest of the United States are to be "adjusted" when it
comes to their inferiority and superiority ambivalence, it
won't be by means of a mental therapy which in itself is
contradictory.

Aesthetics makes the essential superiority and inferiority
feelings in man a working team, a team of oneness. We can't
kick out either Jamison's arrogance or his shyness. They are
both part of him. They are to be made one, and they can be.
Right now, they are in conflict; that is, submissiveness and
domineeringness are close in Jamison's mind, and yet they
are separate. Mr. Jamison wants them to be close; he also
wants them to go away from each other. Togetherness is
fighting separation in his mind. He is having a bad time.

Aesthetics here should be seen as a possible job of engineering. It is clear that Jamison has to feel yielding and
managing at once. Otherwise, he will shuttle unheathily.
The question Jamison and other people face is: Can, in one
mind, feelings represented by superiority exist with feelings

represented by inferiority? Can we be both humble and bold at 3:30 P.M., Tuesday?—Only art shows that the answer is, Yes. If metaphysics, logic, ethics, psychology, can say yes, too—it's because they are, this while, what art is.

Take Whitman's *Song of Myself*. Whitman yields himself to what he sees; to earth, to people; and he is proud doing so. Art shows we can be proud in seeing clearly, without rigmarole, or pretense, that we are less than we can be. Art makes for pride in the fact, even when that fact is against ego in the narrow sense, or 2-A. (Self having false importance by being opposed to the world is termed by us 2-A.) In Whitman's *Song of Myself*, a man becomes exultant through modesty, modest through exultation. The intense, wide, great fact sweeps Whitman truly; he yields and he has a feeling of deep independence and pride. Where even a Whitman does not feel this, it's because art is not complete. As far as Whitman is an artist—and this is very far; and as far as he gives himself, without interior vanity wriggling, to what is, he feels that *he* is, and he is proud. Jamison should know this.

If a person feels inferior, the first question to ask is, What does he feel inferior about? I don't believe that psychiatrists have asked this question rightly. If a person is unable to do something, or if he doesn't know something, and he knows this neatly, definitely, he will not feel inferior in the morbid sense. He would feel at least he knew himself; and would be proud of that. In other words, in yielding to the facts about himself courageously, truly, there would be a self-approval. Further, if what he desired were good, and he really desired it, he would also approve of himself. Every true desire has action going with it. In following, honestly, steadily, without trickery, a true desire, we feel proud. All this means: yielding to the facts can make us proud.

In aesthetics, there is more true yielding to the facts than elsewhere. Suppose a writer were confessing in his manuscript something which was actually so, and offhand seemed depreciating of him. Having the courage to say what was true of himself, for the purpose of saying it truly and having it known as it was—would he not feel proud? The real critical feeling is always proud: whether of oneself or of others. The real critical feeling, however, seldom occurs.

If knowing oneself were to make inevitably for inferiority, certainly many people should be told not to know themselves. But even the most gentle psychotherapists would hesitate to say people should not know themselves. Behind this hesitation is the feeling that when people know themselves, they truly can approve of themselves because they know what they are. *No self can truly know itself and be ashamed.*

When a self knows what it is, wholly as an object, the thing felt is also the thing feeling. Jamison, deeply, deeply, is after this. If he reaches it, he will be doing the aesthetic thing. For in aesthetics, the self finds its freedom by seeing what it is as an object like other objects; and while there is this seeing, there is the healthy, intense, tremendous feeling of the self as existing, acting, free. The subject has become free by meeting the object wholly. You find this in a baby who knows it's Edgar at fifteen months, because it has met enough objects with not too much of the corruption which later may take place.

Inferiority is really guilt. It doesn't come from your job, as such, or wife, or family, or your acquaintances and friends. Jamison is looking either upon the world as a thing to conquer, handle, exploit, or upon himself as someone to be punished for wanting to be monarchical. This is what goes on deeply. Jamison thinks by respecting something else, *he* is less Jamison. It isn't true; only aesthetics can make it entirely not seem true.

It is difficult really to welcome and use art wholly. A person can't be aesthetic without giving his perceptions entirely to the world. He can't be an arrogant, acquisitive self; and as life now is, it is so easy to want to be. Yet it often happens—and in most lives—that in a person's being really modest, he is proud; that, in a successful not-imposing of himself on objects, he has a sense of well-being.

Suppose we take Rosalind Hines, honestly listening to great music. Rosalind has her interior mishaps, and her inward insufficiencies. Still, something in her wants to listen to Mozart as Mozart, music as music, with the possibly acquisitive Rosalind Hines out of it for a while. An eighteenth-century Austrian affects her (the world had affected him). Through Mozart, Rosalind sees the universe for a while come into form in the concert hall. The music has taken her; form and earth have taken her. She yields. She also feels free and proud. In proportion as she is stirred, swept, moved about by sound in great, wonderful order, she is *more* Rosalind Hines, not less.

It is hard, however, while being deeply affected by things to feel we have ourselves intactly. Even Rosalind may have some unconscious qualms after the great Mozartian conquest of her mind. "What happened to me?" she may ask unknowingly to herself. "If this strange external force can do so much to me, where am I, just I?" It is easier, though, to yield to something like music than to something which can more readily and plainly question the complacent and hidden ego. Even so, persons often do not like the fact that music moves them deeply; does something to them unmistakably, thoroughly.

This job of taking care of the warm "oneself" while doing justice to other matters, is truly too philosophic a job for the present day psychiatric equipment. Persons advising other persons will say, in an effort to stabilize selves: "Be yourself"; "Assert yourself." They will also say: "Be interested in other people"; "Think more of other people." When a psychotherapist talks this way, he is affirming conflict; for what a man wants to know is *just how* he can be himself, assert himself, and at the same time be considerate and think more of other people.

Louis Robinson, for example, of Syracuse, New York, like all people, talks to, with, and about himself. Sometimes, in these thoroughly intimate conversations, Louis Robinson asserts: "To hell with other people; I'm out for Number One." On other occasions, the somewhat civilized Mr. Robinson says: "This is too bad, thinking of myself all the time; why don't I forget myself and become interested in other things?"

Should a psychiatrist point out "narcissistic trends" in Mr. Robinson's interior cogitations, he's really telling something in technical language which Mr. Robinson has agonizingly known all along. Sometimes, it *has* seemed best to forget other people, and to concentrate energetically on his own well-being, comfort, importance. It seemed to be the one thing to do. What the soul of Louis Robinson is after knowing is, just how he is to be himself and yet give what is coming to all else. A psychiatrist might likewise point out "masochistic" or "inferiority" feelings in Mr. Robinson, for sometimes the Syracuse man feels humble and wants people to help him, and wants to be nice to people, and wants to be punished for not being nice. Therefore, as to Mr. Robinson: advice given to him either that he assert himself or think less of himself, only prolongs the see-sawing existence of the assertive and deferential sufferer. If a way were shown to Louis Robinson—and this would be the one useful kind of advice—by which he could be himself proudly *by* giving everything that was coming to them to other people and things—that way would be aesthetic: nothing less.

Harold Jamison and Louis Robinson are meeting the same troubles. Harold Jamison has what Louis Robinson has; and self-difficulties are present in Wilkes-Barre and in Syracuse. The instance of Jamison shows the dilemma in terms of power and weakness; that of Robinson, in terms of selfishness and unselfishness, injustice and justice. Still, the Jamison situation and the Robinson situation are akin.

Opposites, therefore, are to be put together in lives in Wilkes-Barre and lives in Syracuse; and lives, of course, elsewhere. An artist puts opposites together; a psychiatrist aims, or should aim, to put personality opposites together. If a psychiatrist succeeds in putting elements in basic opposition together, he would be doing as an artist does.

Where opposites exist, and are not one, there is conflict. Every kind of conflict is, in principle, alike. Opposites in the self are not made by us; we have them by being alive. How our opposites are in relation shows itself in what we do; in the manifestations of daily life. We all of us begin with our selves, and our selves have opposites. It is possible they will work against each other—this is what most largely happens; it is also possible they will be integrated, together, a one.

A person is separate from all other things and together with all other things. To understand opposites in a self, the meaning of *together* and *separate* must be seen. (This meaning is like that of *same* and *different*.) The meaning may seem abstract, and may seem hardly worth going after by a psychiatrist; yet if he fails to go after it, he is evading the entirety of his function. All art puts *separateness* and *togetherness* together. All selves want to do this.

Take a common instance showing the *separate* and *together* problem. Five household objects are in a corner of a moving van. They are seen by a boy, Albert. They are a clock, a table, a chair, a bed, and a lamp. These objects are huddled together in a corner. Albert doesn't think they look proper or good, and hardly anyone would think so. They are close together, all right. But their closeness makes for clashing. The lamp seems to interfere with the bed by hanging right over it; the clock is on the chair, and doesn't belong there; and the table has the bed right up against it. Yes, the things are near to each other; you could almost say they hug each other; but it's their nearness that seems to make them fight. Albert doesn't like the looks of the five objects; even though he wouldn't say it was a bad arrangement of separateness and togetherness.

And then the things in the moving van reach Albert's home. They are put carefully in a room. The bed is farther away from the table; and the lamp is not so near the bed; and the clock is far from the chair. But Albert likes the way they look, better. What has happened is, that because the objects are more separate in a certain way, they are more together. They are close because they're apart. In other words, separateness is not fighting togetherness.

All of us, in a way, are separate from the world. We seem to end with our bodies. If our neighbor, only half a foot away, has a nail in his shoe, we might know about it; but we don't feel it the way he does. If a bed companion blows his nose, our nose is unblown. A blister on a finger touching ours is not our blister. And we seem to have a whole secret manufactory of all kinds of views, impressions, perceptions, outlooks, considerations, desires—all for ourselves, alone. So we are alone in our blood and our bones and our thoughts. It seems we are separate, if we want to feel that way.

And yet we can look out. Not a thing fails to act on us, once we think about it. To think about something means that it acts on us; for when our thoughts are about anything, this thing has changed our minds. We cannot live without ever so many objects, from everywhere. The ground we walk on is unthinkable as not being. Our food is a neighbor which becomes ourselves. The air is a universal indispensable. And we need people. We may even need them to despise them. Everything is around us, indefinitely close, indefinitely inescapable, indefinitely changing ourselves, becoming ourselves. This means we are not only *separate*, we are *together*.

When things are well or beautifully arranged, in every instance, the side of them which can be seen as separate goes along rightly with the side of them which can be seen as together. We saw this with the five objects first in the moving van and then in the room. No matter how many objects are concerned, two, and only two, opposite things are involved. When we talk of the composition of materials, say, the problem is how to place these materials so that their separateness does not conflict with their togetherness. For *all* objects can be seen as being away from other objects, discordant with them; or as close to them, mingling with them serenely.

So the problem that faces a self is how to make its separateness at one with its togetherness. This is the problem which is underneath all others. It can make for agony and it can make for triumph; it can make for painful jumpiness or mobile composure.

There were five objects involved in the first instance I gave of everyday composition. The following is an instance of two objects: A drum and a clarinet are playing at once. The way they play is plainly different. If the drum tries to play exactly what the clarinet is playing, the result is not good. If the drum plays something too different, wrongly opposed to what the clarinet is playing, the result isn't good, either. It would be disastrous if the clarinet were playing *Tales of the Vienna Woods* and the drum were doing something with *Turkey in the Straw*. It would be disastrous also if the clarinet were playing *Turkey in the Straw* and the drum playing, as much as possible, *Turkey in the Straw* the same way. In the first instance of disaster, separateness would be working against togetherness; in the second instance, infelicity would come from togetherness as against separateness. Still, it is possible that, as can be seen very often in halls where music is played, the clarinet and drum can play different things at the same time (or, if one prefers, play different ways); and it is possible that the difference *make* for togetherness or harmony. In all beautiful arrangements, difference works with sameness, separateness with togetherness.

According to Aesthetic Realism, the self is trying to come into composition with the world, and at the same time be different, individual, separate, free. In the instance of drum and clarinet playing well, the clarinet could be seen as helping the drum and the drum as helping the clarinet; that is, the drum could be seen as independent while having the clarinet help it, and the clarinet independent while having the drum help it.

The world *is* helped by our being in it, for without our personalities, the world would not have used every possibility it has; and the world can be seen as helping us. The fact that we need the world does not mean that we are not free; for when we need something to be free, the need is not disabling.

We can see ourselves as separate from, and as together with, the world. When we see our separateness simultaneously with our togetherness, and working as a neat team, or as one, we are adjusted aesthetically, that is, really. For every self can see what it is, at once as separate, together, and both.

There is aesthetics in numbers. The self can be likened to an addition or a subtraction. In us, always, things are added, subtracted; included, put aside. The two sides of us can be seen as two numbers present in us. We can call these numbers 5 and 7. In the neurotic mind, the presence of 5 is in tormenting conflict with the presence of 7. The unstable person thinks that in accepting 5, he must do away with 7; and in welcoming 7, he must banish 5. So, at times, he welcomes 5 and shows 7 the door. But 7 still persists in being around. So he greets 7 warmly and acts coldly to 5. But 5 won't stay away either, for long. Under many disguises, with many transformations, with many embodiments in ordinary life, this shuttling, fickleness, indecision, is what goes on in the nervous person.

Now 5 and 7 must both exist. They are both indispensable. Neither can be seen as not present; neither can be shown the door. The question is, how can both be welcomed? How can the separateness and the togetherness be, at once, neatly maintained?

Simply by seeing them together as 12. Suppose 5 and 7 are seen as 12. You can see 5 separately in 12. You can see the disturbing elements of 5 destroyed, because when 5 has added 7 to it, 5 is destroyed by becoming 12. You also can see 5 as completed by becoming 12. Furthermore, you can see 7 separately in 12. You can see 7 as destroyed by having 5 added to it, and changed into 12. You can also see 7 as completed by having 5 added to it. And, as I said, you can see 7 and 5 quietly, harmoniously, serenely, as one, in 12.

The destruction of 5 by 7 in 12 is an aspect of the separateness of 7. The destruction of 7 by 5 in 12 is an aspect of the separateness of 5. When these numbers become 12, they can be seen also as together. And when a number is seen as completed by the other, there is also separateness with completeness. Anyway, the making of two warring numbers, 7 and 5, into 12, implies separateness and togetherness working together. Here mathematics can be seen as art.

If, instead of the numbers 5 and 7, deep notions of freedom and security are troubling a person, the solution is the same. A neurotic cannot feel he can be free and secure at once; he does not feel he can be free while accepting "discipline" or security.

Timothy Watkins wants to feel he can do as he pleases; that he can relax just like that; that he does not have to put his nose to the grindstone constantly. Yes, Timothy Watkins is against what he sees as restrictions. But, troublesomely, Mr. Watkins finds also that he wants order and routine; that if he does not do something at a specific time, he doesn't feel so good; and that the notion of insecurity frightens him; and the lack of a "system" irks him. And he feels that if he "plugs" for freedom, routine will go to the dogs, or worse; and he will be a disorganized person. Yet he feels, too, that if he chooses routine unquestionably, he will lose his personality; will be smothered by a pattern; crushed by a grind; become a dull human mechanism.

The question confronting everyone is: Is it possible for a human being to do truly as he pleases, to give adequate regard to the intense uniqueness of the moment, to show his instincts (including the primeval), his impulses, his drives, his untrammeled personality—and at the same time satisfy his sense of order, of precision, of stability, of responsibility, of justice? Aesthetic Realism says, Yes; and wants the yes implemented.

For, if the world does not permit freedom and routine to function simultaneously, while making a person want both, it is profoundly inviting ethical chaos, psychic disturbance, universal neurosis. An agonizing see-saw would follow; the world would be unjust. The drive towards freedom and the drive towards precision exist deeply and permanently in the human being: neither can be eradicated; neither can be played off against the other; neither should be nor has to be.

Lacking the aesthetic attitude, persons sometimes lop off some of the drive towards freedom, sometimes lop off some of the drive towards order. Persons vary from the rippling, blown wave to the fixed rock. There is a sad shuttling through life. It should be seen that none of the basic impulses is bad. The discomfort does not come from the impulse itself, but from its disproportionate setting off against another impulse. Who would say that freedom is a bad thing? Who would say that order is a bad thing? Who would say that these weren't basic states of the human mind? If eye and toe can go together in a human body, why can't abandon and restraint?

The only reason why people think that freedom and order can't go together is because they look on opposites necessarily as antagonistic, not as useful to each other, or kind to each other. Negative and positive in the electron are opposed to each other, but they certainly couldn't get along without each other; they certainly are inter-helpful. Woman and man are in a sense opposed to each other, but they certainly can be useful to each other. Sky and ocean are quite different, but there is a kind of general assistance given by one to the other.

One of the most necessary alterations of the present day human mind, is the changing of the feeling that opposites have to fight, that they can't exist as one. Many, many people seeing opposing drives in their minds, feel they have to choose one or the other; and curse the one they don't choose. This is deeply foolish, but it goes on in every State of the Union, and elsewhere.

Aesthetics is not foolish in this way. It points to glorious good sense. It points to an exciting friendship of different ways of mind. Every aesthetic thing, or beautiful thing, or artistic thing, has freedom and order; has to have it, or it wouldn't be aesthetic. A beautiful thing made by man shows that the world gives persons an unlimited chance for tingling good sense. Does a great painting have freedom and order? If a painting didn't have freedom in it, could we call it great? If it didn't have order in it, could we call it great? Does it have freedom at 4:10 P.M. and order at 4:20? Hardly. It has freedom and order at once. And one feels like asking, What is it that painting—coming from the human mind—can do which the human mind itself can't do? A person can ask about a picture, What has it got I can't have—or shouldn't have?

A novel, in essence, has the same thing as a painting. A novel is one thing and many things, that is, it is a whole and parts. And whole and parts are working together. In a good novel you see a certain precision, "has-to-be-ness," or inevitability—that is, there is order in a good novel. And in a novel, too, you feel the characters act freely, the writer is not constrained; there is growth and there is strangeness in the novel: what this means is, the novel has freedom. The freedom and order are to be seen in every chapter; indeed, they can be seen in every sentence. Freedom and order, in a good novel, have their hands, in friendly fashion, on each other's shoulders.

It can be said definitely that wherever there is composition making for beauty, the problem of the neurotic mind is solved in outline. Even if the composition is in a very small field, that presence of freedom and order at once can be seen. Perhaps this can best be exemplified in a single line of poetry. I choose a line from Shelley's *Ode to the West Wind:*

Oh lift me as a wave, a leaf, a cloud!

This line has a definite order: in a certain sense it is as definite as bookkeeping. It has ten syllables. These syllables can be divided into five pairs of two each. The first syllable of each pair is unaccented. The second is accented. (So the line can be read, though some might demur at accenting the word *as*. The demur here I think is incorrect.) The line is what is technically called an iambic pentameter; that is, a line of ten syllables, five feet, with the accent falling on each second syllable.

With metrical scansion, the line appears as:

Oh lĭft | mĕ ás | ă wáve, | ă léaf, | ă clóud!

The line arranged this way still has all its freedom. There is a metrical beat, a pause, on the word *lift;* on the word *as;* on the word *wave;* on the word *leaf;* on the word *cloud.* Yet there is motion in the word *lift;* there is uncertainty in the word *as;* there are ripplingness and speedy curve in the word *wave;* there are height and lightness in the word *leaf;* and there are greater height and airiness in the word *cloud.* The line rises from the word *lift.* There is a going towards the sky from the word *wave.* All this happens *while* the words themselves, like grenadiers, or bricks, or pillars, are precise, fixed, methodical, even statistical. All this comes to the fact that in the line of Shelley I have quoted, the mind of man can find security and adventure, exactness and unrestraint. The line is, in the best sense, mightily adjusted; all the psychiatrists in America can learn from it.

A great deal has been said of the closeness of life to art. The question is, whether art gives order, intensifies life, makes it greater. If art makes life greater, cannot what is in art be used as a means of making life more sensible? Life in other words, makes art; cannot art be used in turn on life; and how?

There is no limit to how art can be used to make life more

sensible. To see art as making life more sensible it is first required of one that he respect art, know what it is, not make it less than it is.

Art, Aesthetic Realism believes, shows reality as it is, deeply: straight. All art does that. The possibilities of reality *are* reality. The more we see reality as having order and strangeness, form and wonder, the more reality we are seeing. Art is a way of seeing reality more by seeing it more as it is.

It is well at this point to take another line of verse, another iambic pentameter. The line is:

> The twisted branches of the knotted oak.

This line has the same meter as the line of Shelley. The feeling or substance of it is different. It doesn't go swiftly to the skies. Its motion is different. Presented metrically, the line is:

$$\breve{}\ /\ \ \breve{}\ /\ \ \ \breve{}\ /\ \ \breve{}\ /\ \ \breve{}\ /$$
The twist | ed bran | ches of | the knot | ted oak.

Again, there is order. The accented syllables fall regularly. There is a statistical division in the line. Still, the line goes all over the place. It seems confused. It is twisting. It curves. It has knots. It seems to be against symmetry. But symmetry is there. The words like *twisted, knotted, branches,* even, are placed in terms of sound with precision. In listening to the line we hear precision and helter-skelterness at once, confusion and correct numbering. The question is, whether the line's being both confused and precise is of reality.

It is. Is not reality confused and orderly at once? Does it not have storms and crystals? Are there not jungles and ordered grass? Isn't the body of an animal organized and changeable? Isn't the sky fixed and moody? Don't events occur both by law and with unpredictability? Isn't the world limited and unlimited? Doesn't mind go by cause and effect, and yet strangely? Isn't everything in reality both strange and definite, existent yet endless?—Well, if reality is two things at once, if a poetic line is two things at once, can't we say that the "dilemma" quality in reality is captured, dealt with wisely, in a line of good verse?

Aesthetic Realism believes that reality as such is aesthetic: that is, it is both free and definite. If we don't see it that way, we are not seeing reality as it is. And since the purpose of psychiatry is to see reality as it is, it should be the purpose of psychiatry to have people (including psychiatrists) see reality as being logical beauty.

All the problems in aesthetics are of immediate, lasting importance for mind. Every aesthetic question is a "must" for human happiness. Let us consider the Shelley line again:

Oh lift me as a wave, a leaf, a cloud!

Suppose I change the line to:

Pray elevate me as if I were a wave, or a leaf,
or a cloud.

It will be seen that by making the line more relaxed, more diffused—less definite—I have also taken away the "lift" or freedom in it. The freedom in the Shelley line depends on its precision, its economy. By altering the precision, adding superfluity, I have taken away the speed, the ardor, the might in motion of the line. Too much in the way of words here makes for too little. The music is gone. Style has left; and with it, the great good sense the line had.—And aesthetic mistakes or deficiencies are like life mistakes or deficiencies. All "adjustment" is a rhythm of definiteness or neatness of self with suggestion or freedom, just as a good line of poetry is.

The psychiatry of the future will look at art zealously, constantly, with the utmost respect and cognitive love. It will find, for instance, in that separation and togetherness in the tango, a guide to the problem of leaving and remaining, far and near, aloofness and huggingness, there is in the self. Every good dance, every good symphony, every good picture, every good short story, every good ballad, will serve as a guide to what humans want, how they can be richly sane, how they can live truly and with meaning.

Every work of art is a problem in being oneself and being other, being *here* and being *there*. As I have mentioned, the solution of this problem is to be found in the procedure of the tango. When the partners are close to each other, they have in mind the long steps away; there are a constant procession and interaction of intimacy, steppings aside, definite departures. However, the intimacy, the steppings aside, the departures, all have one purpose. They all help each other. There is not a rift among them. Their being different makes them the same in so far as their being different has one end—the order and excitement of the dance.

Beauty has not been respected sufficiently. The word *beauty,* even today, has a delicate, frail ring to it. If you talk about beauty, you are regarded by many as not being tough-minded. This should stop. Beauty has to be seen as complete logic, good sense carried further than usual: resplendent sanity.

The moment when beauty comes to be in a mind, is a moment where unconscious and conscious have met well. Beauty shows what we want; and the unconscious is, most deeply, what we want which we don't know we want. The unconscious is also what we don't want which we don't know we don't want. The unconscious is always looking for an expression or embodiment, which we can *see*. What we haven't been aware of, or what we are not aware of, we become aware of as we give aesthetic form to things. It is important to see that every grammatical sentence has a kind of beauty to it; and that when we freely use a good sentence, or talk with form, the unconscious desire for order in change we have, has been embodied in such a way we can consciously be aware of it.

It is a belief of Aesthetic Realism that the unconscious and conscious are acting together in mid-afternoon when we rather calmly talk of ordinary things to acquaintances; and that the unconscious is every moment of our lives functioning, and possibly functioning with order.

Psychoanalysis has helped to make a disjunction between flesh and form. The sensual has been opposed to the logical. The fact that in a painting of Rubens, say, a fleshly, naked woman can be given form, points to the possibility of seeing the voluptuous as intellectual. The reality that made an attractive body also made possible the logic that may be in a mind looking at that attractive body. One of the purposes of art is to have the intellectual felt concretely, even sensually; and to see the sensual as having possible form. Aesthetic Realism says it is one person who can desire a woman and theorize about cube roots. Aesthetic Realism says that the body of a person functions in both desiring a woman and theorizing about cube roots; and that since the body does, the self does.

No person will be at ease, deeply, or fully happy about sex, unless what his body does is at one with form. Wherever sex makes for division—no matter how much a person may know physiologically about it—it hasn't been seen wholly as it is. Sex in man goes towards aesthetics, and has to go towards it.

I have dealt earlier, with two fairly ordinary human beings. These persons, Harold Jamison and Louis Robinson, had problems which in their largest meaning were the problems all art faces. The same kind of problems is had by Hilda Rawlins, distressed young lady living on Central Park West, Manhattan. Miss Rawlins' distress arises from her not being able to manage the problem of unity and diversity in her. Sometimes, Hilda has a corrupt and intense drive towards the unity, the purity of herself. It is then she doesn't want to see anybody. She wishes to stay in bed. She is not interested in the events of the world, or in the events of her friends' lives. Newspapers, to her, are abhorrent. The idea of seeing a show is repellently remote, hardly to be thought of. The notion of going to a party is painfully impossible. The reason for all this is, that Hilda Rawlins wants to have herself "definitely," unstainedly, unalloyedly. Her unconscious feels that the only way to have herself unpolluted by externalities is to deny externality; spurn it, put it out of her life, even annihilate it.

Still, her larger unconscious self knows that this is no way to attain the unity of personality, no way to integrate, sustain selfhood. For in Miss Rawlins' mind, as in other minds, there is a co-existent tendency towards manyness, the heterogeneous earthiness of things. Hilda isn't calm about this tendency, either; for she sees it as the enemy of the tendency towards unity, and doesn't want to see the two tendencies together.

On June 4th, Hilda went to bed feeling—quite sincerely —ill, and told her mother she did not wish to answer telephone calls, receive visitors, or read letters. Even books were looked on with disfavor by the profoundly recoiling Hilda. She remained in bed until June 9th, talking to no one except her mother, and with her curtly. Glumly, she received medicines given to her by a young lady hired for the occasion. Hilda's bed was her universe, with the addition of a stretch of floor and the bathroom. Outwardly, she wasn't happy; but the narrow unconscious, or 2-A, had taken her over, and that, in its subterranean fashion, was triumphant.

Nevertheless, Hilda, being human, had that in her which needed more than herself. The fight between the two aspects of herself was always going on, and had been going on. On June 9th, the strength of the unconscious forces altered. The fight had been going on, unknown to Hilda. The outcome of the fight, however, seized upon her. On June 9th, Hilda had a sudden desire to see people, to talk to them, to have them near, near to her. She flung the bed clothes off her. She called up friends. She talked buoyantly, raptly. She went out. On the subway, she was interested in everybody. She wanted to grab everybody to herself. If she didn't know *everything* about a person, she felt bad. She was tremendously agog and curious.

At a party, Hilda had a smile for everyone. She asked questions eagerly. She showed untiring interest in everyone to whom she was talking, and she talked to many. She wanted to put her arms around the whole, encyclopedic universe. This breathless participation of Hilda in everything she met went on for four and a half days. Late on June 13th, Hilda felt strangely tired. She went to bed feeling sad. A vague fear was in her mind. She had faintly, but pervasively, a headache.

The next morning, Hilda declined an invitation. She talked somberly to her mother. She was interested in death, and talked about it with Mrs. Rawlins. The next days, Hilda was mournful. She wasn't impolite, as she had been before; but she was confused, waveringly aloof. Once, with her aunt who came to see her, Hilda was abrupt and rude. Ten minutes later, she meekly apologized. Life at this time for Hilda was criss-cross, winding up and down, unformed. She began to think of God, religion, and even thought of going away somewhere to lead a selfless, religious life, doing nothing but helping other people.

Three moods were present in Hilda Rawlins' self. One of these moods was fiercely exclusive; it wanted to achieve ego contentment by keeping out, forgetting, negating. The other was excessively acquisitive, grabbing disproportionately, possessively aware of all things unknown, all things not Hilda. The third was a bad mingling of the first two, making Hilda tired and mournful. In this mood she wanted to present herself "selflessly" to "God"; she could lose her apparent outward self, but have her unconscious ego; the fact that this was not acceptable to her whole personality "slowed" her up.

Had Hilda been aware that she could have herself as one thing, while it was meeting all kinds of situations and persons and objects, Hilda would not have had to stay in bed, would not have had to be rapturously grabbing, and she would not have had to be confusedly, incompletely religious. Hilda's self, like all selves, is an aesthetic proposition. By this I mean the questions she had to answer about what she was, are the questions a working artist has deeply to answer. Hilda asked herself without knowing it—and therefore did not completely ask it—How can I be a unity with detail? How can I be in motion, yet stable? How can I be perfect and imperfect? How can I be known and unknown to myself? How can I be I and other than I? How can I be a changing composition and a fixed singleness?

At every moment in her life, the whole self of Hilda was a definition and a mobility, an intimacy and a remoteness. Hilda's life, however, had made it so that these two aspects of herself were seen as separate selves. Hilda was never able to see, just so, that her meeting of people, her listening to them, her reading of books, was the *means* of having herself as such. Hilda wanted to be Hilda and nothing less, or more; she also wanted to be popular, go out, experience things. She had never asked clearly: Is the Hilda that acts with people *just* the same Hilda that thinks to herself? Is the Hilda under her skin, so warm, so taking-care-of-herself, the same Hilda that laughs at another's joke, pours tea for a strange young man, calls up a publisher on behalf of a good cause? She hadn't asked, was it the same Hilda who allowed her hand to be held by Stan Hayes for fifteen minutes, as the Hilda who thought about Stan Hayes while she was lying in bed? She had never asked was Hilda's Hilda the same as other people's Hilda?

The self is indefinitely deep and indefinitely extensive. It is vertical and horizontal. It is an ineluctable unity while it is constantly mobile. Hilda had not seen that the deep Hilda was also the extensive Hilda; that her vertical self was also her horizontal self; that the unity of Hilda was also her mobility. She had placed the static aspect of her personality against the dynamic.

There is not a pair of opposites I have used which is not relevant to Hilda's pain and pleasure, depression and exaltation; and also to the procedures and aims of art.

Art is internal and external. The repose a person feels in aesthetic creation comes from his, for the time, feeling he is what he is and also what he is not. Ego and otherness don't fight for the while. The artist feels he has reached form in the deepest places of his personality, because things outside himself have been seen courageously, truly, respectfully by him.

Neuroticism is corrupted knowledge. Art is complete knowledge. There is a tremendous correspondence between the very unlimited depths of personality and the astonishing universe in its suddenness, its ordinariness, its surprisingness, its concreteness, its boundlessness. The depths, the real depths, of self, are the world. The further we know what these depths are, the further we know what reality is. The last point in the unconscious of the human being meets the meaning of an everyday object in its completeness.

Could, therefore, Hilda see an inkstand or a friend or the sky utterly, she would be having herself. If she is afraid to meet an object utterly, it is because she is afraid that in doing so, instead of having herself more, she would lose her precise and warm Hilda-ness.

If one meets an object utterly, he sees it with unrestrained verticality and horizontality, definition and comprehensiveness. As our mind goes towards an object, works on it, so our mind is. We are the way we know.

Now Hilda had the vertical aspect of herself and the horizontal. Everyone has. The vertical line is a symbol to the unconscious of the self alone; the horizontal, of the self going out. Our selves go towards the precision of a line seen as nothing—for a line can be thought of as not being at all —that is, simply as a line. The down and up motion of a line is like the ego given to nothing but itself. The horizontal line also is like nothing, but represents the ego going out, as an *off-set* to verticality. Were the vertical line to become one with the horizontal line, narrowness, width, and height would exist at once; and further, were width and height to become one, the motion continued would make for a square, then a cube; and if a point in a line were completed, with both dark and light, it would make a circle.

What I have just written is, of course, abstract. Still, it can be said that the self is a point; a line, both vertical and horizontal; a square; a cube; a triangle; a circle. Somewhere, this is practical.

The personality of everyone is both solidity and space. One way of saying space and solidity is mind and body. At any moment, if we try, we can see our feelings, which are in a sense all we know, like space; they are not solid, as feelings; they can't be touched, as feelings. And we have a body. The feelings of our body, which is ourselves, are form; the body can be seen as weight.

In aesthetics, various geometric forms meet. Solidity and space also become one. In that aspect of ourselves which is our body, it is clear we can find all the forms I have mentioned: a sphere, a cube, a cone. In the space quality of our feelings, we can find all the other forms: the point, the line, the square, the triangle, the circle.

The aesthetic problem I have accented with Hilda Rawlins is that of singleness and manyness, or oneness and diversity. In her, or concerning her, are all other aesthetic problems. The things that make art, go together. If they are present in a person, they are present in their multiplicity and completeness.

If a person, for example, were to be completely happy, body and form would be entirely at one. The most graceful body acts *as if it were not a body*. When a person is happy, he is likely to say: "I feel light as a feather." However, he knows that he's present to himself and all others in his, perhaps, 160 pounds. In all bodies, there is a tendency to absence of body: that is, form.

Further, it has been said that a completely good digestion would mean one we did not have to be aware of; one we did not have to think about at all. Yet, it is apparent, it would be well for a person having a good digestion to know that he had it. In this situation of being able to be unaware of a bodily state and yet to know that it exists, there is that beautiful combination of naiveté and subtlety, spontaneity and awareness, unconscious and conscious, that makes art.

And then there is the problem of slowness and speed—

in everything and everyone. Sometimes, Hilda talks too fast. At other times, words come painfully, draggingly. What this means is that in her there is a warring of basic speed against basic slowness. An aspect of rhythm, or of form in time, is the feeling of speed in slowness, slowness in speed. When music is good, there is a sense of motion and of pause. A play is good when we think things are happening, and yet there is something meditative, large, easy, spatially quiet. When we feel that something is speedy and quiet at once, we feel something beautiful. That is why, if Hilda comes to be entirely "well," she will have put in her personality a presence at once of slowness and speed, meditativeness and agogness, akin to that which we can find in a good concerto, in a good one-act play, in a good bit of choreography, in a good moving picture.

Sometimes, Hilda has yearned for what has been called the "simple life." She also has wanted to be in a constant round of New York social complexities; wanted things to happen; wanted to see new things constantly; wanted to be in a whirl of excitement, going places, even intrigue. Well, this desire for both simplicity and complication is also seen in what art goes after, what it has to meet if it reaches what it goes after. Every work of art has largely succeeded with the problem of simplicity and complexity. Some works accent one, or seem to be one, offhand; but they all have both.

For how can a thing really be simple unless there is a chance, felt somewhere, it could have been, or is, complex, too? Simplicity, without the likelihood of intricacy, would hardly be satisfying. If, for example, a symphony seems complex, it is simple also as much as its complexities have been arranged rightly. And if a song seems simple and is a good or great song, its simplicity must have suggestion, many sides, richness to it, if its simplicity is to be other than thin, pretty-pretty, false.

The self has in it the drive towards simplicity, for it must be one. It has in it the drive towards multiplicity, for the world is various, and the self grows by meeting more and more and arranging this more and more.

It is incumbent, therefore, on Hilda Rawlins, that she feel herself to be as simple as a pebble and as complicated as a Demerara jungle, at once. The self is that way: wants to be that way; has to be that way. The problem of simplicity in the self won't be dealt with sufficiently if Hilda decides to go to some farmhouse, eat cream, avoid complicated books, eschew the telephone, go about in dungarees, and lie on the grass looking at nothing but the blue sky. She won't become really simple by making much of nakedness, "nature," and undisturbed devotion to the soil. That is not the simplicity the human personality is truly satisfied with.

It should be asked: Does the self want much diverse experience? Ah yes, in all of us can be discerned, affirmed, a desire to avoid intricacy, to make life as neat, as simple as possible. But if we don't stop looking at ourselves, we can also find a desire for unlimited experience: "for life and more life and yet more life"; for subtle and delicate adventure. These possibilities of the self are both to be met. So what are we going to do? Be simple in the summer and complicated in the fall; avoid intricacy in the morning and welcome spiritual adventure in the afternoon? This won't work. People have tried it and come to dislike themselves for their pains. The metaphysical, or aesthetic obligation faces us of being simple and intricate at the same moment, in the same hour, in the same day, in the same life.

The history of art shows that there is a true beauty in simplicity and a true beauty in complexity. A novel like *Robinson Crusoe* is beautiful. Tolstoy's *War and Peace* is beautiful. The simplicity of the Twenty-third Psalm is good;

the ornateness of Swinburne's chorus from *Atalanta,* "When the Hounds of Spring," is good. Complexity, however, is also in Defoe's novel; and simplicity in Tolstoy's multitudinous work. The Twenty-third Psalm has in its plainness a richness, diversity, unexpectedness of rhythm. Swinburne's "When the Hounds of Spring" has, along with its swift ornateness, its flashing changes of rhythm and word, a driving simplicity of structure.

In mind, wherever simplicity does not have richness to it, the simplicity is thin, not real. Our unity must come from a multitudinous welcoming; otherwise it is too easy, exclusive, timid, artificial, unhealthy.

And Hilda has wanted the strange; and she has wanted the homely, the "comfy," the close. She has had thoughts of spending the rest of her life with her mother and a cousin in some neat, unpretentious place. She has also wanted to go to Africa, to Fontainebleau, to Rome, and see the sights and objects there and in other places. She enjoyed having tea and cake with her mother one day, and had a decided yearning to visit the interior of Australia the next.

These things happen: they are a phase of the "realism-romance" problem as it is in the human mind; it is also the problem of ordinariness and strangeness as we find it in the history of art. And all great art or true art is strange and ordinary, wonderful and matter-of-fact; strange, perhaps, because of the *way* it is ordinary; matter-of-fact because of the *way* it is wonderful.

There is not a basic problem that the minds of Harold Jamison, Louis Robinson, and Hilda Rawlins face, which is not deeply, most clearly, a problem of art. When willed beauty—which is art—is understood, it will be seen as always with us, never rightly to be put aside: inevitable. Beauty is good sense. It is hard good sense. It takes all of us in. If we wish to be really well, let us understand it.

4

The Organization of Self

The Organization of Self

A LONG with the commonly expressed desire to be "adjusted" there is the desire to be "organized." Being organized is certainly considered as a necessary achievement, but the precise meaning of the terms "organized" and "organization" are not too eagerly sought. I have not found much precision in the dealing with various fundamental terms: and "organized" is one of these.

When a person desires to be "organized" he feels that he can be more comfortable, respect himself more, and do away with some of the things displeasing or perhaps feverishly annoying him. In the going towards organization, however, he may decide to destroy things which are necessary for organization to be real. The common procedure in seeking method in self, or discipline, or order, is to exclude; to decide that some traits or attitudes are villainous, deleterious, and have to be put out of existence. Such a procedure, as I have implied, is very dangerous. For true order, true discipline, true organization, is not only denial, it is inclusion; it is not only diagram, it is imagination; it is not only pattern, but color. The neurotic is just as much after organization as anyone; he is so insistent on an idea of organization that he is willing to destroy, at various times, some of the things which have to be organized. He is ready to give up comprehensiveness for pattern.

We make organization stand for the unity to be achieved.

The unity is considered as apart from the manyness which is to be brought into order. There is a fear that if we *include* this, then an efficient arrangement within us will be interfered with. We hold ourselves, therefore, immune, as much as we can, from certain experiences, people, or objects. In doing this, while we think we are adjusting self, we are crippling it.

The first thing necessary in coming to an organized attitude towards the world is to include all the materials needed for organization. We could hardly build a complete chair without enough lumber; we could hardly construct a machine without including all its parts. We, therefore, come to an idea of organization as meaning unity through comprehensiveness, selection through inclusion. Were we really to organize ourselves, we would go through the process by which a picture becomes a stirring composition, a drama neat yet opulently representative of life, and a poem taut yet replete with unexpected suggestion. For the idea of organization is one inseparable from the logic of aesthetics. If a person is to be organized he has to be one and many; he has to be simple and complex, a point and a series of relations.

Edgar Hutchins, living in the Middle West, is taken periodically with the desire to organize himself. He has a notion that many of the things he has been doing are incorrect and —though the God of his Episcopalian fathers is no longer his—evil. When Mr. Hutchins is going through one of his self-critical and reorganizing periods, the chief thing in his mind is how to do away with traits or habits. Were he asked to reorganize a factory or a machine, he would in some fashion try to see the factory or machine as it was. But Mr. Hutchins, when it comes to reorganizing himself, goes by a previous notion of what he is and should be. He has come to a pattern before he has been willing to reach full knowledge. How can one, in other words, really reorganize oneself if one is afraid or unwilling and therefore unable to see oneself?

The question is, Can one organize oneself or reorganize oneself without knowing oneself? Let us assume that a person thinks that he wishes to bring order and accuracy into his self and yet is afraid to see all of himself; for he unconsciously thinks that if he sees every detail of himself he might find something which would distress him. Edgar Hutchins is one of those persons who wishes to bring form to his life and yet does not wish to see fully what that life is. For what does it mean—to know oneself? How can we do this while we don't know even what should be known? Mr. Hutchins does not care to see what he is in relation to objects in general; he would see this as metaphysical, useless—definitely impractical. What he wants is the following of certain formulas by which he can be toughened and take on a formidable symmetry to meet the contingencies of existence. Still, Mr. Hutchins *is* in relation to a large and multitudinous world. Can our middle western American, therefore, organize himself while unready to accept the terms of that organization?

Life in itself makes a constant demand for organization. There may be demands which we, wishing to be neat and practical do not think worth seeing; we go ahead as if they were too remote to be considered. But in the self there is no real remote and no near; what we may look on as distant may be really of tremendous immediacy. It seems, therefore, that prior to any self-organization, the willingness to see what oneself is—no matter where that willingness may lead

—is necessary. Aesthetics has in it the interaction of immediacy and meaning beyond; of nearness and distance; of the familiar and the romantic. Life at its beginning, and in essence, has in it such an interaction. When our midwestern man of business, Edgar Hutchins, was born, the interaction of remoteness and immediacy began. What a baby feels first is its own body, its self; but while it does that, it has no awareness of self in the sense that it has later—in the sense that the worried Mr. Hutchins has it now. The baby feels itself but does not see itself as an object. This means that it has no sense of "I." How does it get this sense of "I"? It gets it in principle by the means which Mr. Hutchins, without knowing it, is spurning; by meeting the world, no matter how outside it may be.

It needs to be seen that for a baby, everything is remote and from one point of view impractical; for the baby had been doing a fairly practical job while within the body of its mother. It was a success and the world was taking care of it; it was exacting its toll from the universe. To a baby just born any object in the room is as remote as Hindu metaphysics, or existence in a galaxy; or the relations of mathematics and dreams to the practical adult. Life, at its beginning, is an interaction of the wonderful and distant with the immediate and intimate. Still, in accepting the remote the baby comes to a sense of self, for it is evident that without external impressions the baby could not be saying "I" a year later. Were Edgar Hutchins, as a baby, to have been kept to himself, simply fed and maintained alive, he would not at the age of fourteen months or so have said "I" and been aware of his life as an object. Why has Mr. Hutchins gone aside from this principle? Is it no longer efficacious? Is he right when he says that we should stick to matters of immediate use and that "we should so organize ourselves that the irrelevant can be rejected at a moment's notice"?

It appears then that the self, as such, depends for its being on things outside it. Were a self to be out of contact with the possibilities of objects there would, in time, be no self. This is true about food; it is also true, deeply, about impressions. This means that when Mr. Hutchins decided that he was to keep himself immune from all kinds of things and nourish his intimate self, he was really working to abolish the life of Edgar Hutchins—intimate self and all. So when, at the age of forty-eight, he is trying to organize himself— as he has tried in the past—and will not do so satisfactorily, it is not surprising. You can't organize yourself if you don't accept all the materials.

Another point in this matter of self-organization is whether emotions are to be organized too. First of all, in most of us, emotions are regarded as interferences with organization and propriety. The difference between the organization that goes on in aesthetics from the organization explicit at least in such matters as department stores, home-budgets, and building-and-loan associations, is that feelings are looked upon as organizable in aesthetics. Aesthetics exists on the supposition that feelings are objects, worthy realities, estimable aspects of the world; and as such can be given precise and fruitful arrangement. In aesthetics feeling and logic make a team; they are not quarreling, competitive boys. When Mr. Hutchins decided to put himself in order, he went about, as in the past, doing it with the assumption that emotions were to be checked, impulses to be docked, and passions in general, neatly to be wrapped and submerged. For, in the Hutchins mind, emotions and organization were like red and green; an Indian brave and a bishop; a storm and fair May weather. The one way he has seen of getting his emotions into shape is by lessening them. It is hardly wonderful, therefore, that since Mr. Hutchins' emotions were just as much a part of him as his conscious attitude towards family, church, and political party, his attempts at self-organization did not even please him.

Every instance of insanity or neuroticism is an instance of disorganization. For wherever there is mental incompleteness there must be disorganization. The insane person has consented to accept a part of his self for his whole self. In doing so he has accepted a malady. In being timid we are not our whole selves. In disliking something because it is new, we are not our whole selves; in being jealous, we are not our whole selves; in feeling that this person or that thing is against us, we are not our whole selves; in not knowing what we should about our life, we are not our whole selves, either. The answer to the question, "What is our whole self?" is a logical and an aesthetic one. The self is a situation and a process; it is a state and a way of motion. When it is seen only as one of these, there may be suffering. When the word "situation" is used, an idea of rest or space is involved; in "process," an idea of motion or time is involved. However impractical it may sound, it would seem, therefore, that to organize a self having situation and process in it, time and space, these mentioned things would need also to be organized. Yet were Mr. Edgar Hutchins to be told that situation and process in his soul were related to his efforts towards self-improvement, he would laugh the aloof laugh of the practical man, but he would be wrong.

To be interested in the organization of one's personal life is impossible without being interested in organization itself. Organization always implies the presence of details and a possible unifying of these details. These details must, in some way, be opposed to each other, otherwise they would be already one. They must have some similarity or their unifying could not take place. In proportion as organization is complete, a self is happier.

In terms of an actual human being, it can be readily seen that from one point of view the details to be organized are all the experiences, impressions, attitudes which are of the person. If anyone looks at himself, he will see himself bristling, radiating, undulating, swarming with a host of responses, impulses, goings forward and withdrawings. Were a self to be organized, a unity would be found among such things as his response to brushing his teeth, meeting his aunt, looking at a building, and suddenly remembering something. There would be a logical junction between himself as dreaming and himself as endorsing a check. There would be continuity between the darkness of his infancy, the darkness of 4 A.M. last night, and the lucidity of a hearty handshake at noon or a staring headline in the evening newspaper. It is apparent that the self is a one; that something ties together an experience of frost, an experience of music, and a wincing at the recollection of someone's name. If we do not accept the opulence of possibilities within us as something which may fortify and accent the continuity or oneness within us, then, despite any asseveration to the contrary, we are really opposed to self-organization.

We come then to the necessity of knowing ourselves by welcoming deeply and exactly the possibilities of the universe. This means that no feeling whatsoever need be looked upon in itself as hostile. Once we decide that a feeling is hostile, there is, to that degree, a consent to the lessening of what we are, that is, a consent to non-growth. Where a person like our Mr. Edgar Hutchins is at fault is in his believing that he can arrive at self-discipline without welcoming a world much larger than the world he is ready to welcome. Where there is fear there can be no real organization.

What can make us less fearful of the prerequisites of self-shaping? We must feel, first of all, that thorough, wide organization is not against us. Could we see that a certain

pleasure follows a real organization of impressions, the unconscious unreadiness to arrive at personal form by comprehensiveness would be lessened. This is tantamount to saying
that unless Mr. Hutchins, or any American, has approvingly
experienced reality as aesthetics, his attempts at self-realiza-
tion will be a failure.

A neurotic is in a painful quandary between security and
growth. He would like to see himself as large as possible, but
meanwhile, he hugs an image of what he is. He thinks that
the one necessity in character-sculpture is to chisel away
superfluities; he does not see that there can be no self-sculp-
ture where the material lacks the adequate dimensions, or
the adequate texture. As the neurotic has come to the belief
that many details are not for him, that they are inimical to
his autonomy, he can hardly grow. He goes deep and then
rises precipitately; he welcomes effusively and then rejects
in horror. Out of all this arises a compound of mechanism
posing as discipline, and frustration posing as discrimina-
tion. The truth is that we are afraid to know ourselves or for
that matter, to know another.

The importance of art is that it enables us to know ourselves thoroughly; without terror. We cannot know ourselves simply by the inventory of impassive qualities. We
must be willing to see our character traits go through fire,
forests, topsy-turviness. Before we can arrange ourselves,
our depths must seem attractive. In art our selves as animals
function along with our selves as calculating. As long as the
calculator in Mr. Hutchins is disjoined from the animal, Mr.
Hutchins won't have his house in order.

Character traits within a person can be seen as remote and
intimate. This division of remote and intimate is fundamental, not only in the self, but in regard to any object whatsoever. An aesthetic creation—any aesthetic creation—is a res-

olution, among other things, of the remote and intimate. When we see a poem carefully, we notice an immediate impact, something as close to us as our noses. If this immediate something were not present, the poem would have no effect on us because the remote, as such, simply leaves us cold. From another point of view, however, the poem is far away, beyond the customary, the familiar, the expected. The poem, stated otherwise, has health in it because the self, being remote and intimate at once, will become organized —that is, consciously, wholly what it is—by finding its likeness in the world it apprehends.

There are instances of mental ailment which are manifested in the patient's finding everything monotonous, boring, lifeless. He cannot abide himself; he wishes to change himself into some remote being like Joan of Arc, a foreign general, a South American banker, or an American hero. Here we have the problem of familiarity and remoteness, or unusualness, finding a pathological solution. Again, as Don Quixote did, a patient may find miraculous, fantastic qualities in a quite ordinary person or object. The like is done by all of us to some degree. It is incumbent on humans, therefore, so to organize themselves that the aspect of their personality standing for the remote function as one with that aspect standing for the familiar and usual.

The realistic and romantic are two concepts which historically and essentially are of aesthetics. A novel, for example, that is great would take persons whom we know in New York, or a small town, or a dull city, or in a hospital, and present them in such a way that we would feel we were seeing things in these familiar persons we had never seen before. The novel would bring the wonderful to the customary. When we do not see or are not ready to see the wonderful in the familiar-real, our personality is not complete nor organized.

There is, for example, Miss Tessie Wilson who is displeased by her environment. She sees it as dull and though
she behaves like a good daughter she feels that her mother
and father are boring, that her relatives are boring, that the
town in which she lives is boring, and that life, as she sees
it ordinarily, is a pretty small thing. She has taken to reading
fiction, which presents life in terms of princesses, heroes
faultlessly attired, raptures beyond the stars, and places different from the town of Titusville. Many women before
Tessie have found that their minds made a leap from the
familiar to a region unquestionably beyond it.

In the sixteen-year-old mind of Tessie Wilson, a cleavage
is proceeding. It consists of a demarcation between, and a
growing incompatibility of, what she sees and what she
thinks she deserves to see. It is very likely that she will meet
a young man who will act towards her as if she were a being
of wonder; for she is now inclined to see love and sex as
making for a miraculous transformation of just dull objects.
The person appealing to the cherished and remote self of
Miss Wilson will, by a logical, spiritual reciprocity, likewise
be endowed with a miraculous otherness. Should Tessie be
compelled to look upon this young man at some time or
other as a hateful person, a person who was an architect of
dreams but also a demolisher, she will become mournful and
bitter. It will not mean that the world she insists on making
wonderful and other will no longer be desired by her. It will
simply mean that this world of her mind is in greater dispar-
ity than ever with the world about her.

Perhaps she will try again, perhaps she will rise from the
depths of bitterness and once more listen to a young man
who acts as if he were her heavenly servitor; perhaps she will
marry this young man. It is likely (for this has happened
many times) that the wonder with which she has endowed
her husband will run out and that she will be forced to rely

on herself, unassisted, in the construction of a strange world; a fair world; a benign world; a romantic world taking the place of the immediate one. By this time disillusionment in all its modifications and vicissitudes may affect the mind of Tessie deeply. Her bitterness may become profound; her dislike of the world possess her more wholly. At this time she may cultivate a tendency to see herself as someone else; to feel that she should have no concern with such things as kitchens and babies and husbands, that she has a mission beyond the serving of food, the kissing of tired husbands and the welcoming of acquaintances.

The actual and familiar will then be in diseased opposition to the remote and romantic. Schizophrenia will have resulted from the consent of a personality to live in a world of her choosing rather than the world apparently chosen for her; schizophrenia will have resulted, in a sense, from an unfortunate disjunction of the aesthetic qualities of distant and intimate, inaccessible and present.

Miss Wilson, like Mr. Hutchins, has been organizing her world too much in terms of an element in all organization —separation or distinction. There is a rich, strange world in Mr. Hutchins' personality which he knows very little about and in so far as he does know it, has kept trim and proper. He has given his attention predominantly, if not utterly, to family, sales, neighbors, lodge, political party, and church. He may never realize that his self has continents uncharted, unexplored, disdained. Yet in him there are strange regions corresponding to the fantastic regions in the mind of Miss Wilson. In Mr. Hutchins' case the world uppermost, given most attention, is a world of acquisition, everyday competition, respectability. He may be said to have tackled existence the intimate way. Miss Wilson, despite her being a daughter and a wife, tackled existence—in terms of preponderant spiritual energy—the remote or romantic way. Mr. Hutchins suffers despite his successful embargo of color and perceptive tropics from acute, if formal misgivings which take shape in the reiterated and tormenting desire for what he would call "some real organization." He isn't meeting life at all points, just as Tessie Wilson isn't. They have organized themselves by leaving out, muting, or condemning. Mr. Hutchins will, most likely, not go to a hospital—not, at least, for any spiritual reason. Perhaps his continuous self-proddings may give rise or help to give rise to some physical ailment; perhaps he will now and then show great irritation with his family, or depression; perhaps he will want to take a rest for a few months. Miss Wilson, on the other hand, may go to an asylum. It is possible that a relative of Mr. Hutchins may even be the official in charge of the asylum to which she goes. Yet fundamentally, the "romantic" girl and the outwardly staid man of business suffer from the same malady of self: disorganization by exclusion.

The work of the Russian writer, Chekhov, is relevant to the lives of Tessie Wilson and Edgar Hutchins. Chekhov dealt with plain people factually, and in seeing with some perspective, keenness, largeness—that is, with aesthetic power—these lives, was able to impart a feeling of strangeness, unusualness, even mystery to the realistic and fairly ordinary. That is what aesthetics does constantly. Wordsworth, in his best poems, sticking to plain people, plain events, simple background, was able to create an otherworldly feeling. If a reader does not see in Wordsworth a matter-of-factness and a wonder, then, I believe, Wordsworth isn't being had at all. When Cézanne paints a common fruit he does not add to that fruit qualities which the fruit does not possess; he sees the fruit accurately—with unrelenting accuracy; nevertheless, through his accuracy a something beyond the fruit, a wonder beyond the vegetable is presented. Familiarity and wonder must be, and have been, present in all true aesthetics.

A common phrase of significance to be heard in America is: "It's the gypsy in me." Stout mothers of daughters, in equable circumstances, have uttered it as have, at least in times of revelry, well-to-do members of respectable lodges, mayors, and vice-presidents of state banks. Everyone likes to feel that he or she is on the side of adventure and that somewhere he or she is living dangerously. The stuffiness of routine has afflicted the executive, the public official, the well-to-do matron, along with the mechanic and the factory-worker. We usually take this yearning for the strange as just the by-product of life and give way to it chiefly on vacations, New Year's Eve, and high drinking occasions generally. Still, wherever there is the manifestation of jest there is the dim foundation of some deeper character tendency. All of us have made for ourselves a world apart from the world closely about us.

Even the circumscribed Mr. Hutchins likes to say: "Life is an adventure." In his more deliberate moments Mr. Hutchins is not inclined to accent the adventure aspect of life, yet it is there. He has, for instance, hopes of seeing Egypt, India, Rio de Janeiro, and has talked of spending a few months alone or nearly so in the highest Rockies. That is the way he has given homage to the idea of a large experience. He doesn't know that he has been curtailing and hindering experience. Neither does he know that what he really wants is fought against by himself. He doesn't see that an adequate idea of experience is required if his life is deeply to please him.

If one looks at the word "experience," he finds again a relation of subject and object. Experience is not merely the presence of a human being where action is. It is an action *as it has been changed into what one is or one feels.* Now, just how much experience, and how thorough, is necessary for a human being? If experience in its largest sense does not come to a person, a formal equivalent of insanity is already present. If we do not experience what we should, we cannot be completely what we should; and if we are not completely what we should be, then we are not entirely ourselves; and in not being entirely ourselves, we are not entirely sane. It therefore appears that a definition of experience is a definition essential to psychiatry. One can observe a fear of experience everywhere in the present world. We are afraid of feeling deeply and clearly. Not to be afraid of experience would be unrestrainedly to desire the exact transformation of activities and objects into our own nature. Where this transformation occurs truly is through the aesthetic procedure. And where this transformation does not occur fully and deeply, organization cannot occur.

Let us take our Mr. Hutchins in one of his proposed travels: a visit to Cairo, Egypt. Our traveler wishes, he thinks, to perceive the glamour, the exoticism, the newness of Egyptian territory but, after all, he brings himself along. When he sees a Cairo scene, something in him says: "It is well for this to affect me so much," but if it goes beyond a point, the Hutchins composure will be interfered with. This means that the Egyptian visitor wants to experience things as long as they do not change him too much. For he is afraid of change. Full experience would be the merging of Egyptian sights, people, history, with the being of the traveler. Our traveler, in his exclusiveness, shuns this experience.

Traveling is often a way, seemingly, of acquiring experience and seeking the new, but really a way of shunning a deep and exact experience. We all know of persons who have constantly to be on the move. They are unwilling to change themselves deeply, for they have an image of themselves which they wish to maintain. Yet they cannot bear the idea of not being in some kind of motion, some kind of transformation. They make up, accordingly, for an unseen wish to remain as one is, by ceaseless bustle which may take the form of travel. Organization is a proper seeing of new and old, of past and present. It implies the viewing of experience as a tremendous give-and-take of self and universe in all its forms. It presupposes an absence of fear of the universe; it presupposes, therefore, imagination.

It follows then that not to imagine is not to experience; and not to experience is not to have the materials for self-completion. When I use the word "imagination," I am, plainly, in territory seen as luxurious, unnecessary, or dangerous. Imagination is connected most often with a Homer or a lunatic. It is quite true that psychologists and psychiatrists have told their patients: "You should cultivate your imagination," but unfortunately a patient most often thinks that he already has cultivated his imagination and perhaps too much so. Now, plainly, if one is to cultivate imagination and yet is to avoid the dangers of imagination, some means where he can do both the cultivating and the avoiding has to be presented to him. Should the psychiatrist, Dr. Jenkins, or the psychologist, Mr. Wallis, attempt to show a patient how to use his imagination, giving it scope and health, both Dr. Jenkins and Mr. Wallis would be compelled to become the philosophic, aesthetic critic. They would have to possess and manifest the criteria by which imagination has value.

Our world, realistically or idealistically, is what we take it to be. It can be shown that if what we take it to be doesn't jibe with what it is, miserable calamity may result. Nevertheless, it is our minds to which and through which the world comes. What goes on in our minds is fundamentally our lives. The way we arrange the innumerable and incessant impressions that we get, is what we are. We are up against the question then of what we can do to give true arrangement to our impressions. That is a problem of organization, it is also a problem of imagination; it is also an aesthetic problem.

5

Imagination, Reality, and Aesthetics

Imagination, Reality, and Aesthetics

I N LOOKING at the life of Miss Vanessa Hall of Cleveland, Ohio, we can say that her life is an addition of two factors: Miss Vanessa Hall and whatever is not Miss Vanessa Hall. When she feels bad these two factors are in some arrangement, when she feels good the arrangement may be different but the factors as a whole are the same. When Miss Hall is puzzled, the factors still are the same. When she is in glee, they have not changed; when she is exultant they haven't and when she is sick they haven't. It, consequently, appears that the life of Miss Hall, as it changes, is a change of arrangement and form. That goes for the lives of all of us.

Since form is decisive, basic, in the lives of Miss Vanessa Hall and all Clevelanders and all non-Clevelanders, the idea of form becomes important. It is that idea of form which distinguishes the imagined world of a Shakespeare in *The Tempest*—which an alienist, too, may delight seeing—and the world of a resident of an Ohio hospital. It may be said of a patient in a mental hospital: "His talk is incoherent, less coherent than it was two months ago." It is apparent that the terms "coherent" and "incoherent" have their aesthetic relevance. When the actions of a mentally ailing person are described as "disorderly," even the word "disorderly" is connected with an idea of form. When it is said of a schizophrenic: "He is diseased in his self-exaltation"; and when it is said of a person in business: "He has a constant, healthy confidence in himself," the diseased self-exaltation of the ailing pauper is taken to be quantitatively and *formally* different from the "healthy confidence" of the businessman. Again the word *form* seems important.

If imagination is necessary and inevitable, and if, nevertheless, imagination may lead to catastrophe, then a careful study of that which differentiates felicitous from calamitous imagination is required. Well, that study, by whomever made, if it is on the subject and thorough, will be an aesthetic study. Is not an important psychiatric question: How can imagination be unhindered and beneficial? I have no doubt that it is.

On what is all imagination based? It is based on something known, that is, something which being an object outside a self, has in some way become that self. It should be seen that there is no experience or feeling whatsoever that does not have something of the known to it. Whenever a thing is known the organism knowing it does something or other to it. We desire to know but we also desire to be pleased. Where a new thing seems to be against our idea of comfort or pleasure, it is quite plain that the knowing will be tampered with. The desire for comfort or pleasure, as such, is a phase of the self in its smallness, in its exclusiveness, in its desire to approve of what it is at the expense of everything else. This desire is ineradicable, basic; it is inherent in life itself. It may be described as the self when centripetal. It is the self as converging. The other desire: for the enlargement, the widening, the radiating of self is related to knowing. This is equivalent to saying that truth and pleasure are simultaneous, inherent, indispensable aspects of what we are.

It has been thought over the years that the tendency towards truth and the tendency towards pleasure, like oil and water, ordinary cat and ordinary dog, ice and sun, must battle and that the poor human soul tossed about in the battle, had to take complainingly one side or the other. Freud's psychoanalytic statements about the conflict between the reality principle and the "id," though seemingly protesting against previous notions of the make-up of self, here at least were in keeping with them; decidedly so. I do not believe that Freud's distinctions among the egos are any too lucid or satisfying. What, however, I wish to point out here is the similarity of Freud's ideas at bottom to those had by a 17th-century divine, an 18th-century moralist, or a 19th-century lay writer on ethical questions. When (leaving aside other matters) Freud stated that one aspect of the ego was intent on nothing but its own aggrandizement, its own power, and its own gratification; and that another was more watchful, more regardful of the rights of others, more timid, he was really stating the old idea that there is a selfish and an altruistic principle in us. Freud, with new terminology, was once more saying that the self, going for truth or reality, was opposed to the self going for lustful joys, power, and the showing of its hate for others when they interfered with its sensual and other satisfactions. Freud has implied that two egos (if not three) are in a swirling battle, chiefly unconscious; and has also implied that the battle was in the nature of things; that one could look at it, give it bounds, but that it could not be done away with.

Freud's attitude towards the egos within us, is neither accurate nor complete. In the same way as medicine is a useful background for the study of mind, so is philosophy; and Freud was one of the many who ignorantly depreciated that close and thorough study of the abstract which philosophy is at its best. Ego, as such, is an abstract idea and it is hardly possible to understand an abstract idea while having an aversion for the study of the abstract itself. The egos within us can be unified and are not—inevitably—at war. The self as desiring or imagining need not be in combat with the self as ethical or considering. The animal in us is ready to go along with the cognitive.

Where imagination is wrong ethics will be. One does not have a disproportionate *picture* of the world without having a disproportionate *evaluation*. Further, where knowledge is amiss, imagination will be. The merging of the joyous, the righteous, and the accurate has been a constant dream of the centuries; and it is one dream that has a basis in harsh logic.

We all of us have pictures of the world in our minds—and these pictures are of imagination; the beauty and rightness of these pictures depend on how much we can see the world as what it is.

One of the earliest and most frequent things that can happen to a human mind is to see the world as inimical. The world is a constant partner of every one of us. We are compelled to have pictures of it. When we remember a tree it is the tree plus ourselves that is in our mind; when we remember a person it is that person plus ourselves which we remember; when we remember a happening ourselves have been joined to that happening. Yet it is likely that the object with which, in some way, we are compelled to join ourselves is disliked or feared by us because we feel that giving everything the object has to it, will interfere with our own comfort, prerogative, importance. We don't have junctions with the world; we have collisions or evasions or quarrels.

Dreams are, of course, the best known evidence of the fact that we must imagine. They show that not only do we get impressions but that we combine them, change them, alter them, transform them—that we make them undergo a profound logical masquerade in our minds. Dreams cannot be fully understood until the imagination, as such, is fully understood. The study of the imagination would belong to metaphysics or aesthetics: and Freud and many others have shied away disapprovingly from this study.

First of all, every one of us has imagined a complete world for himself or herself. That world has constantly to run up against the world as it fully is. Our picture of the world is unceasingly in contact with that world from which the picture came. And we all of us have a philosophy. One doesn't get a philosophy by studying it in a learned establishment; one has it by being alive. Is it not important, then, since a philosophy of this kind is inevitable, that it be made as nearly as possible adequate? How can that adequacy be reached?

A most obvious requirement for adequacy in any field at all is the desire for adequacy. We have two general impulses in us: one towards the broad and comprehensive; another towards the narrow and concentrated. I have mentioned previously various conflicts arising from universal points of view. One pair of universal views may be described as the specialized and the expansive. We are all specialists from the beginning in so far as we must specialize in ourselves. The self is, in one sense, the last thing in particularity and uniqueness. This particularity or uniqueness has the job, equivalent to life, of imagining, that is, having *to make act in it* a comprehensive, variable world. The self, however, feels secure when it is intact; and intactness it is likely to see as being achieved only by narrowness or specialization.

In a previous writing *(The Aesthetic Meaning of Psychiatry)*, there was Mr. Daniel Parkinson of the 18th century. Mr. Parkinson imagined a world but imagined it preponderantly by means of one symbol. Imagination fiercely narrowed is equivalent to mania. Imagination of the healthy kind has in it concentration. It must be able, for example, to see a scene with a fierce stripping of needless details, to see a world as symbolized by one thing or a group of things. A symbol is, from one point of view, always concentration. But whereas the symbol used by the miser Daniel Parkinson tended to annul other symbols, a symbol in true imagination will, in its compactness, make for suggestion and richness and universality.

An obsession is a kind of concentration. As I shall show later, obsessions are symbolical punishments that we give ourselves because we feel that what the obsessions symbolize has been neglected by us. It is a kind of diseased concentration making up for an evasion or dislike of objects in their inclusiveness. Where imagination does not possess both compactness and expansiveness, it is that much diseased.

It is true that we imagine what we want. It is also true that one of the hardest things to do is to know what we want; for what we want is our very selves. Whatever we want comes from objects and therefore we find ourselves wanting the possibilities of objects and still perhaps hating those objects. We want to be pleased by things in the world and yet we may hate the world itself. This makes for a terrific interference with the imaginative process. For there can be no healthy imagination that is not based on belief; and there is no sound belief possible without a love for reality; and there is no love possible without the desire to know.

Psychologists of various types—behaviorists and psychoanalysts and orthodox psychiatrists—have dealt with mind but have not, I think, seen the very wonder of mind at its simplest. If one talks of the wonder of mind it is likely that one will be seen as a rapt mystic or some fuzzy pursuer of non-certified dreams. Nevertheless, the having of the slightest impression is, strictly speaking, a matter of wonder. The fact that one can have within his mind a picture of a lake three miles wide which he saw three years ago, is a matter of wonder. For the customary, approved notions of the possibilities of reality do not take care of that problem of dimension and representation that is within the everyday fact of a person's having within himself as he walks a picture of a lake, or a mountain, or a railroad. Were the idea of common wonder more accepted there would not be such a pained, dismissing attitude towards dreams. We must take a wider, deeper, more adventurous, yet more matter-of-fact standpoint as to mind itself.

At the present time in America, wonder and matter-of-fact live on two sides of the railroad. A person behaves with groomed propriety outwardly; but in his bed, or in revery, or in just thinking to himself, there is another world. And these two worlds are seen as neighbors who need never meet. Imagination and aesthetics make for the meeting of wonder and matter-of-fact and therefore if we do not respect imagination and aesthetics consciously, we are permitting the seeds of personality disjunction to operate.

For example, there is Julius Harris, a worker for the federal post office. He is a methodical servant of our government in the post office of Troy, New York. He married early and he has no good, evident reason for leaving his wife. He is a respected member of the post office force of his city. He "kids along" with his fellow workers and sometimes with the patrons of his post office. He has set for himself a notion of social propriety. He likes to put on a dignified front in every situation. He wishes he could have more money, but he feels himself secure. Four years ago Mr. Harris found himself going without sleep for a whole night. But he appeared at work promptly and went about his business. However, the sleepless nights occurred more often. His wife noticed them but he jestingly said: "I guess it is because I know my work too well and really don't have enough to do. I have more energy, maybe, than I can use." When he couldn't sleep, Harris, at times, would start writing. He has had thoughts of writing for many years. He has written some poems and short stories and has studied books on the art of writing. He is quite aware that there is a world of imagination and art.

Despite all the writing that Julius Harris has done, there are some thoughts in himself that he has never looked at. When he was a child he imagined that he was a king of a large island in the Pacific and that whenever he needed them he could summon people from a country nearby and order them to do as he pleased. But if he became tired of them, he could dismiss them to the country where they belonged, just like that. He also imagined quite often that every person in the world was dead; only he was alive. Furthermore, despite the fact that on the whole he has been a meek and faithful husband, he has imagined strange places where he would be alone with the most beautiful women in the world, and in any number. He has imagined invisible penthouses where the most prominently alluring females of the universe were at his beck to do what he wanted with. These internal mental procedures of Julius Harris have gone on for many years. They have been so common that he has not even noticed them. When he writes stories, he sees to it that he does not write about himself. He writes about life in Florida, which he once visited; and life in New York, usually from a satirical and comic point of view. And he has gone in for a strange kind of allegory. He wouldn't think of writing about the post office for anything. He is fond of telling jokes and can be neatly cynical. However, the insomnia of Julius Harris is growing worse.

Imagination, like some other things, begins at home. It is a picture of the world and like the world it must have its immediacy and its distance. It is not something which can be used to make up for the reluctances and deficiencies of self; it must start with the self. But for imagination to start with the self, that self must be seen as of a piece with other things; and Julius Harris is afraid to let imagination implicate *himself*. There is a life of marriage and post office which he is aware of; there is a life in himself and elsewhere which he doesn't want to be aware of. Not wanting to be aware of this life in himself, he makes up for it by manipulating pictures that rise from himself, but do not really show it. His insomnia comes from the fact that the evolving life in himself is at odds with that which he chooses to see as what concerns him. He acts as a friend to people and as a sensible hail-fellow-well-met. But there is a life going on day by day which he has put aside. There is disjunction in the imagination of Julius Harris, and this disjunction has made for his insomnia.

Imagination has fear in it, but it has also the most rapturous desire and the most unlimited hopes. In all hope and fear there is imagination because both hope and fear are pictures of possibilities; and wherever there is a picture of possibility there is the mind molding the world to its purpose.

The mind is in an unremitting, inevitable career towards adequacy. Art and imagination are, like a human self, a matter of including, selecting and shaping. The difference between the imagination of art and the imagination of everyday life is that where in art imagination serves to show the self by showing the world, imagination in "life" is used to make the self comfortable, without necessarily showing it. There is a use of symbol in art which is meant to illuminate and widen the meaning of objects; but symbols, other than accurately artistic symbols, may be used to present yet conceal the ideas affecting a self. The unconscious *in art* is not frustrated or stunted; it is not reluctantly put into action; it is not a means of concealment. It is often so in "life."

For example, Henry Hillard at one time failed to make the statement that would have helped a friend in an emergency. Had he done so Hillard's position in life might have become a little less respectable and comfortable; besides he was jealous of this friend and did not want to please him. When Hillard failed to show courage and fairness towards a person he knew, he thought outwardly: "Well, why should I take a risk for a fellow like that? I have enough trouble taking care of my wife and children, let alone yours truly." But the lukewarm, if not treacherous, friend found himself counting the number of cars that passed a certain point in the afternoon. For some reason he could not go back to lunch, but had to stand at a corner and count just how many motor vehicles went by. He looked at his watch, saw it was 2:40 P.M., and rushed headlong to his office. He found himself, though, at other times compelled to count cars; and once he felt an odd impulse to count stairs. Now Hillard's mind had gone through a kind of poetic simile. The poet welcomes a simile, even though he finds himself driven to accept it, but he sees the simile as *of himself.* He does not look upon it as a weird intruder into the territory of a planned life. Hillard had avoided details and a fair telling of something in which he was implicated; he chose to make it something foreign and unrelated to him; he let it drift because it would disturb him. Yet the disturbance continued though our self-justifying American lawyer did not see himself as worse than other people when he did not go out of his way to tell the facts which would have helped a man he had known for a long time. Mr. Hillard hardly saw himself as a "poet." But, not being able to face the demands of his unconscious as to a certain situation, he went "poetically" through a painful symbol of atonement in outline. His unconscious seized upon the "simile" between clearly presenting details about a happening without murkily dismissing them and going through the one by one counting of moving cars.

A good many "counting compulsions" are a kind of simile-substitute for something we cannot see directly or where it starts. The imagination of Mr. Hillard was fearful. He was not wholly interested in presenting the world clearly and originally and truly; he was interested in being comfortable, but there was more than the desire to be comfortable in an ordinary sense. For sometimes we are only comfortable when we have punished ourselves. This means that Mr. Hillard's imagination was an evasive mingling of the desire to enjoy comfort at the cost of another, and the desire to punish himself for that enjoyment. It was a neurotic compulsion but, as all neurotic compulsions have, there was imagination to it. Had the imagination included both conscious and unconscious, motive and procedure, object and shape, situation and self, it would have been aesthetic imagination. It would not have been painful; it would not have been unhealthy.

Imagination, where it is not corrupt, never arises from failure or frustration. Accurate imagination is courage and sight and joy. The imagination that is fond of detours, given to evasion, and is bent on concealing as much as illuminating, is something other than creative procedure.

A notion has been fostered by Freud and others that art is a substitute for an inability to act; that creation is the resort of the sexually frustrated. This notion, in itself, is enough to make one suspicious of the comprehensive insight of Freud or anyone else advocating it. In the same way as logic may be used by the political blusterer or by the charlatan, or by the adroit defender of doctrines personally agreeable, so imagination can be used for skulking, or ignoble, or weak purposes. Yet it is certainly unwise to attack logic because

the appearance of logic has been given by the adroitly ma-
neuvering. In the same way, imagination should not be
judged by its corrupt mishandling.

Freud does not see that imagination which is complete is
already courage. As I have pointed out, imagination, like
knowledge, is always a matter of object and person. Since
to use imagination on the world implies a comprehensive
love for the data that the world presents, there is really no
evasion of reality in the imaginative process. When a mind
arranges the facts which the world presents to it, it does not
mean that this mind is fleeing from these facts. To make
creation the same as escape is one of the most harmful things
that can be done. It is incumbent on every student of mind
to distinguish between the imagination of a Defoe in *Robinson Crusoe,* or of a Thackeray in *Vanity Fair,* or of a Bennett
in *The Old Wives' Tale,* or of a Browning in *The Ring and
the Book,* and the "imagination" that is carelessly used to
cover every aberration from factual perception. Further, in
order to understand that incomplete, impure imagination
which we may see in the mentally distressed, we must first
see where it is not corrupt. That again means a respect for,
and a study of, aesthetics.

All neuroticism or insanity has in it incomplete or corrupt
imagination. I have mentioned the instance of Mr. Hillard
who used an unwilling imagination in such a way as to make
cars objects which had to be counted. There is Luther Davison who quite often sees the eyes of persons about him
staring fiercely and accusingly. Now Luther has a deep
sense of having done something wrong. He cannot, nor does
he wish to, see what that something wrong is. He cannot see
the thing symbolized by his distressed vision. Could he see
that he hates or has a contempt for people and that something in him is telling him that he is guilty in doing so, then
the compulsory symbol which is the accusing eyes of the

people he meets, would not be necessary. The imagination of Luther Davison arises from an *unwillingness to see,* not from a willingness. Could he accept symbol and thing symbolized, then there would be a mingling of unconscious and will. And where unconscious and will are at one, the premises of art are present.

We have pictures which are pictures not so much of what we want to see as of what we don't want to see. We go through imaginative painful rituals called compulsions, not so much because we wish to imagine truly—which would mean to see truly, but because we do not wish to imagine so. These pictures or obsessions, and these compulsions are compromise junctions of a troubled and dim self with an unwillingly and partially seen world. For example, in the picture which a mother may have of a child lost or run over or injured, there is the imaginative substitute, and the punishing substitute, for the deep feeling which the mother has that the child is not a person in its own right and that if it exists at all, it exists as an annex of herself. The mother has the guilt feeling arising from the fact that she does not wish to see her child as an outside object. She punishes herself and makes up for the unwillingness to see her child wholly, by thinking of the child as dead or lost. This is imagination but it is the imagination of running off. The two parts of the imaginative process, the symbol and what is symbolized, are disjoined. They act together, but there is an unwillingness to see them together. Another example of compulsive imagination is to be seen in the young lady who cannot resist immediately removing a bit of paper that may have fallen on a table, or a speck of dust that she sees on furniture. She must be cleaning her home unremittingly; she cannot stand a greyish appearance on a white or polished surface. She is atoning imaginatively and somewhat painfully, for the unwillingness to show, reveal, or purge herself.

I have used the word "symbol" quite often in relation to the general meaning and activity of imagination. The word itself was in rich existence before psychoanalysis or even current psychiatry. It is always well, when a word is used in a new field, to make its new meaning harmonize, if possible, with the meaning it had in the past. There has been a large to-do about symbols in contemporary mental therapy. But, as elsewhere, the word has been given too narrow a meaning. Everything can be a symbol. When a symbol is used by a person there are three factors in it:

1. Something bound up with the person's particular existence;
2. An intermediate something which is coordinated with the person's particular outlook;
3. The world itself, which somewhere is present in every instance of a symbol.

A symbol everywhere is something used to stand for something else. The purpose of a symbol may be various. We may use a symbol to heighten the meaning of the thing symbolized, we may use it as a substitute for the thing symbolized, and we may use it to conceal the thing symbolized. By the ailing mind a symbol is used, it is true, as a thing standing for something else, but also as a means of *concealing* that for which it stands.

What does it mean when it is said that a symbol stands for reality as a whole? It means that every thing, including a thing used as a symbol, in some way or other, is representative of the possibilities of reality as a whole. For example, if a person fears suddenly that he is going to be drowned, just what does the drowning symbolize? Is it a hidden desire for sex, as some have said? But is sex here the *final* reality to which the symbol points? Now, by none of those who have dealt with sex as a basic and constant and ramified drive in the human ego, have I yet seen sex called The Ultimate Reality. Is it possible that sex itself is a symbol? I think it is. Well!—Could the fear of drowning be a symbol of something else besides sex—even though that symbol, it is true, could include it? Is it not likely that the person who had this fearful vision was expressing a relation to something larger than bodily junction as such? Cannot the unconscious imaginatively and terrifiedly present through a symbol, a picture of a personality in relation to the whole universe? What hinders the unconscious, which after all was caused by the universe in its entirety, from presenting in outline some feeling about that universe? Yes, if it is possible for two eyes to see an outline of the sun, why cannot the eyes of the unconscious perceive in outline existence as a whole?

When, then, is imagination a beautiful and orderly and sound thing? If it is to be orderly, it must have what all order has; it must have unity and detail which serve each other. Further, of course, it must be based on fact. In order, however, for imagination to be based on fact, there must be a belief that fact is free; that knowledge is on one's side; that reality is a companion not a rival.

6
Some Definitions

Some Definitions

I HAVE now reached the point where certain key definitions are in order. These definitions will be in keeping with terms already used, but will, I believe, expand their meaning.

1. REALITY.—I have already remarked that the notion of reality as customarily used is too small. A definition can err just as much in not being *comprehensive* enough as in not being confined enough. It is the purpose of a definition to give everything that a thing has and nothing that it hasn't. It is apparent that the word reality is as wide as any word in our language. It follows then that to deal with it accurately one must give everything to that wideness.

A working definition of reality is: *Everything that can affect one.* Somewhere in the cause of neurosis and insanity anything can take a part; for, whether we like it or no, any phase of the world may operate to change us. The mind, whether it can manage successfully or not all reality, is still affected by it. If this is so, we cannot be too comprehensive in dealing with the causes of mental mishap.

It follows from my definition that as soon as a thing affects one, it is real. This means that a mistake, a delusion, or illusion, in so far as it has an effect, is real. Furthermore, any feeling, no matter how unknown or how remote, if it has an effect on a self, is real. An idea as such is just as real as

a mother, and a dream is just as real as an office to which
one goes daily. In fact, as soon as we state a thing it becomes
real, because in stating a thing we are being affected
by it.

2. FEELING.—Every reality, in so far as it meets a mind,
causes feeling. There is no such thing as mind without
feeling and there is no such thing as feeling not caused by
some reality. A definition, then, of feeling is: *Any situation
of mind taken by itself.* Life is a constant interplay of reality
and mind, and any result of that interplay can be seen
as feeling. The question, therefore, of the unconscious,
is whether there can be conditions of mind or feelings
which are not seen. I think the answer undoubtedly is,
Yes.

3. INSTINCT.—The word unconscious is associated most
often with psychoanalysis or psychology, and the word instinct with biology and physiology. The word instinct is
looked on as something Victorian, and the word unconscious has largely superseded it for modern psychiatric purposes. There would be nothing amiss in this if the two
words were still seen as related.

It needs to be pointed out that all of the unconscious, in
so far as the unconscious is an incitation to behavior, is
instinct. In the minds of many the concept "unconscious"
and the concept "instinct" have been placed in different
mental localities and have been given different percep-
tual wrappings. It is necessary here to make a junction between psychoanalysis and strict biology or, if one prefers,
physiological psychology. My definition of instinct is
simply: *Desire not seen as an object;* and if the unconscious
is *desire,* then instinct and the unconscious are largely
equivalent.

4. DESIRE.—All feelings are desires. There is no feeling which does not have its aspect of *going to* or, if one wishes, its dynamic aspect. Every person, at any one time, has innumerable desires, for he has innumerable feelings. Somewhere in every feeling there is what can be called a position of the self towards its continuance or discontinuance; its enlarging or its lessening; its maintaining or its changing. This desire is of the feeling itself. Desire, then, can be defined as: *Feeling thought of as a cause.* All instinct, the unconscious as a whole, all feelings, all mind are made up of desire.

5. WILL.—Will, like instinct, is one of the older terms. It doesn't have the modern dapper appearance of unconscious, complex, repression, and so on. I may mention here once more that the discoordination of older and newer mental terms has been hurtful to the seeing of mind and disorders of mind in perspective.—It needs first to be seen that all will is desire. There has been a disposition to look on will as something opposed to desire; to see desire as some shapeless thing, furious thing, disorderly thing, which is in a state of war as to will. What is the difference, however, between desire and will? Certainly if a self has will, it has not lost desire. It is evident, in fact, that the desire has grown stronger in will, not weaker. What, therefore, has been given to desire to make it will? Is there anything really "new"; anything decidedly altering? Not at all. The only thing that has occurred to desire in its becoming will is that it has been seen as an object. As soon as a desire becomes conscious it is will. Will can be defined therefore as: *Known desire,* that is, desire seen as an object by the possessor of desire. Will, like desire, can exist without its being completed in action. For example, a person may have a desire simultaneously to get a glass of wine in a nearby restaurant

and to stay at home; and he may have a will to see a friend or go to bed. A corollary from what I have said is that an unconscious desire is one which, for reasons of comfort or ignorance, or both, has not become a will.

6. KNOWLEDGE.—The desire for knowledge is as definitely a desire as the desire for drink, or love, or political power. One knows a desire and one desires to know a desire. Knowledge in a certain sense is unavoidable. To be alive is to know. Knowledge as such is: *Reality had in mind.* I am not now talking of quality or size of knowledge; I am talking of the thing itself. If a person imagines he sees a green skeleton, the possibility of a green skeleton is had in mind. There is some knowledge there. If a person drinks wine there is some knowledge even if it is only the knowledge that the wine tastes so and so. There is no feeling without knowledge.

7. PAIN AND PLEASURE.—All desire is a *going from* or a *going to,* and this implies that state between *going from* and *going to* which is *remaining. Any feeling thought of as something which a self wants to go from, not be in,* is pain. It is not the immediate cause of the feeling, it is the position of the self as to a situation. The first half-pound of meat may be pleasing, the second displeasing because the position of the self has changed. Pain also can be described as any condition of the self in which it does not want to be. Pleasure, then, is: *Any condition of the self in which it wants to be.*

8. THOUGHT.—In the same way as the question arose, Can there be feeling which is unknown, the question can be asked, Can there be thought which is unknown? The answer here is Yes, too; for thought is: *Any instance of mind seen as in action.* A situation of mind is feeling. That which makes

one situation grow into another is thought. There is, though, no essential difference between thought and feeling. Feeling, thought of as moving, would be given thought; thought, seen as resting, would be given feeling.

9. REPRESSION.—The self meets its own desires. The meeting of desire by the self is a cause of pain and pleasure. When the feelings of the self, which are unknown to it, want something, and the feelings of the self that are known to it, for whatever reason, find pain in this desire, there will be the attempt to modify or mute those things in self which are painful to it. It should be seen here that repression, as such, arises from a desire. Repression can then be described as: *The lessening, muting, or annulling of desire.*

10. CONFLICT.—*A position of the self which, meeting another position, causes pain* is a conflict. Conflict may also be described as the having of desires which in their contact make for pain.

11. HAPPINESS.—Happiness is *the feeling that the self is at one with reality as a whole.* The feeling that the will of the self is at one with reality makes for dynamic tranquillity. This is what each self must have as its purpose.

7
Love and Reality

Love and Reality

THE SELF by its very nature is compelled to love reality. The self has to aim after happiness and there is no happiness except by the successful love of reality. Were the self really to get what it wants, its various phases or possibilities would be working as one; and what it was after as a whole would be working as one with all other things. The self, in other words, must find some means of saying that something other than it, is for it, is approving of it.

I am quite aware that if Jim Haskins were told he was trying to love reality as a whole in caring for Miss Edith Ritchie, he might say "Balderdash"; "Nothing of the kind"; "Quit your kidding." And for that matter if the more learned professor of chemistry, Andrew Harding, were told he was in pursuit of reality as a whole in courting the daughter of his teacher, Professor Simons, he, too, might say, "None of these soaring, needlessly philosophic outlooks." Still, sometimes the only way to be completely factual is to be philosophic. There was a time when Jim Haskins had not heard of Edith Ritchie. He now thinks (and in fact has told Edith) that if she loves him, "The world is mine." Sometimes Jim is swept by a feeling which goes beyond his toes and his ears, and which he regards as the grandest thing in the world. He does not see this feeling as close to the material in his philosophy course at college, but it is. For Edith Ritchie, as she may deserve to be, has been taken by him as a symbol of the whole world and when his self meets through her body the self of Edith Ritchie, something of that world which she symbolizes comes to him; not lucidly perhaps, not cognitively, not in the form of a spiritual blueprint; but still, however accompanied by fuzziness, that something represents the world. Love is a tremendous instance of that insistent possibility of symbolism of which I have spoken. Indeed, sex is basically philosophic.

Why, if Edith should be aloof or deny herself to him, may Jim be swept by a desolation that seemingly is limitless? Why should no other body have the meaning for Jim that the body of Edith Ritchie may have? Why has a biological entity taken on the vastness of import, the inescapable undulations of meaning which the biological entity called Edith Ritchie has taken for another entity called Jim Haskins? Plainly, the cause is not body, or even self, in its ordinary meaning, for other bodies and selves have psychologically or biologically what Edith Ritchie has. And therefore, that largeness of meaning which has been given to this particular self or body is a symbolical largeness of meaning; that is, it stands for something. What is that for which the self or body of Edith Ritchie stands? Where are the boundaries of the thing represented in Jim's mind by this one person? Does it end with a state or a country or a family or an ocean or even the sky? There is no ending in Jim's mind of the thing represented by Edith, for she stands for everything. Everything is another term for the world or reality. Jim may be in a confusion as to the boundaries of his deepest desire, yet beneath the confusion that desire has universality.

Logically, relations need not be particularized or lucidly bounded to exist. We may be affected by something without knowing that it exists or knowing its shape. Jim Haskins, without knowing it, is concerned with a certain relation of general and particular, of great importance in logic and aesthetics.

Jim Haskins marries Edith Ritchie. The object Edith Ritchie now becomes, as far as human law permits, the object Jim Haskins. There is still, however, a third partner to the relation of Edith and Jim. That partner is the world as a whole. If Jim, through his love for Edith, hates this third partner he will become sulky, even though apparently dependent more and more on Edith. The same goes for Miss Ritchie. Too often, however, two people come together in the marriage bond, or otherwise, and use their high estimate of each other to depreciate, and even hate, the world in general. Here it must be insisted on that hate for the world in general is failure in life—no matter what else happens.

The purpose of love is to feel closely one with things as a whole. I have intimated before my vigorous disbelief in the idea commonly had that sex governs our attitude to things. Sex is the intense, inescapable, tremendous representative of the necessity of a person to complete himself by seeing that whatever else exists is related to him; and indeed is he. Sex, seen fully, is intellectual, has knowledge to it, is philosophic. It is the symbolic, joyful junction of two bodies or selves: symbolical of the joy there would be were a self to accept the world entirely and see its freedom in doing so.

Ronald Hill was a moody young man who despised his uncles, the people he met, people in general; he thought himself a profoundly distinguished being whose attitudes had a dimension to them that could not be discerned elsewhere. Though Ronald proudly lived in this exalted, sequestered island, when eighteen he noticed that the desire for woman was strong, mastering. He used to talk contemptuously of women, saying: "Liz is a light weight"; "Hannah knows nothing but the powder on her nose"; and "If Margaret knew more she would know as much as a half-witted man." He saw women as playthings to be manipulated and twisted by his own masterful, spiritual cunning.

Surprisingly, nevertheless, he found himself once sobbing on Hannah's shoulder, weeping that he needed her always, and hoping that she would never leave him. When Margaret was once curt to him, he got into a terrible fury and threw a stone through the garage window. Two weeks later he humbly phoned to Margaret and asked whether he could see her. To her he said that night nothing else mattered but her, and that however the world went, if he had her he would be happy. He called her an angel, said she was wonderful; but when he went home he masturbated, thinking that she had been cleaning his shoes, wiping his lips after he had eaten heavily, and lying face down on the floor permitting him to walk over her. When he came to see her the next evening he was humble again. At about ten o'clock he was weeping on her shoulder and saying that he was a miserable being and that without her he was as lost as a "beer bottle at the bottom of the ocean." Margaret permitted him to touch her body pretty much as he pleased, and in a close embrace Ronald had an orgasm.

Fifteen minutes later somehow Ronald and Margaret got into a discussion on politics. Ronald, in an exhibition of pompous, sarcastic intensity, called a certain senator who supported trade-unions, "A no-good, hypocritical, nincompoop, hell-bent on getting to the White House by a road of union membership cards and union dues." (Ronald was a kind of master of a regimented, withering rhetoric which placed together tremendously gorgeous words with words of foul content. As he put it, he "liked to throw mud under the stars.")

Margaret said: "Senator Haines, I don't think, is as bad as all that. After all, Ronald, he may really believe in unions."

Ronald answered: "Look, mouse, you have been hornswog-gled hook, line and stinker, by all the liberal droppings you've read. Your beautiful staring eyes take in everything from those stinky-pinky red sheets you read. I don't see why women should be let alone with politics anyway. They'll be taken in by any Greek-letter faker with a whining, bleeding line." (This was Ronald at his rhetorical piercingest. As he put it, he liked "to put together James Joyce and a truck driver in negligee.") His eyes now blazed triumphantly, maliciously. Margaret was taken aback by the attack on her intelligence. He seemed to be gazing at her from a cruel mountain top. She began crying. "Ronald," she whimpered, "that language to me, do you think it's right?"—"Look here, Margaret," answered Ronald, "if a gal starts crying just because a political statement she makes is demolished with both barrels, without tear or favor to Eve or Steve or Old Mother Hubbard herself, well, I just think that crying, sigh-ing, curved ignoramus—(snapping his fingers)—I say that if that shown-up non-Adam starts shedding the big worry tears of ignorance, why then I, Edmund Burke on the ram-page say: 'Let her shed.' " Margaret was silent for a while. She looked at him in surprise. She rose from the couch they had been lolling on and stood up.

She said: "You think you're damn brilliant, Ronald Hill. It may be true that you know more about books than any person in this fair-sized city, at least your age; and you can quote your Joyce and your Rimbaud in your bad French, but when you quote Ronald Hill to me in just that way you're going to do it from now on when I'm not around. Get out." She shook, but held her place. Ronald sat open-mouthed a moment; his eyes narrowed; he clenched his fist; in a minute he walked out.

Margaret did not hear from Ronald for six days. On Fri-day afternoon he called on the phone. He said to Margaret who answered the phone, "I'm coming over." Margaret answered: "Not if I can help it," and put down the receiver. On Saturday morning she received the following note:

Dear Dramatic Marge:

I do profoundly suppose that intellectual coruscation may be attended in this vale of fears and valley of mistimed sallies with cerebral suffering, Schopenhauer de luxe.

Please see me, please see me, please see me, please see me, please see me, please see me, please see me, please see me, please see me, please see me, please see me, please see me.

This night ere the dusk falls over mournful politics and never-to-be-running Ronald at 7 o'clock, your father's time, I shall ring the bell.

Please see me, please answer the bell, please smile, please forget, where are the woes of yesterfear?

Yours, but not mine,
Ronald

At 7 o'clock, with the precision of a nautical instrument, Ronald rang the bell. He had been hovering around the corner for about twelve minutes and had timed his first-class wristwatch immaculately. Margaret answered, after an afternoon of swaying thoughts. Her mother liked Ronald for he had always been polite to her: in fact he was always polite to older women. Margaret had not told her mother just what Ronald had said, she had only mentioned that he had forgot himself and insulted her. Her mother had replied: "Why, dear, every young man, no matter how nice, can forget himself now and then." Anyway, at 7 o'clock the thoughts of Margaret had swayed to the answering of the bell. Ronald, as a matter of course, was invited to have dinner. At the dinner table he was meek, offered information and opinions as if he had received a favor, and said very astutely that he felt Margaret's sociology course at college might be the means, in time, of her helping to eradicate a few of the more ugly spots in America—"and that takes in our city, too." He was particularly courteous to Mrs. Milton, Margaret's mother. On the whole he did little talking. He acted the part of a penitent who knew dinner could be important.

After dinner Margaret and Ronald went into the living room. Margaret was silent, so was Ronald. Finally he said: "In the best Rumanian, Margaret, I'm a heel." Margaret, after some seconds said: "I wouldn't put it just that way, Ronald."

"I could put it worse, dear."—"You don't have to try." Then there was silence for about ten minutes. Suddenly Ronald began sobbing strongly, clutched Margaret's shoulders and buried his head in her breast. "I need you Marge of Marges, more than I need myself. Yet something makes me want to throw you away, as a stupid angel might his wings. But you are not stupid, angel; you will have your wings forever. You will have yours while mine are in an ashcan in the City Hall into which fat Mr. James throws his Republican cigar butt. I'll need you forever, even when I'm dead." And then in a shrill voice he said: "Even when I'm dead, even when I'm dead, even when I'm dead," and he sobbed unrestrainedly. Between sobs he muttered: "Angel, angel, angel." And then, with his head on her breast, he was silent. After a few minutes he rose, said with great politeness, "Margaret, I can't stand it any more, I'm going now. I'll see you and you'll see me even if I don't see me, or Mimi." Margaret, surprised, said: "Goodbye."

Ronald could see Margaret as someone to whom he must give unlimited devotion or as someone on whose body he was treading. Though his self did not consent, the body of

Ronald went drivingly towards certain objects: in this instance, the bodies of girls about his age. Older women did not cause such a body drive, therefore, there was no conflict, and Ronald could be constantly polite. He saw the whole world as an interference with the liberty of himself. To give himself to the world meant surrender of his self-sovereignty, yet he was compelled to give his body, at least outwardly. Margaret and Hannah represented outside objects to which he was driven; but the world of which these objects were a part was looked on with hatred by Ronald as an oppressor, invader of his own world. He was driven to read books, yet he hated the world which they represented. That is why, while walking over a bridge, he threw a book he had been reading with intensity ten minutes before, into the river he was crossing. At times he could not read books at all. While this was going on he would take long walks, and give himself to his own meditations. He hated the world, yet he was driven towards particular objects in it, like girls and books. When his body, after an orgasm, had symbolically been given to one of these outside objects—Margaret—Ronald felt unconsciously that he had yielded up the kingdom of himself. He had to crush that which was the cause of his own shameful submission. She to whom he had surrendered was a feminine, zealous student of social problems. The political discussion was seized on by Ronald as a means of regaining his sovereignty. His unconscious had to bear down hard. He had gorgeously to elevate himself, and contemptuously to shatter a hitherto successful opponent. Ronald was up against the tough question of just how to give oneself to a person while hating and fearing the world she represented. He did not know how to answer it. He swung from insolence to humility; from triumphant malice to tears. In disliking the universe he could not like Margaret and at this age he could not manage to dislike.

In my experience I have met men who masturbated after having been with a woman. The solitary masturbation proved to them that the force to which they had yielded, to which they had yielded with a deep hate though apparently with orgiastic abandon, could be manifested by themselves to themselves. For these men reasoned that in submitting to a power which was not they, they were saying that they were dependent, humiliatingly attached. The masturbation stated that: "I don't need her, I can do that myself." There was a young man, who after showing ardent, sweeping devotion to a girl, found when reaching home he had to go to the bathroom. This young man associated being alone in the bathroom and defecating, with his own triumphant autonomy. When his parents or others had been oppressive it was in biological procedures of the bathroom that he found solace for the onslaughts of his ego. Though he had enjoyed the carnal satisfactions of sex, he felt, nevertheless, that he was giving up something. He restored that something to himself in the bathroom.

There are women who, after sex, have felt depressed and sulky. The depression and sulkiness have the same cause as the like feelings in men. Their bodies have yielded but they themselves have not; and they have seen this offering of body as insulting to an intactness of personality. A woman often alleviates this situation by the changing of the man into a person who, belonging to the woman, represents her own individuality; therefore, yielding to him is an act of power. But where the man is seen as a stranger there is a keen attitude of self-disapproval, which may take the form of morosity, quarrelsomeness and retaliation. The feeling that a man belongs to one, is owned by one, has likewise its painful, guilt consequences.

Wherever sex is separated from other attitudes and activities of personality there is psychological trouble. Sex should be a means of accurately approving of the whole self. If a woman or a man, though apparently loved, is a means of disapproving of the world or of oneself, there will be displeasure with, or hate for, that man or woman. A woman may find it necessary, unavoidable, seemingly ecstatic, to give her body to a man and yet hate him for it. It often happens in marriage that a woman, bound to her husband, needing expression of her body, and finding the only means of doing so in a man she still sees deeply as a stranger, will hate her husband for it. Sometimes she will punish her husband by means of a child. She will show affection to a child as a way of giving pain to her husband. But at times she sees the child as a stranger and the husband as belonging to her. At this time, without knowing it, she may pain the child.

Love and marriage, in the contemporary world, are attended often by desires to possess, desires to hate, giving of one's body without the giving of one's self, anger, shame, misery. It is all because that third partner in any relation of two people is not seen for what it is and not loved. One cannot really love a person without loving reality, just as one cannot love oneself without loving reality; and as a logical corollary, one cannot love another without loving oneself. The last statement may be made clear by the following observations. If one does not love oneself and one appears to be loved by another, then that which one is not able to do is being done by another. Now this other person is either wrong or right. If he is right, then the person who doesn't love herself doesn't know herself. But a person who doesn't know herself cannot be honest, and it would follow then that a dishonest and therefore weak person is loved. This, strictly speaking, is impossible as I will show. On the other hand, if a person is wrong in loving a person who doesn't like herself, then the other person is really pitying, and to pity in this instance is to be contemptuous.

Love is a tremendous field for that agonizing interaction and simultaneity of superiority and inferiority common to contemporary human beings. A human being is compelled to love or approve of himself, but if he does so by means which his critical unconscious cannot justify, he will feel inferior and pained. Self-love, unless it is truly based, is also self-contempt. It follows then that if love for another is really another form of self-love and untruly based, this love for another will be a factor in profound pain.

Selma Gaylord, like all human beings before her, had to find herself pleasing in her own eyes. Whether she knew it or not everything she did had as its deepest and ultimate purpose the being able to look at herself and to find what she saw good. She met Ted Wendling. Ted met her on June 12; and on June 16 he called her "Wonderful." Selma wanted all her life to be called wonderful and here was someone whom she had not known at all five days before using this proud adjective to describe her. Selma had not gathered satisfactorily the data making valid the term "wonderful"; but neither had she given up the idea that she might be deserving the adjective. When she heard Ted use the word she was not in the mood of a churlish inspector of phraseology. For her own peace of mind she had to justify her existence and here was someone doing it for her in a most torrential and unhesitating style. When Ted, the same night, said that he needed her more than he needed anything else in the world, Selma felt a responsive, immeasurably deep glow somewhere in her body. For here a person who was nowhere less than a week ago, was saying that without her his existence would with difficulty continue. However,

Selma, at moments, was aware that men could tell stories and that Ted was beating the drum of adoration perhaps too regularly. But Selma and Ted continued to meet and Ted persisted in using the words: "wonderful," "adorable," and —in letters—"divine." He kept on saying that without her his life was empty, not worth living.

The night that Selma met Ted she was critical of him. She did not like his ways so much, he seemed somewhat awkward, he was not the best-dressed person in the hall, and he did not talk with the courtly grace of a Leslie Howard, or a gay philosopher on a white horse. She felt, too, that there was a clumsy eagerness on his part. She wished that his eyes were a little different. But as the days went on and as Ted kept displaying his devotion to her and insisting on her indispensability, the defects noted at the beginning dissolved in a mist of transmutation, forgiveness, praise. For here was a person sent by the world to corroborate Selma's hopes that all was well with her and that she could assert herself as a triumphant, unblemished being in a puzzling and wide world. Ted came to stand for the world as benign; for a world that recognized the distinction of Selma Gaylord; for a world with which she could come to joyous terms.

With the months, Selma no longer saw Ted as an object like other objects. She divided the world into three parts: herself; Ted; and everything else. She grudgingly admitted the existence of everything else. What was strange in Ted she lessened, altered. As Ted insisted on making his life hers, she came to see him as being herself. What Selma did not know, as all this went on, was that she was really loving herself with the participation of another.

Like many others, Selma loved Ted, not because of what he *was,* but because of what he was *to her.* In fact, as far as she was able, she kept away from seeing what Ted was in relation to everything else. If she thought of her lover in terms of other things, other people, it was essentially because she had to think of these things and people in order to feel Ted as to herself. The chief reason she loved Ted, then, was not because he was a person having the universe in him, a person with bones, flesh, mind, and possibilities, but because he needed her and therefore provided evidence validating her self-love. Selma said to Ted: "My one wish is to make you happy," and Ted said to Selma: "I would give my life to make you happy." But if Ted were happy and Selma felt that she was not the cause of that happiness she would not like it. (Ted would not like it either if Selma were happy and somebody else had brought happiness to her.) Selma was really interested, not in Ted's happiness, but in the fact that in being able to make him happy she seemed important in her own eyes.

Once Ted went on a trip to Springfield, Massachusetts. Selma bade him goodbye with the appropriately large emotional ceremony. She told him: "I hope you will have an interesting time, Ted, and don't come back just on my account." But when Ted wrote her a short and apparently hurried letter in which he said he was busy and "things are more interesting up here than I expected," Selma didn't like it, although she did not affirm to herself just so that she didn't. She had a kind of pleasure when, in the next letter, Ted said he was feeling blue and "the people up here don't seem to know what it's all about." Selma wrote in her next letter: "I know, dear, that being in a strange city may make you feel blue, but, after all, you know you're there for the best so don't mind me and don't come back until everything you went to Springfield for has really been done. I don't want you to lose any opportunity just because, you know, I can't carry on so well without you. When we get married, all our difficulties will be like last week's rain." When Ted, a few days later, wrote: "I've met a real live number, a fellow who knows the score"; that this man had been in show business, that he (Ted) was going to visit his family that evening, Selma, without being too clear about it, didn't like it so much. When she was depressed she felt it was because she missed Ted. She did not know so well she could be depressed because Ted could be happy in one way or another without her. She did not know that she could be affronted because Ted could be having a good time without her playing the big role. When she grieved she felt she was worrying about Ted.

Selma went through the procedures and states of mind which many lovers have gone through. Strictly speaking, those procedures and states of mind are not of love at all. When a person loves another, that person is interested in the other's happiness *without any reservations whatsoever.* To love a person is to wish to please that person; but one sees oneself as cooperating with the whole world to please—not as being in competition with it. Selma's mind went through something like this: "I want to please Ted, but if anything else can please Ted, then that means he needs me so much the less. If he needs me so much the less, then I'm not as good as I thought I was. Therefore, if anything brings happiness to Ted where I'm not concerned, I shouldn't like it: I'm against it." Now Selma, in all her respectable, seemingly devoted romanticizations, could never sharply articulate her real attitude to Ted. If a good deal in Selma's mind was love, then love is a quite ugly, a quite diseased, quite hurtful thing. To know and feel the self of another is a beautiful thing. To see another person as having meaning and beauty and power is a lovely procedure. But to see another person as having meaning, having beauty, and having power because one can use that person as an argument in behalf of one's self-love —that is really to despise a person; to hate him; to de-individualize him.

In the love that is accurate, jealousy is not possible. Jealousy is a feeling of pain caused by the fact that a person who means something to oneself should mean something to another. Suppose Ted Wendling is cared for not only by Selma Gaylord, but by Ricarda Dale. Selma has said that her chief interest is to make Ted happy. If Ted gets any real happiness from meaning something to Ricarda, then there is no reason for pain to Selma. If Ted does not get any real happiness from his being cared for by Ricarda, then Selma should commiserate or pity Ted for he is doing something which is bringing him harm. Now pity, wherever it occurs, means a seeing of weakness in the person for whom it is shown. We cannot love weakness because weakness is not beautiful and only the beautiful is lovable in itself. If we love weakness, it is not the weakness that we love, but our use of weakness to make ourselves strong. We find then that if Selma were loving Ted in himself she would see Ted's relation to Ricarda as bringing either pleasure or pain, good or bad, growth or harm to him. If it brings him pleasure or good or growth, she should be happy because of it. If it does not, it means that she was mistaken in her love for Ted because he is weak, does not know himself and therefore cannot be seen as truly lovable. That is the accurate outline of the jealousy situation possible in Selma's mind.

However, it may be said that jealousy will occur. The question to be asked is: "Does the jealousy arise from that in a mind standing for love or that in a mind which is against love?" In every instance, despite the sultry, seemingly noble literature written around jealousy, the thing itself, no matter how frequent, is a bourgeois state of mind, a possessive state of mind in which self-love truculently and imposingly stalks and maneuvers as love for an object. We can be displeased with a person because that person prefers a cheap quality in another rather than a real quality in ourselves. But if he does so, why cannot we come forth in a straightforward fashion and say: "This person is capable of weakness, of blindness, of shortsightedness, of selfishness"; and therefore say that in so far as he is capable of these unlovely qualities, that much we do not love him. Is it possible that we can really love a person whom we think to be unfair to ourselves and therefore unfair as such? This would mean, if it were so, that we could love an unfair person, an ugly person. *This is impossible.* If we think we love such a person it is because we have taken him for something else and therefore the graceful thing to do is to admit it and say it wasn't love in the first place.

Getting back to Selma: Selma was jealous of Ted because a person she had built up, acted not in accordance with the specifications which she had given him. If Ted were unfair, then that capability for unfairness was in Ted before he met Selma and before he met Ricarda. If Selma did not see it, then she did not know Ted and this means she could not love him because it is absurd to say that a person can love something which he doesn't know. If he thinks he does, he is really loving something else. Selma's self was hurt because someone she had constructed to represent, externalize and justify herself, had the boldness to interfere with her arrangements and the architecture of her vanity. I must be clear here. Where there has been jealousy in drama, in the opera, in the novel—as in the instance of Selma—it was not the love in a person that supported it, it was the lack of love associated with perhaps some of the real elements of love.

A person is everything that he is and nothing else than he is. His possibilities are part of what he is. To say that one loves a person is the same as saying that one loves what a person is, and this, in turn, is saying that one loves everything he is. Consequently, love is in exact proportion to accurate knowledge. To say that love—as many have intimated—is based on mystery, dimness, blindness, blurriness, though it may sound fetchingly "romantic," is really to do away with the true mystery, the true expansiveness, the true grandeur, the true intensity of love.

Every perception is made up of what we are and what the object is. If a person has a perception of another, then that perception, as in the instance of the perception of a brook, or a steamer, or a house, is made up of what the person brings and what the object is. This means that if Selma Gaylord has a perception of Ted Wendling which is not accurate, then what Selma has done is to interfere with what Ted is by bringing something of her own either to lessen or to make greater something beginning in Ted. Now if Selma sees more in Ted than what is coming to him she is, strictly speaking, pitying him. For whenever we give to a person praise, or devotion which is not deserved by him, there is pity attending the offering. If Selma does not see Ted accurately and does not give something which is coming to him, then Selma is grudgingly unfair. Injustices to a person consist in every instance of either denying something to a person which he deserves or granting something to him which he does not deserve. It is clear that in order to avoid the injustice of denial or the injustice of excessive granting, a person must be known wholly and exactly as he is. Otherwise, we shall, in the long run, either pity that person or be unfair to him.

Love, certainly, is not pity. Love, certainly, is not grudging. The conclusion, then, is that love is the giving to a person of all that which is coming to him or her; nothing which is not deserved; everything which is. For that, a constant, comprehensive, intense desire to know a person is necessary. In the history of the relation of selves and of men and women, such a desire has often—exceedingly often—been lacking.

I do not agree with the meanings given by Freud and others to such matters as the Oedipus complex and the Electra complex, because I believe that the terms mentioned are both too narrow and too inclusive. Nevertheless, there is a similarity in the relation that a young man may have to his mother and the relation this young man may have to a girl; and there is a similarity between the basis of a girl's feeling towards her father and her feeling towards some male with whom her life is involved. The fact is that, deeply speaking, there is a likeness in the relation between mother and baby, brother and sister, young man and girl, father and son, brother and brother, sister and sister, and so on. Wherever two lives are deeply involved; wherever two selves seek realization through each other, the situation is, basically, somewhere akin. In each instance, there is a process of having another person belong to one and a process of belonging to another. The self goes forward and the self recoils, wherever, while trying to maintain its own power, intactness, or supremacy, it finds another self necessary to its existence. Every love relationship is a moving equation of dependence and independence, of giving and conquering. And in every instance where the giving and conquering are in some lopsided arrangement, there is pain given and pain taken.

I have dealt with the instance of Selma Gaylord and how she was displeased when her lover, away from her, seemed to be faring pretty well—despite her absence. The displeasure of Selma Gaylord is fundamentally like the displeasure of a mother of whom I was told. This mother, Mrs. Harrison, had a son who went to Cincinnati. She told him to take care of himself, not to be homesick, and to do everything that would enable him to achieve his life's purpose. Her son, Richard, wrote: "I weighed myself yesterday, mom, and I find I weigh two pounds more than I did when I left home. I guess the eating in Cincinnati is agreeing with me. I took

a walk by the shores of the Ohio and went back feeling life
was pretty good. When I got home, my landlady offered me
some food; but all I had was a glass of milk and an orange.
I've been sleeping pretty well and I think Cincinnati is
going to do mighty fine by your wandering boy."

Mrs. Harrison, like Selma, didn't see it so clearly, but she
wasn't pleased when her boy told her he was gaining
weight, was feeling good, and was receiving such unobjec-
tionable articles of food as oranges and glasses of milk from
his landlady. Somehow she felt that all of Richard's health-
building activities ought to be initiated and managed by her.
She was displeased, and somehow in her next letter to Richard she inserted a splenetic air which Richard observed and
at which he was surprised. He didn't see why his mother had
to remind him in just that tone that he owed $80 to his uncle
(his mother's brother). He got the idea somewhere that his
mother was not too pleased he had found his life in Cincinnati suitable to his welfare.

Richard was right. Mrs. Harrison—like Selma with Ted
Wendling—wanted her son to be happy, but happy only
through *her* means. She wished to be considered indispensable to her son. She mistook this desire to be considered
indispensable, for love. A good deal, then, of mother-love is
based on vanity and absence of an unlimited desire to make
the object of such love happy. That Richard could find good
food and good lodgings in Cincinnati, away from her, was
looked on as an affront by his mother. To be sure, Mrs.
Harrison had no conspicuous inclination to look at this fact
clearly; she took out her displeasure with Richard by trying
to make him uncomfortable as to other matters, such as the
money he owed. But when her vanity, clothed as mother-
love, was injured by Richard's ability to find tranquillity and
satisfaction away from her, she retaliated just as a girl loving
Richard might when *her* self-consideration was attacked.

Strictly speaking, there is no such thing as the Oedipus complex as an isolated entity. It happens with most human beings that the first object of what is called love is a parent; and one reason for this is that the parent is the first person whom the child meets. If a child were to meet another person—and this is possible—then that sense of needing and being needed would arise from a person other than the mother and father.

Now every human being, in a love relation with someone, when he comes to be in a love relation with someone else, has to coordinate the new attitude with the old. The drive towards unification of our principal feelings is inevitable. Whenever a person has a new emotion of magnitude, something must happen to a previous emotion of magnitude. One of the procedures commonly followed when a new emotion arises, is to liken it to, and assimilate it with, an old emotion. One, then, does not need the concept of Oedipus complex to explain such a necessity of likening and assimilation.

Also to be expected, is that the person use the old emotion to belittle or depreciate the new, or the new to belittle or depreciate the old. A girl, then, who thinks that her mother belongs to her will use the feeling that a young man belongs to her either to combine the two emotional situations or to play off one against the other. The procedure can be explained without using terms borrowed from Greek tragedy.

A boy can be vexed that his sister, as to whom he has a sense of possession, should find happiness in another. A sister can be vexed with a brother for a similar reason. Love, historically speaking, is based on a feeling of possession which, in turn, arises from the feeling that a person's life is incomplete without us and that because of what we are the person we love exists. Therefore, wherever the basis of that possession is interfered with, there will be a feeling of injury. It is clear that once possession and love are regarded as equivalent, any feeling whatsoever implying possession is like any other feeling implying it.

As I have pointed out, there is a desire on the part of every human being to be independent and yet to have his existence justified by something external to himself. This means that wherever we are needed by someone we feel that this someone is saying the world is approving of us, and that therefore our specific self is given approval. Still, we feel that where the person who belongs to us is other than ourselves, this otherness is inimical. This means that where possession, the logical end of which would be the complete absorption of another by ourselves, is interfered with, we resent it. At the same time if this desire for possession reaches completion, we come to a feeling that we are really losing ourselves, and that therefore our sense of painful, guilty isolation is not assuaged. Persons, therefore, can simultaneously be driven towards a complete possession of another—lover, son, brother, sister, father—and at the same time be greatly pained by the feeling that in doing this they are only accentuating their own separation from the world.

We love because we desire to be entirely ourselves: everything we can be. We are interested in sex because sex is a means of fulfilling that desire to be entirely what we can be. When Selma Gaylord went through her evolution of mind as to Ted Wendling, her fundamental desire was to be and to live; and, of course, implied in the fundamental desire "to be and to live" was the desire to live pleasurably or joyously. One reason for my insistence on using, at this point, simple terms, is the wish to tie together contemporary psychological terminology and the great expressions of feeling to be found in the great literatures of England, America, and the world. Only by having a common vocabulary can an accurate coordination take place between the insight of say,

Shakespeare in *Othello,* La Rochefoucauld in his *Maxims,* Dostoevsky in his *Crime and Punishment,* Ibsen in his *Hedda Gabler,* and Chekhov in his *Three Sisters*—and the full import of a case-history of the immediate present. Were I to be content with the fact that love in *Faust* is expressed in language other than it is expressed in a psychiatric finding, I should countenance that expression of words with double motive, which in other connections, I have described as making for that compulsory togetherness and conflict which is neuroticism.

There are many persons who are in some way like Ronald Hill; like Selma Gaylord; like Mrs. Harrison. Persons who do not know themselves well enough (and most persons don't) will see love as a chance for the possession of another person, and for the triumph arising from managing him. The question is, Does love have to be possession, hidden management, darksome resentment, inimical confusion? It doesn't.

There are two sources for every emotion; these sources are the two ways of self. As the world has been, it is easier to get to satisfaction of a kind by not seeing the tremendous and subtle and wonderful reality outside oneself in its completeness, its exactness, its tireless change. So we decide to get soothingness and power by not seeing it. And we have done this in love. But the very fact that it has made for perceptible and obscure misery shows that people don't want to lessen reality in coming to tranquillity in might for themselves. What's in people may; people as whole beings don't.

There is a possible (as purpose it is inevitable) true triumph in fleshly majesty of the self through the seeing, the dealing with another self as wholly it is, in its limitation for a time, and in its hate of limitation. A self can say to another being, "Through what you do and what you are and what

you can do, I can come to be more I, more me, more myself;
and I can see the immeasurable being of things more wonderfully of me, for me, and therefore sharply and magnificently kind and akin."

Love, like God, is in progress. If loving a person truly
implies loving the wholeness of things truly—and it does—
then, since there is no limit to how much we can authenti-
cally love the wholeness of things, there is no limit to the
successful combating of the pretenses, the petrifactions, the
antagonistic murkiness, the acquisitiveness which have attended the doings of one self with another in amorous territory. The purpose of experience is knowledge; and the purpose, or rather the very substance of knowledge—though
this is not consciously seen often—is the having of a state of
self in which there's the pleasure of a great definiteness of
personality with an unhindered flexibility of personality.
That is the personality as accomplished aesthetics.

This situation is equal to rapturous, factual cognition; and
this rapturous, factual cognition is a love of what's real,
attended by enough of the facts and enough shape to them
or organization of them. Further, this authentic love of reality, or things, must see this reality as unified, personal, concentrated. Expansion goes with concentration. And so, it
can be said without verbal overbrimmingness, that an adequate, pleasing relation with things implies a concentrated,
deep, flexible, comprehensive relation to a thing as person
or self. Such a relation, represented physiologically or in
terms of touch and the other senses, when physiology is
right, is love.

Something of this love as accomplished or complete is
present in the relations of people as we now see them. Tom
and Mary are going for it. Just as we can see the wholeness
of one hundred in the imperfection of 30, or 42½, so the
wholeness of amorousness as truth can be seen in the fum-

blings and retractions and muddle of love as a sociological happening. The value of a love situation, therefore, is how truly or willingly or with how little unnecessary opposition, Tom and Mary, say, *do* go after what they really mean. This going after what Mary means or Tom or Kathie or Dan, does exist; but a going after something else exists too. It is the tangling of the two purposes that makes for the painful "paradoxes" of love that we see everywhere.

If Tom and Mary see themselves as having an immeasurable lot to do with all the things they know and all the things they don't know, and their desire to be just themselves is not seen as fighting with their deeper desire to be all themselves, Tom and Mary will not only be in love, but deeply moving and alive and forming in love. (The "in" of in love is quite often a fixity like that of being in a room one can't get out of because what's outside the room is feared.) Knowledge of anything or everything is inevitably knowledge of oneself, and oneself as loving and love. Let us say that Tom and Mary know this and are happy knowing it. Then they love because Tom is Tom-and-Mary and in process of being Tom-and-everything-else, and so is Mary. And being this, they help all the presumed Toms and Marys there are.

8
Inhibitions, Frustrations, Sublimations

Inhibitions, Frustrations, Sublimations

THE "BLOCK" using of the term *libido* in contemporary
psychiatric thought is to be censured. There is nothing,
I believe, in the term *libido* which could not be covered by
the term *desire*, or *desire* supplemented by some equally
common term. It is only when an adequate notion of the
nature, the variations, the contradictions, and ramifications
of desire is had, that the term *inhibitions* can rightly be
presented. It needs to be seen, first of all, that the word
inhibition itself partakes of the nature of the term *desire*. It,
therefore, follows that if the term *libido* falls under the term
desire, in a certain sense, the term *inhibition* also is related
to the term *libido*.

In Freudian terminology, the word *libido* has come to
mean those forces which drive an organism or self towards
gratification from objects—usually sexual objects. Without
overdoing the matter, it seems to me that Freud, as I have
implied, has been very slippery and too conveniently flexible in his use of the term *libido*. There are drives in the
human organism. These drives may have their origin in the
life of animals and of men hundreds of thousands of years
ago; but the fact remains that all these drives are a phase of
the desire to live as such. Freud would agree that whatever
the *libido* was after, it is after pleasure; but it can be shown
just as well that the desire to live is the desire to live with
pleasure; because where life attains pleasure, there its desire

to continue is that much strengthened. Logically, there is no such thing as the desire to live without pleasure, because pleasure itself is the organic affirmation of the correctness of being alive. Out of all of Freud's somewhat elusive employments of the portentous word *libido* remains an idea of *a self bent on pleasing what it is.* I deny that, despite the impressive lexicon of Freudianism, anything more, fundamentally, is to be found.

Desire may be defined as: Feeling seen as cause. There is, however, a cause, not only for our action, but also our inaction. It needs to be seen, therefore, that when we abstain from something there is also the *desire to abstain.* When a child doesn't take food from the table at 1¹ A.M. just before lunch time—however that desire has come to be—*there is a desire not to take food from the table.* One of the incomplete, somewhat muddled notions now prevalent and helped by the psychoanalytic vocabulary, is the notion that desire is something simply tigerish, aggressive, purple, fleshly, sensual. Desire, however, has its less melodramatic aspects; it has even its monotonous aspects. The desire not to eat meat is just as much a desire as the desire to eat meat; and the desire to think well of oneself in not making advances to a girl is just as much a desire as the desire to approach the girl like a social conqueror. Desire, in its very nature, like all other things, has its negative side. Its negative is an aspect of its positive; just as in the atom, *which preceded sex,* the negative is simultaneous with the positive. Abstinence did not arise from a puritanical injunction against expression; *abstinence can be a phase of expression itself.*

For in not doing something which we see as ugly, there is just as much expression as in doing something. In fact, all doing of one thing is the negation of the doing of something else. Were there this essential notion of the inseparability of positive and negative, we should not have this needless hostility between abstinence and expression. For example, when a writer refrains from using a fancy word or a needless sentence, or when a painter refrains from adding a surplus color or an excess touch, we do not say that in abstaining from this needless sentence, or needless color, the writer or artist has failed to express himself by being abstinent; the abstinence clearly can be a part of his expressing himself accurately—the only kind of real expression. If accurate expression is the only kind of real expression, and, as is clear, accuracy implies some kind of abstinence, then expression itself implies some kind of abstinence.

What the human being most deeply desires, what is its most profound *libido,* is the completing of itself, the coming to be everything that it can be. In the same way that it would be unwise to accept $70 if it hindered one from getting $100, so it is wise—in keeping with the most profound desire of all—to sidestep one thing at a certain time so that a larger thing may not be lost. Certainly abstinence here is not a hindrance to expression. Abstinence, like selection, can be a means of losing something; but like selection, it can also be a means of stopping the loss of something.

Wherever there is inhibition, there is, strictly speaking, the checking of one desire by another. For example, if a child were visiting the house of an aunt it hated and that aunt offered food to the child, the child, if it were hungry, might want the food very much and at the same time would not want to take it, because in doing so it would show approval of a person it hated. Let us assume that the child did not eat the food. In that case the desire to satisfy its own sense of self-respect and spiritual revenge would win out. This might happen at, say, one o'clock in the afternoon. But the child, not being able to leave the house, becomes much hungrier at five o'clock in the afternoon. Again it is offered food. The same problem exists, but this time the child takes the food and lets another desire take precedence over a simultaneous opposing desire. In the first instance, the child may be said to have inhibited a desire to eat. In the second instance, the child may be said to have inhibited a desire to maintain its dignity and to get spiritual revenge.

Let us assume, again, that a man thinks he has been lied to, made fun of, held in disrespect by, his wife. He feels that his wife, having injured his spiritual worth, should not be approached in terms of love by him. He maintains an aloofness for, let us say, five days. At this time he is gratifying his desire to retaliate and to maintain his sense of his ethical dues. He is inhibiting a desire to have the body of his wife near him and the desire to possess that body. In other words, this man is gratifying and inhibiting at the same time. On the sixth day, the desire to retaliate fades somewhat and the desire for contact with the body of his wife grows. At this time, though the desire to retaliate has not left him, it has given precedence to the other. The desire for retaliation then is inhibited and the desire for sexual contact gratified; but there are still inhibition and gratification at the same time.

All inhibition is also gratification, because if there is a real desire to abstain, then the satisfaction of that desire is the *gratification of the desire to abstain.* Inhibition does not exist as a thing in itself, just as the outside of a plate of tin does not exist without the corresponding side we do not see. If we see desire as present at every moment in life (and it is), and in everything we do, then the true fulfillment of desire can be called expression. And a life that is successful can be called a life fully expressed. But wherever there is expression of one thing, there is a repression of another thing. The implications of art, which are also the implications of life, have in them both expression and repression.

A perception is intense not only by what it includes but

by what it leaves out; and the leaving out is a kind of inclusion. Therefore to talk of inhibition as an evil in itself or as necessarily an escape, is unwise; for inhibition may be a means of complete, that is, accurate expression.

In order to judge of the evil or good of inhibition or of frustration, it is evident that some notion of what the ego as a whole is after must be had. Freud, it is my belief, had no such notion; and his writing, therefore, on inhibition, frustration, and sublimation, is that much inadequate. The question needs to be asked, Just how is a self frustrated? Is it possible that in seeming non-frustration in sex a phase of the ego more profound is frustrated? This, to me, is the important question, Just what is being frustrated in the self? The word *frustration* (related etymologically to the word *fraud*), comes from the Latin word *frustra* which means "in vain"; or *frustrus* which means "deceitful." It needs to be asked, Just what is the self doing "in vain" and just what is "deceiving" it?

Frustration may certainly be considered a cause of neurosis. If something more essential to the stability of the self is unexpressed and something less essential expressed, it would follow that the self would feel ill-at-ease and defrauded, at least to a degree. However, if in not expressing something less essential, the more essential aspect of the self is not defrauded, there might be unease; but there would be less disturbance of the personality than if the more essential aspect of the self had been submerged. We arrive then at the question asked also by the Greeks and asked somewhere by all mankind: What is that which the self is most profoundly after? Where achievement of *that* is frustrated, it would seem *there* is the greatest frustration. It is a little curious to place the question of the *summum bonum,* the highest good, as medieval philosophers phrased it, next to a problem raised in contemporary psychiatry, but it is necessary. Without a notion of the *summum bonum,* the final aim, the end of man to which all his specific purposes are subsidiary, we cannot talk other than superficially about frustration.

The highest purpose in general of man is to live accurately and comprehensively. If sex is a means of his doing that, then sex is beautiful, ethical, lovely, on the side of God, man, and the angels. If sex is that which prevents man from living accurately and comprehensively, then it is not only not on the side of God and the angels, but also not on the side of man. Of course, sex in its fullest meaning is not against man's living accurately and comprehensively, just as food isn't; but sex, like food, must be seen critically and completely.

Freud has likewise often used the term *sublimation.* His most succinct definition of sublimation is: The process by which the "sexual impulses . . . are diverted from their sexual goals and directed to ends socially higher and no longer sexual" (*A General Introduction to Psychoanalysis,* 1920, page 8). Sublimation, apparently, is a means of taking sex when it cannot be gratified, and changing it to some more respectable activity like engaging in athletics, writing a book, making a speech, being kind to a relative, or working in a trade-union. In this sense there is really no such thing as sublimation. The ideas of Freud on the subject are, to me, inexact, ill-based.

Despite all the talk of sublimation, I have not seen any acceptable validating of its existence or description of its meaning and procedure. To say, for example, that nature was sublimating when it made man out of the ape; or that it was sublimating when out of paleolithic man, it made the person who thought about the technique of music, or the nature of logic, or the meaning of history—is, it appears quite certain, rather foolish. Why cannot the progress from ape to logician be a going from less energy to more energy? Apparently, the arising of intellect from the senses is something which happened without any desire to deny the senses: what really occurred was the *completion of the senses by intellect.*

The implication by Freud and others that intellect is something evasively opposed to sex is harmful and superficial. Sex represents a great energy; intellect represents a great energy; but there is no more reason for them to be in conflict than the clear blue of a sky and the heavy green waves of ocean. Nature wanted man, if one wishes, to copulate, fornicate, couple, express *libido,* desire body fiercely; but it is just as apparent that nature wanted man to get to the multiplication table, to find an alphabet, to get to grammar, to write history, to get joy from logic. Was neolithic man, when he approached the alphabet, running away from the fact that he wanted to lie with a woman in a cave? Is it not possible that the reality which made a man of fifty thousand years ago bear a child on a woman also of fifty thousand years ago, was just as courageous when it made that man come to a notion of form, utter words, love primitive wisdom, see meaning in the sun? The question that Freud and his advocates must answer is, Just why neolithic man, who did not have the reason for sublimation that a tormented New Yorker has, came, nonetheless, to mathematics, writing, and larger thoughts.

Freud has been guilty of a great logical misstep or, if one wishes, immobility. The fact of the matter is that sex and other activities are all manifestations of a reality big enough to take them all in. For example, let us call reality as a whole, A. Sex we shall call, B; other activities, C. Now B and C, that is, sex and other activities, both represent A, reality as a whole, and both come from A. It follows then that if sex and other activities come from and represent A, reality, they have something in common. But, of course, that does not mean that C, other activities, has to come from B, sex. It simply means that having A in common they will have something in common among themselves.

Sex has been such a tremendous, mysterious, omnipresent thing it is no wonder it has been given a separate world. It is no wonder people have been frightened, mystified, spiritually intimidated by the idea of sex. But that is because a conspicuous force is more likely to frighten and mystify than a force equally great which is less conspicuous. Reality is just as tremendous as sex. The fact that sex can intimidate and frighten, simply points to the wonder and power of reality itself; and should not be used to obscure the meaning of reality in general. When one is tremendously excited, moved by femininity or masculinity, one is honoring with one's body the power and immediacy of existence itself. It is existence that is captivating us, driving us, tormenting us, and alluring us.

I say, definitely, there is no such thing as sublimation. The first desire of a child is to know its world. The fact that a recently born infant grabs an object, is part of the desire to know. The fact that a child will try to distinguish sounds and colors and shapes, is a part of the desire to know. The desire to know, at no time, whether at birth, or at twenty, or at forty, or at sixty, or at eighty, is a sublimation. The desire to know is nothing less than the desire to have the reality of the world adequately in one's mind; to come to a oneness with the world which biologically gave us our very existence. And that desire to come to a oneness with the world which made us—taking form as the desire to know —is not a sublimation, and never has been. It is a primitive, irreducible, tremendous drive in its own right. It is an oceanic thing; and a sharp thing. Certainly it has to do with sex; but it is just as logical to say that sex is the embodiment of the drive to be at one with reality, as that the drive to be at one with reality is a sublimation or evasion of the sex-drive. It is not by superficial chance that the tree of knowledge in the Garden of Eden was called the tree of knowledge; or that, in the Bible, *to know* was the same as to have sex. Those who wrote the Bible, whoever they were, felt somewhere that sex was the outward presentation of the desire to know; they presented sex as the desire to know when this was a terrifically impelling thing, driving the body. Sex is the inevitable manifestation and honoring of the drive of every organism to come to some adequate relation with its source.

When, in Babylon or Egypt, scholars there, considering the shapes of land, thought of the shapes alone and came to the forms of line, angle, triangle, circle, they were not necessarily "sublimating" the physical things from which they came to the idea of shapes. To arrive at the abstract from the concrete is not a "sublimation" in the somewhat elusive Freudian sense; for in this sense, the "sublimation" hints at a weakening and an evasion of what went before. The abstract can be seen as a strengthening of the concrete just as much as a weakening or denying of it.

Freudian thought has attempted to show that if a person writes a poem about love, the writing of the poem is a going away from the power of love itself. This is decidedly foolish. Why cannot thought about sex add to the strength of sex in its full meaning? Why need the attempt to give form to a sexual situation be a drawing away from that situation—as is implied in a good deal of psychoanalytical writings on art and other subjects.

An action is completed when it is expressed, not evaded or diminished by its expression. Of course, here we come to just what expression is. Expression is never evasion or "sublimation": it is completion. And while persons in the psychoanalytical profession do not know this, I think their usefulness is meeting large handicaps.

For it should definitely be seen that the basis of sex is to be found in the world as it was before sex came to be. Sex with all its romance, complications, unease, fury, is an aspect of that *positive and negative, like and unlike, same and different* interaction to be seen everywhere in the universe.

There is a general dialectic or rhythm in the world, a completion of a thing by its opposite. This dialectic may take the form of sex, but preceded it. This dialectic, one phase of which is sex, is present in its entirety in the human being; because the human being has within himself the reality of rocks and space and motion and water and force. To say that sex precedes reality is like saying that the tree is greater than the mountain on and from which it grows; or that the leaf is greater than the tree from which it comes. We must understand sex in terms of a constant process to be found in the atom, in the chemical elements, in plants, in animals, and in man as a whole.

The fundamental motion of sex existed implicitly in inorganic things before it existed in the organic. This means that sex is a manifestation of the world where it begins. And the world where it begins, and still is, should be used to explain sex; the contemporary interpretation of sex should not be used disproportionately to explain the past world and the world which persists. The atoms and the forms in the body and dress of Miss Harriet Simpson may, considered abstractly, be less engrossing than the alluringly clothed body of Miss Simpson; but is it not more likely that these atoms and forms can explain causally the effect of Miss Simpson, rather than that the sexual impact of the girl explain the atoms and forms? "Abstract" electrons did not have to be sublimated to exist in the body of Miss Simpson.

That being both within and without another body which is a basic situation in sex, is also a basic situation in knowledge. Whenever we know something, we give ourselves to that thing, and that thing gives itself to us. Both knowledge and sex, in other words, are expressive of a fundamental interaction of reality. This does not mean that knowledge is subsidiary to sex. For example, if a person has a knowledge of the existence of Mt. Monadnock in New England, this person, in so far as he is affected by the mountain, has given himself to it. On the other hand, in so far as the mountain is in a person, the person has taken the mountain.

If Richard Hart remembers Mt. Monadnock, what he is doing is giving himself to Mt. Monadnock and yet he is having—for he remembers it—Mt. Monadnock within him: the mountain is part of his memory, that is, part of himself, and, in a certain sense, even part of his body. This procedure of being affected by objects and affecting objects, if it takes a complex, organized form, certainly need not be a "sublimation." Knowledge is an outgrowth, if one wishes, of the eye and the ear; but the eye and the ear are not "sublimations" of the sense of touch: they are intensifications, completions of the sense of touch: they are continuations, not evasive rivals.

The only way we don't escape from reality is by welcoming all of it. Where we welcome part of it disproportionately, it means we evade another part. In order, therefore, to understand what escaping from reality in any manner means, one must have an organized knowledge of it. To say that the desire to understand love, to describe it, is a "sublimation" of the inability to enjoy it, is just as silly as to say that the desire to describe to a friend a dinner a person has enjoyed, comes from an inability to enjoy the dinner. I believe all those who take seriously the idea of sublimation would grant that persons have been with a woman, and yet have been impelled to describe their feelings. For example, it is well known that Byron was not monastic. It follows, therefore, that perhaps his describing of the love of Don Juan and Haidée is not necessarily a sublimation. What is found constantly is this: One feels something; there is the desire to *complete* the feeling—by expressing it.

There has been a good deal of talk, which to me is portentously silly, about sex desire or *libido* being sublimated by trade-union activity, charitable activity, painting, interest in science, dancing, writing, and the like. These questions arise: When savages danced, just why, being naive as they were, should they have to sublimate sex? If sublimation is a process coming from contemporary repression, just why did that unknown painter who conquered a mammoth beast have to paint that beast in a cave in southern France? Can we explain primitive songs in terms of sublimation? Can we explain a lullaby in terms of sublimation? What shall we say of Alexandre Dumas who possessed many women and yet wrote, by himself and in collaboration, hundreds of volumes? Isn't it possible that—what with the desire for food, including food for children—a man could be interested in trade-unions and even become a leader, without necessarily wishing to sublimate sex? The whole idea of sublimation, to me, won't stand against the rush of all the facts. The existence of the idea depends on a pedantic choosing of facts and aspects of facts, hardly representative of the whole matter.

What is forgot by the sex-emphasizers is the fact that in a certain sense a person can use sex as a means of "sublimation," when he is unable to express himself otherwise. For example, John Harris was not permitted to attend a certain exclusive meeting. He had hoped that he would be able to be there. He was not chosen, and he took out his disappointment by sleeping with his wife more often that week than perhaps he would have done otherwise.

It happens very often that because there is nothing else to do, a man spends more time with a wife or a woman he is living with, than otherwise. I have known of one instance where a man frankly told me he would not have been with his wife so often if he had more money to go places. In other words, he "sublimated" a desire to do something else, by sleeping with his wife. In order to understand the whole business of "sublimation," the desires of a human being must be seen in proportion and must be seen completely. In so far as any desire is good, it works along with any other desire that is good. If writing a book and sleeping with a woman are both good, there is no real conflict. If it is right to organize a trade-union and it is right to enjoy the body of a female human being, again there is no real conflict. Love, and music arising from love, do not have to fight each other. Furthermore, in the same way that an article in a newspaper is most interesting to a person who has witnessed what the article tells about, so reading about sex very often is most interesting to people who have participated in it.

The brain of man exists as much as his generative organs. There is a relation between the two. The brain of man was a later production of evolution than the generative organs, as such. As I intimated earlier, it seems uncritical to say that when nature arrived at the complex brain and nervous system of man, it was in an effort to evade or "sublimate" his life as a reproductive being. It seems logical that a later, more complex manifestation of the possibilities of nature would include previous manifestations of nature. That is, the brain would include the meaning of sex, and complete it.

If nature simply wanted man to reproduce as such, just why would it give man the possibility of reasoning subtly, writing delicately, perceiving accurately? It is true that the act of sex has come to have more and more relations with every other purpose or every other act of man. Can this not mean that from the very beginning sex had a relation to every other possible activity of man; and that all these activities could lend strength and meaning to each other? The act of reproduction is creation; the writing of a book is creation; the finding of a new chemical substance is a kind of creation; the leading of a trade-union can be creative. Can this not be because creation is implicit in reality itself, not because other kinds of creation followed when sexual creation was difficult or impossible?

Freud had no real knowledge of literature and art; he had no real knowledge of economics or politics; he looked on metaphysics disdainfully; and he saw the endlessly multifarious world of objects too narrowly. Sex, it is true, is related to literature and art and economics and politics and metaphysics and logic, but what this means is that Freud was inequipped to understand sex. After all, truth works both ways. If a man is inequipped to understand the true source of a poem because he does not understand sex, isn't it also likely that a man may not understand sex because he does not understand the true source of a poem?

Sex, in other words, can help to explain the origins of beauty and trade-union activity and friendship and scientific thought; but a knowledge of beauty and trade-union activity and friendship and scientific thought is necessary for a complete knowledge of sex. The last kind of knowledge the psychoanalytic practitioners, I am afraid, do not have. They need to have it, otherwise they cannot approach the problem of sex fully armed. I believe the whole notion of frustration and sublimation, as psychoanalysts now have it, needs to be "ditched."

If there was more illumination than otherwise in these

wavering concepts, of course, such a stringent statement would be unjustified. But the psychoanalytic writings have helped to further a neurotic state on the subject of sex and other activities of man. Wherever necessary activities are seen, not as completing each other, but as intrinsically in conflict with each other, the neurotic condition is supported. I do not see the eye as necessarily in conflict with the penis, nor do I see the enjoyment of sex as opposed to the enjoyment of a good paragraph of prose. I cannot see why a person may not enjoy Beethoven without thinking that he is evading the enjoyment of another human being. I do not see why the release of conversation has to be at war with biological release. I believe that they both, fundamentally, without either being an evasion of the other, represent the possibilities of man.

At this point, let me take the specific instance of a person listening to Beethoven's *Moonlight Sonata*. There is a great huddle of thought on the subject of music created by psychoanalysts who temerariously have attacked the art problem. First of all it is said that music like Beethoven's *Moonlight Sonata* can be an aphrodisiac; that is, it can incite to sex. On the other hand, Beethoven, it has been said, wrote the *Moonlight Sonata* because he had to "sublimate" repressed sex feelings. We have, therefore, a "sublimation" acting as an incitement to sex—as it does in Tolstoy's *The Kreutzer Sonata*.

Whether aphrodisiac or sublimation, or both, Beethoven's *Moonlight Sonata* has mathematics to it. The notes in all their tearfulness, lingeringness, mysterious heart piercingness, have definite quantitative relationships all through them. So we find both sex and mathematics in the *Moonlight Sonata*. The Freudians would say that the sex explained the mathematics, if they considered the mathematics at all (which they do not). If sex and mathematics can appear in the same reality, then, as in the case of any other reality which has two phases, one can be used to explain the other. Sex, therefore, can be seen as illuminating mathematics; but why cannot mathematics be seen as illuminating sex? If mathematical quantities can lead to sex feeling, does it not follow that there is something of sex in mathematics itself? If there is something of sex in mathematics itself this means that since sex can be found in the non-sexual, the non-sexual is sexual, and the sexual is non-sexual. This means that reality can be used to explain sex and should be so used.

When one finds sex in everything, what really one is doing is saying that sex is not sex alone; that sex is really a way of looking at something larger than it. If one can explain a room by means of a chair, one can also explain a chair by means of a room. The second procedure is not welcomed by psychoanalysts.

Furthermore, it is not true that the sexual is the first or most meaningful manifestation of the child. One of the earliest things that a kitten wants to do is to open its eyes; and the corresponding thing is what a child wants to do. A good deal of what the child does, which has been called latently sexual, or just sexual, by various writers, is simply a phase of the child's wanting to know itself and the world. When a child listens to sounds, in the first weeks of its life, its great desire is to come to be itself by accepting the presentations of the world surrounding it. When a child is curious about a strange thing, it is trying to come to a sense of its own individuality by trying to find out what something different from itself means. The child's first desire is to know the world in which it has been placed; because through knowing the world, it feels it is affirming its own existence. It will desire to please itself, certainly; but its greatest desire is to please itself by becoming at one with what, by birth, it is forced to meet. By being at one with what it meets, the child affirms its life. The desire of the child to affirm its life is its greatest desire. A child's desire to affirm its life by knowledge will go on as long as life goes on. This desire is fundamental; it preceded thumbsucking, masturbation, "anal-erotism," possible hatred of its father, possible desire to know its mother sexually. This desire, furthermore, being pervasive, universal, tremendously deep, need not be "sublimated." Sex is a phase of this desire; sex should go along with it. In so far as sex goes along with it, the desire to know, to be at one with the world in all its depth and ramifications, is never evaded; for successful sex means successful knowledge.

9
The Child

The Child

CHILDREN are included in the census of America. From the viewpoint of the dispassioned census, they are quantitatively as important as persons six, seven, eight, and even forty times their age. The census of the United States has gone ahead on the quite accurate presumption that children are persons, no more so and no less so, than human beings older than they. The procedure of the census is here quite justified.

As soon as a child is born he has all the appurtenances and qualities of personality that a professor has, or a broker has, or a grandmother has, or a general has. That personality may be dim, unmanifest, encompassed by the clouds attending inactive perception; yet it is there. A person is a reality which, being an entity or world, sees and must see, is related to inexorably, that other tremendously multifarious entity, the world. It is to be expected that when a new entity, a baby, arrives in that larger entity, the world,—the baby do all it can to establish its own existence by being able to make, all the time, happier and freer and more accurate relationships with the universe into which it has entered.

A baby has been born. That baby may be called Joseph. Joseph will not know just where he is; but he will want to find out. He has needs. Those needs, if met at all, will be met by an arrangement of the larger world and himself. When Joseph's needs are met, a feeling, however unexpressed, will occur amounting to: "We make a team." Joe will want to eat; there is food in the world. Joe will want to see; there are things to be seen, and there is light in the world. Joe will want to crawl, and walk, and run; and there is space in the world to be crawled in, to be walked in, to be run in. Joe will want to touch; there are things to be touched. Joe will want to love, and there are things to be loved, whether he successfully does so or not.

Joe doesn't know what interferences he will meet in the process he has tackled of completing himself. He doesn't know this now—while in the room in which he at this moment is. The room Joe Johnson is in is neighbored by other rooms, and surrounded by all kinds of things, which, if he lives, he will have to find out about. He doesn't want any unjust interferences in the job of establishing and completing the particular world that he is. If there are interferences, or what he takes to be interferences, he will do something about them. What things will help new-born Joe to become himself, he will like. He will go for them if he can. If he can't, though he may not know anything about it, he won't like it.

Somewhere in Joe now are drives, inclinations, attitudes, which may be shown when he is twenty, thirty, forty, or sixty. In the same way as the possibility of a huge, various oak is in the acorn, so the possibility of a various, complicated structure is now in the perhaps gurgling or whimpering boy, Joseph. What is the full meaning of that which Joe murkily, unwittingly, but inevitably is after?

There, of course, are parents and others around Joe. He will distinguish them fairly soon; he hasn't—as yet. These parents feel that Joe belongs to them. He came from their flesh. Legally he is theirs, and they are responsible for him.

They know that Joe is theirs. If asked, they would most likely admit that they do not know what Joe means. In some ways, they are just as ignorant about Joe as Joe himself. Joe's parents, Helen and Robert, don't fully know what they are about. In fact, they weren't sure a year ago just whether they wanted the child called Joseph Johnson.

Joe's parents have their own worries. They are quite proud that they have a boy. They are kindly disposed towards that boy. However, they have their own lives to live; they hope that Joe will be a help to, an adornment of, their own lives. Joe's parents don't see Joe as the census-taker would: an indefeasible, sovereign person in his own right. How can they? The little human has to be in bed, can't see, he goes with exceeding blindness towards a breast and towards space. He whimpers; and there are strange curves on his face. His hands go up and down, this way and that, in the air; and his toes and feet make motions. He doesn't know what it's all about. How can this new, completely ignorant being, be a person in the sense that a diplomat is, or a president of a baseball club, or a grandmother, or his own mother? But Joseph Johnson is. If he were killed it would be murder; if he died the United States census would be one less. When he looks into the dark, it is he that is doing it: that he represents man, is a man, and is a person.

Joe will come to his senses. He will find out that black is different from white; that purple is different from pink; that milk is different from furniture; and that his father is different from his uncle. He will find that when snow falls, it sounds different from when a dish falls. He will know his own voice is different from the voice of his mother. He will distinguish the rain from the water coming out of the faucet in the kitchen-sink. He will smell leaves, milk, and garbage; he will distinguish the taste of oatmeal from orange juice. He will touch walls, flowers, chairs, noses, toes, and himself; and he will come to know that these things "touch" differently. He will take part in this world-exploration and self-exploration with great eagerness.

Joe doesn't want to die. He may have cried for whatever reason when he got his first touch of the world; but he does other things than cry now. He isn't against the world. The world and he are pals; though Joe may have a puzzling pal and, at times, a painful one. But there is a tremendous contract between him and that world, a contract dating back to a long time ago; and this contract Joe doesn't want to break.

Sometimes Joe's mother, Helen, has been irritated with him. Joe couldn't understand why his mother, Helen, should be irritated with him (just as Helen's husband hasn't understood why she has been irritated with *him;* and Helen hasn't understood, either). Sometimes Helen's irritations would occur without notice, just when she seemed to be pleased with the growing and exploring Joe. It just didn't make sense. Here was some being, an important being, smiling at him; and then, some moments later, maybe just because a doorbell rang, or because something in the kitchen went wrong, acting as if she didn't care for Joe at all. This sudden change from smiling to unconcern bewildered Joe and hurt him, just as it might somebody much older.

Once Helen, on a hot day, slapped Joe's face; and in the evening took him on her lap and showed him off to her uncle. But Joe remembered he had been slapped. He had been in the hot weather, too, and he didn't like slapping any more in hot weather than in cool weather. Helen had her troubles; but what Joe saw was that she made many changes in her attitude towards him; she could change just like that, from a flower into a big pin that stuck him. Sometimes it seemed as if Joe meant the whole world to her; at other times it seemed as if a friend of Helen's, Ada Jones, was more important than Joe. Anyway, Helen could talk to Ada Jones for hours, while Joe was in the room; and Helen did not seem to know that he was in the room trying to find out what Helen and Miss Jones were up to. It all was baffling; it all was painful; it all didn't make sense; and Joe had to do something about it.

He did. He felt he had two kinds of mother; in fact, that he had two mothers. One was on his side. This mother smiled at him, called him darling, worried if something fell on his finger-nail, saw to it that he ate the right thing, and that nothing bad happened after he ate it; put him to bed and stayed in the room after he was asleep (even when he wasn't asleep, but when Helen thought he was). This mother, it appeared, couldn't live without him. He was more important to this mother than all the Miss Joneses in the world, no matter where they came from, or how often. This mother seemed to exist for the purpose of being nice to Joe. Joe came to feel that this Helen was his, that she belonged to him, and that, without him, she couldn't be at all. He loved this Helen; she was on his side; she seemed to grow out from him. She existed so that he could like things.

The other Helen was pretty mysterious, pretty distant, and Joe came to feel she wasn't on his side at all. This Helen could suddenly take him out-of-doors as if he were some package she had to get to the outside. This Helen could say: "Run along now," just when Joe felt he was showing her the most important thing there was. This Helen seemed not to care whether there was anybody like Joe around or not. This Helen seemed like a tall building at the other end of town which seemed to stand there unconcerned with what happened to Joe. This Helen tried to make Joe do things when he didn't want to do them, and he didn't know why he should do them. This Helen seemed to have a pleasure in making Joe feel bad. This Helen could cry and say to Joe when he came up to her: "Look, don't you see I want to be alone? Why don't you go out and play like a nice little boy, your mother has troubles enough." Joe would go out to play, but he felt that this Helen didn't want his help. He felt deep down he could help Helen, though she was grown up, a big person, and used words he didn't understand. But just at that time Helen chose to think that Joe was something like a pretty important cockroach, or like that tough-looking policeman he saw one Saturday afternoon (sometimes he felt Helen was a policeman).

Then there was Robert. Robert and Helen would put Joe to sleep; and sometimes Joe got out of bed without his parents knowing it, and opened the door a little and saw and listened to what was going on. Once he saw Helen on Robert's lap; and once he saw Helen slap Robert just the way she once slapped Joe. Once he saw Helen and Robert talk, and he heard the word "dollars" come up very often. He knew that dollars had something to do with the pennies Helen gave him; but he felt that when his parents talked of dollars he wasn't in on it at all, and that he was pretty unimportant. Once he saw Helen rush up to her own room after her face had become, the little boy noticed, pretty red, and when she looked as if she were ready to cry. Once when Helen and Robert had a fight, Helen went out for two days; and Robert said to Joe (whom she didn't take along with her): "Well, I've got you, little chap, anyway."

Robert's attitude would change, too. Sometimes Robert would spend a lot of time with him in the park; and Joe's father wouldn't mention Helen at all. Sometimes Robert would give him a nickel and a dime and get him ice-cream cones and nice chocolates and so on. Once Robert got him a drum, and at various times other toys. But quite often it was Robert who said: "Don't you think you'd better go to bed, Joey? Run along now." Once Robert put him across his knee and spanked him; for the life of him Joey didn't know why. The night before Robert had talked about "dollars" with Helen. Sometimes Robert, too, would act as if Joe weren't around in the slightest. Robert didn't make sense, either. One Robert could say: "I have you, Joe, and I'll see to it that you get something out of life." One Robert could beg Joe to sit on his lap. One Robert could get a sailor suit for Joe, put him on his shoulder wearing the sailor suit, and walk down a whole block with everybody in the neighborhood seeing Joe on his father's shoulder. But the other Robert wasn't like that at all. The other Robert seemed more interested in "dollars"; this Robert could talk about a Mrs. Devlin to Helen and forget Joe was in the room. So it seemed that one Robert belonged to Joe, was on Joe's side, liked Joe; and the other was somebody far away who didn't like Joe and could act like a policeman, or a giant, or just like anybody else who didn't care whether Joe felt good or bad. Joe felt he had two Roberts, two fathers on his hands. One father belonged to him, the other was a stranger who was against him.

Joe kept on growing. When his mother pleased him, his mother was somewhere part of him; when his father pleased him, his father was part of him. When they didn't please him, they had to be dealt with; and the best way of dealing with them was found at night when Joe could say that he had got rid of the awful part of his mother and the awful part of his father. When Robert and Helen kept on quarreling, Joe's life within himself, which came to be more and more important after the age of two, seemed more than ever necessary, more than ever justified.

After all, Joe had to live. He didn't want to think that he was living in the world where those two big people in his life quarreled. At night, and sometimes in the bathroom, Joe could forget all the things in the world that were against him and didn't make sense. The world when it was painful, the way his mother and father could be painful, was around him in the daytime; but there was no reason why this puzzling and hurting world had to follow him to sleep. However, Joe couldn't sleep all the time; and he had to come out of the bathroom after a while. He was aware that these thoughts he had in himself weren't very much cared about by Helen and Robert. They were interested in having his face washed, in his not having a bellyache, in his going to the bathroom in the right way, in his not dirtying his clothes, in his not making too much noise, in his being able to walk, in his going to sleep at the right time; but they didn't seem to be worried much about what Joe thought of himself inside. Well, if they weren't worried about what was going on inside Joe, Joe wouldn't tell them. In fact, Joe later felt a little good that he could have things happen inside him which his mother and father didn't know about. That made him important to himself;—and he felt that no matter how unkind the world was and how awful, he had something inside him he could go to. (Joe didn't put this into words but this is what happened, anyway.)

Between the ages of three and four, Joe had decided pretty definitely that his mother and father weren't altogether his friends. They didn't seem to care for him in just the way he cared for himself. They wanted him to be a good, strong boy; but Joe was after bigger game. He didn't like the idea that they wanted him to eat right, but didn't care what he felt at night inside himself. Joe didn't want to tell them by now, but still he felt that they ought to ask *some questions*.

In time, Joe didn't like the idea of eating the food two people like Helen and Robert gave him; two people who didn't care for Joe inside and out one hundred per cent. Joe was hungry, but he felt he had to show Helen and Robert he didn't want their food so very much. He took his time about eating, and played around with his oatmeal before he put the spoon into his mouth. Helen became angry and said: "Joe, do you have to play with that oatmeal? Isn't it good? Take it like a good boy, now quick!" Joe took it quickly this time, but he felt that it was right to annoy Helen. He would show her, he would make her see that there were things about him she hadn't thought about. If she didn't think about what went on inside him, at least she would have to think about why he didn't eat the oatmeal quickly.

Once, after a very bad quarrel of Helen and Robert, Joe ate his oatmeal and twenty minutes later vomited. The quarrel had occurred the night before and Joe had dreamed about gangsters shooting across the street with him right in the middle of the street. He didn't know why he vomited, but he still remembered his dream. This vomiting of Joe distressed his father and mother and the boy didn't like it entirely either, though there was some pleasure for him in doing it. Joe continued to give trouble to his parents, and his parents continued to give trouble to him. Nevertheless, as things go, they loved each other and Joe saw home as the place where he had to be, and couldn't see himself anywhere else.

Joe's thoughts went on. Other things pained him. He had quarrels with little boys and girls and sometimes he would rather be with those boys and girls than with his mother and father. There were other adults whom he came to know; and these, like Helen and Robert, could please and displease. Things more than ever seemed to be for him and against him. The solution he had come to continued and was enlarged. There was the other world and there was Joe's world. Joe's world he could manage with apparently complete administrative powers. When things got tough elsewhere, Joe's snug and intimate universe was used more than ever. But something in Joe, though the solution seemed to be the only one around, didn't like the idea of the separation of worlds. At times, without knowing it, he felt he was cowardly and wrong in dealing with the tough world by making a more manageable and kinder world within himself, for himself.

Joe didn't want to give up that second interior world, but when the shame grew intense he didn't know what to do. Joe didn't know it, and Helen didn't know it, and Robert didn't know it, but when he got tantrums Joe was really protesting against the fact that he had to keep his worlds apart. He was dissatisfied with himself; and he fought his mother and father and what they represented for making him do something which made him dissatisfied with himself.

Joe's tantrums were seen as unhappy, worrisome incidents in the life of a not completely well-behaved child. When Joe once took a dish, threw it on the floor, got off his chair, stamped his foot, and said: "I wish I was dead. You don't like me, I wish I was dead,"—and ran outside, the happening was regarded as a culmination of undesirable maladjustment. Joe was really protesting, though, at the fact that his universe was not coordinated and that he couldn't make it so, and that Helen and Robert weren't helping him.

Joe went to school. He left his home for a while, and that home he saw as good and bad, for him and against him. He was interested in the other boys and the teacher but after all, he carried with him the deep memory that things which pleased him could also pain him. Joe wanted to learn, but when he learned he knew in his fashion that what he was learning came from a world which could be against him. This world was everywhere around him. It could give him pleasure, but he didn't trust it. Well, if he had to meet it, he at least could fight it and show that he was around fighting. He began to show off. He even used his parents as a means of showing off. He got into a fight with a boy, Billy, and said to Billy that just as he could punch Billy's nose, so his father could punch Billy's father's nose. One day he had a scrap with Billy and made Billy run away. He felt triumphant, important. That night when his father came home, Joe noticed he was pretty worried. Somebody, where his father worked, was worrying Robert and Robert was complaining to Helen. Joe felt that in a way he could protect Robert, too. He felt that he could do some things his father couldn't because he made Billy run away. His father, though, was having a hard time where he worked, with this Mr. Richards, who seemed against him.

Joe asserted himself more and more. He wanted to show his parents the things that he knew. He began to think of himself as a general and as a pirate. He began to think he was smarter than the other boys. He would show people he was somebody. But beneath it all, the world that was entirely his own went on. He took it for granted now. It was right to have things in the night-time different from things in the day-time.—Joe was now seven years old.

Joe Johnson is fairly representative of the boys and girls born and growing up in America and elsewhere. Joe's father, Robert, once had pretty much the same situation to meet, as did Joe's mother, Helen. Joe didn't start out with the idea of dividing the reality in which he participated; he was compelled to do so. In accepting this division of reality he was making trouble for himself later, but to divide the world seemed the one thing to do.

If mother and father will not accept the whole being of a child, the child will retaliate and not accept them and what they stand for, entirely. He will change his disappointment into a kind of triumph, because disappointment can't be let go at that; and the alteration of tragedy into victory, if possible, will be achieved.

A child, fundamentally, doesn't want to escape from reality. The notion that an infant, just so, wishes to evade the actual conditions of existence is not true; because these conditions of existence are not seen as against him. If Joe Johnson meets inward trouble in his later years it won't be because of "infantile regression": the infant isn't so bad that the word "regression" has to be put next to him. Infants want to be reasonable, realistic in the best sense. A neurotic, therefore, does not go back to an infantile procedure, *as such;* he rather *persists* in doing something his ego, or in Aesthetic Realism terminology, his 2-A, saw as necessary or gratifying, in his earliest years.

Every person will at some time or other, when he is in a tough spot, use a solution which has been found efficient a long time ago. The child is indecisive when it eats food and at the same time dawdles with it. Here the child has found a solution for the problem of how to accept something, and yet show that he is against those from whom he accepts that something. The solution here is similar to that taken by a person who, wanting to visit someone and yet feeling that he shouldn't, comes late. The coming late is the acceptance of a situation and the showing that one doesn't entirely approve of it. This doesn't mean that there is an "infantile regression." It is a persistence, as I have said, and not a regression; but it isn't an inevitable persistence, either. An answer to a big, unavoidable problem was once found, and the answer can still work. If a person, for example, uses the fact that three and four make seven (which he learns while a child), it doesn't mean that he is going back to childhood in a regressive way when he uses the fact that three and four make seven at the age of forty-three. Let us not calumniate infancy.

In this world children are up against things. They come to various methods of dealing with unwelcome or unfair situations. If these methods work at all they will continue to be used. At any moment in the life of a man, an impression occurring at the age of four may join with an impression occurring at the age of thirty-four. Children are after wisdom, and a bit of wisdom, once found serviceable, will be clung to, retained, in one form or another while life goes on. There is, furthermore, a wisdom in children which is not seen as had; that is, it is not known to be possessed. Children are really desperate to see the world as pleasing; and their desperateness is part of a wise hope. The meaning of learning is intensely strong in childhood. The desire for order is intensely strong. The desire to see the world as good and beautiful, is intensely strong. But of course children, like all beings, are changeable by what they meet. They have possibilities which find mighty pervasive opposition. The character of this pervasive opposition it is our job to know.

2. LUELLA, RAMPAGEOUS AND PROFOUND

Luella Hargreaves, age five, is a difficult child living in Philadelphia. She has nearly the whole repertoire of procedures that a troublesome child can have. At times, though, she has the most delightful smile, a smile so sunny and pleasant that persons who do not know the annoyingly imperialistic Luella would think she was hardly other than angelic. And this smile is not insincere: sometimes the troubled personality of Luella does come forth serenely and looks with childlike, bland satisfaction at things surrounding. Luella is quite apparently an intelligent child, too. The kindergarten she goes to has issued reports to her mother of her keenness, even though the kindergarten has also reported that Luella will suddenly do such things as pinch the calf of a child next to her; put chewing gum on another child's dress; and suddenly yell she has to go to the toilet. The question is whether the angelic smile manifested by Luella at intervals is representative of her, or whether it is an indication of a hypocrisy of which the young and wily Luella is a master. The question also, therefore, is whether the tantrums, the pinchings, the yellings, the contrariness, the general adroit devilishness of Luella are really she.

Luella's mother is Lucia and her father is Hibbard Hargreaves. Luella is their only child. Hibbard Hargreaves is a lawyer, a graduate of Harvard Law School; and Lucia, before she married, had thought of writing. In fact, she has written various things in print here and there. Both Hibbard and Lucia are sticking to their individualities. In order to stick to his individuality, Hibbard has found it necessary at times to outmaneuver Lucia and attack hers; Lucia has found it necessary to employ the same procedure. The perceptive Luella has seen the maneuvers of her mother and father, has seen victories, defeats, skirmishes, drawn battles; has felt secret operations in the air; and has been pervaded with the aroma of spiritual battle, retreat, and siege. Luella has been used—as Joe Johnson was used—by both mother and father. Her parents have thought of divorce, and have even discussed it; but though there have been clawing and scratching and hate, victory is seen as possible by both of them and divorce is not imminent.

When Luella was born, her mother already knew that in a fashion she hated her husband. Even before she gave birth to Luella, there was a desire within her mind to use her coming child against her husband. Lucia did not take her pregnancy gracefully. When she became aware of it, she felt: "God damn it, I guess writing will be harder than ever." She went through her pregnancy, saw meaning in it as it approached culmination, but never was entirely for it. She decided that her child was to be a "prime article,"—as she put it to one of her friends. During pregnancy, she read books on child care. Somewhat she wanted to be a good mother; but Lucia was disappointed with Hibbard, disappointed with her "luck," disappointed with the earth she was on. The wise volumes she consulted on child care did not do away with that large disappointment.

When Luella was born, Hibbard felt proud; but he also felt that he was more tied than before to the woman he had once described to himself as a "glamorous bitch." The fact that Lucia was a mother made him think of her in more endearing terms than ever; but the new closeness heavily overlaid the uncertainty and antipathy, did not banish them. Luella became a kind of weather between the sky of Hibbard and the ocean of Lucia. The child was a province contested by two sovereign powers, bound by a treaty neither wanted fully to maintain.

From the very beginning, Luella participated in sudden, subtle sunshine, showers, storms, droughts, and unsettledness. Luella was an apprehensive child. She grew up amid kissing and hating; she grew up amid clawing caresses and caressing clawings. She felt there were spikes in gloves; and that a rose without a thorn had something the matter with it.

At the age of ten months, while in the nursery, she heard her mother throw a book to the floor and shout to her husband: "Well, for God's sake, Hibbard, let's call it off once and for all, and you can have Luella if you want her; I'm through." Luella did not know, to be sure, what the words meant; but they did sound pretty strange. Before Luella could talk she had heard some of the meanest things possible said in the most discriminating and elegant manner.

Once Hibbard and Lucia were by her crib.

Lucia said: "Well, Hib, I guess she's getting to look a little more like me these days."

Hibbard said: "Maybe you should have asked the little darling's permission."

"How do you know, Judge, I haven't?"

"If you have, then Lu is certainly a distinguished person, because you don't ask permission about anything from anybody else."

"Well, if you think that maybe I believe my daughter is a privileged person, maybe you're right. She hasn't had the time to be selfish; she hasn't had the time to learn how to draw up briefs which puzzle people; she hasn't had the time to go into politics just because a wife isn't desirable some of the time."

Hibbard forgot himself and raised his voice. "God, Lucia, do you think this is the place, and this is the time to say things like that? Jesus Christ, Lucia, can't we have our quarrels without getting the kid in?"

But Luella heard some of the conversation; and heard the raised voices. Despite the care of the parents not to have disagreements too close to the child, they did.

They both had discussed the welfare of their daughter: even Hibbard had read books on child care. They knew that a child was to be an individual; they were prepared to give it its freedom; they wanted it to learn about sex as efficiently and as early as possible. They were not prepared to scold it; they did not wish to tyrannize over it; and, in their ways, they wanted it to be happy. Its food, its sleep, its dress, its education, and its psychology were attended to in the modern fashion. But Luella was subtle: Lucia Hargreaves felt that her husband, Hibbard Hargreaves, was her enemy; and Luella, in her fashion, found out this was so.

At the age of fourteen months, Luella began to talk. One day, early in her third year, Luella cried and said: "I don't want to be here."

The nurse asked her: "Why, Lu? Why don't you want to be here?"

"Daddy isn't here."

"But your mother is here."

"Daddy's got to be here, too," and Luella cried more strongly than before.

Ten minutes later there were no tears on her face and she was smiling. A few days after, Luella was crying again. The nurse came in and asked: "What's it about?"

Luella didn't answer.

"Now what are you crying for?"

"Mamma's got to go, too."

"Got to go where?"

"Where daddy goes."

"Ah, that's silly."

The crying went on: "I want mamma go where daddy go."

Luella had by now the sense that the chief persons in her life were against each other. About this time a feeling of her own individuality had come to her. She knew that she was Luella Hargreaves, a human being. She felt that there was an I and that there was something else than I. About the time that this sense of her I came to her, there wasn't much reason to believe in the symmetry and justice and comeliness of that which wasn't herself or her I. She had a dim awareness of the falsity between her mother and father. She had perceived a little that she was a territory swept across and desired by both the clasping, warring powers. The apprehension of the battling duality of things was keen, if not conscious, in the little girl's mind. Simultaneously, then, with the recognition of the fact that there was a difference between her body and the world about her, there was a perception of the fact that this world, where it began for her, was divided, too.

Luella could not have much respect or love for such a silly, quarreling world. Earlier she did have. She knew, as all infants know, that through meeting this world, the coming to be of herself, her individuality, depended. Despite the suave bellicosities, and sometimes the flaring antagonisms of her mother and father, Luella saw her way, clambered her way, heard her way, touched her way to self-apprehension. This she had to do. She was a keen child and the impressions of the world went towards her; and she met them eagerly. Through taking to herself the externalities of reality, she came to know what she was; came to see herself as an entity in a universe of entities and combinations. But her conscious introduction into the world was not auspicious. Her curiosity was great, her disappointment was also great.

Both Lucia and Hibbard would flatter her. When she said: "I wish I was in the sky, I would tear your button off," this was taken as a very bright, poetic statement; and it was. What wasn't seen so well was Luella's desire to take away something, vengefully and correctingly, from her father. When Luella asked, at the age of two: "What's underneath your hair, mommy?"—this question was looked on as "cute"; and it was. What wasn't seen was the desire on Luella's part to get more inside her mother than the child was.

Anyway, the little girl couldn't see the world as entirely pleasant. Like Joe Johnson she interfered with the process of welcoming the world trustfully and eagerly. She, too, made a world for herself in opposition to her father and mother and everyone else. She began to be suspicious of the offerings of reality, she saw reality as an unfriendly interference. But she didn't like the seeing of existence as unfriendly. Beneath her recoiling from things, she wanted the love and belief in them she had in her first months of life. For, as I have said, no one can love the world more than a new-born child can. The very existence of the very self of the child depends on the successful love of objects by the child. There is no greater stake in the world than the existence of our selves as such; and this is the stake present in the life of the infant in its earliest days.

Lucia and Hibbard made much of the growing Luella. The child was "damnably clever," as a friend of Hibbard's once put it. Luella said that the hat of an aunt of Hibbard's looked like a towel. She asked once if people could wear shoes on their heads. She asked whether, if she kept it up, she could pull every hair from her head. She once told a little girl who had come to the house, that her father couldn't go to as many places as Hibbard could, because her mother didn't let him the way Luella's mother let her father. This was taken as quite funny and Luella was looked on as clever, much too clever.

Between the ages of two and three, Luella cultivated, quite noticeably, some hardly endurable qualities. Once, at the supper table, after having been silent in a sweet way, she began energetically pulling at the table-cloth. "Stop that, Luella," her mother said.—"I want to see what's underneath," Luella yelled; "I want to see how the candles look when they fall."

Luella was prevented from pulling the table-cloth from the table and from bringing the candles to the floor. There was nicely restrained consternation among the guests. There was silence for a while. Lucia, after taking her daughter's hands away from the table-cloth, stood over the child. Luella then uttered a yell distinctive of her, having in it both Indian warlikeness and a strange pain; said good-bye with a peculiar formality, and ran upstairs.

Luella stayed in her room and when her mother came to see her later she was fingering tranquilly a picture-book.

Her mother said: "Well, Lu—." Luella interrupted her, saying: "I had to do it, Mom, and you know I had to do it." There was a look in her face as if she meant it. Lucia saw that look and couldn't say more than: "All right, go to bed. We'll see later."

The next morning the child did not want to talk about it; and neither did her parents. Lucia knew that Luella meant it when she said: "I had to do it"; and Hibbard got the idea by this time likewise. The sudden demolishing activities of Luella, they felt, did come from a deep source and in their fashion her parents respected that deep source. They didn't know what to do about it.

Luella's father and mother knew that she was nervous, knew that she was maladjusted, knew that she wanted to bring attention to herself, knew that she was tyrannical, knew that she was destructive; but didn't know why. They had spanked her, they had disregarded her when she didn't eat, they had let her go to her room, and they had taken no notice when she was conspicuously misbehaved. They had taken her to doctors, including two who were esteemed for their knowledge of children's maladies. They had tried to deal with their froward and unpredictable child sensibly. They are thinking now of placing Luella with another family related to them, or even in a nursery away from family. These two last measures are not considered too happily by the troubled parents. To use them would mean acknowledgment of defeat in a way that is hardly attractive to either. Meanwhile, the five year old goes her sporadic, staccato, and disconcerting way.

Father and mother are willing to make concessions to their rampageous child: they are willing even to grant that they have made mistakes; they are aware that their own lives, singly and together, are partly the cause of Luella's displeasing manifestations. They wish to understand the belligerent child; but they cannot go beyond a certain point; and the self of Luella insists that they do.

Lucia can't see that what Luella has wanted, is, basically, what Hibbard has wanted, and what she herself has wanted; that is, to be loved and still to be seen as a perceptive entity, as a being in herself; as Lucia without any family reservations whatsoever. Despite all the strivings of her mother and father, the child is still deeply seen as a biological incident, as an appurtenance of their own lives, as a field for the playing of their own personal histories.

The reason Lucia can't love Luella is the reason she can't love Hibbard. She cannot give herself to Luella except as her daughter; she cannot give herself to Hibbard except as her lover or husband. In other words, she can't give herself to either husband or daughter but as an enlargement of herself. Hibbard has his way of fighting this situation; and Luella has hers. As I have intimated before, we cannot love anyone truly while we don't see that person not only as ours, but as a stranger. For, as soon as we love a person because that person is ours, we are esteeming ourselves in a new way, and do not see the other being as wholly free. Luella, being insistently and keenly human, wants to be loved as a free person, not as a caressed province; her father and her mother want to be loved that way, too.

Luella, like Joe Johnson, knows that there is something inside her, something she is which her mother and father should see, welcome, bring forth, honor, and develop. It is this mystery in herself which troubles the child and which she wishes to come out in the open, happily and effectively. Luella, like older people, is up against the question of the fate of her whole personality. That personality is *the thing* in her, however intangible and inaccessible it may be.

Luella knows that she has a self, that this self is frantically beating at doors, fumbling with locks, restlessly trying to meet the sun; and to emerge. Her parents think of her from themselves out, are interested in having selected aspects of her self to function and be manifest. To be sure, the father and mother have thought considerably of personality; and they have said quite often to their friends that they do not wish to interfere with the personality of their daughter.

But they have already interfered, because of the way they look at *themselves.* Lucia wants to love Luella—but her notion of love is to have the person loved, subtly and preponderantly, subservient to herself. She felt this way before she married; before she became a mother; and there has been no reason in her life to change this attitude. Despite her modernity, to love a person means to her having that person gratifyingly subsidiary to her own life. She thinks she is greatly honoring a person when she permits that person to participate deeply in her own existence. But when that person participates, it is still as one human she has conquered, and taken to herself.

Lucia has tried to make a conquest of her daughter in the way that she has, up to a point, made a conquest of Hibbard. Hibbard has objected in ways that he doesn't fully know; and so has Luella. All this has troubled the mother, and she has had periods of profound misgiving. There have been times when Lucia has looked on herself and not liked what she saw. Hibbard also has disliked what he is. And these two beings, elevating and isolating themselves, conquering and pervading, have tried to take a new human being unto themselves—meanwhile distrusting the strange world she represents.

Well, when Luella pulls at table-cloths with company present, and wants to see candles fall, she is announcing to her parents and to others that this procedure of two adults won't do. She is staging an unconscious revolt against the spiritual acquisitiveness and also spiritual aloofness of the two most important beings in her life. If she annoys others, it is because she has been deeply disappointed and aggrieved by the two central representatives of that existence which takes in teachers, schoolmates, guests, relatives. She is saying to her parents, that the world which has been presented to her, through them, is a world she doesn't like and won't accept. She can't write letters to congressmen, nor does she know how to reach God successfully; and she can't leave home; so she yells, stamps her feet, asks strange questions, makes disconcerting statements, and annoys generally.

The great number of books on children points to the fact that there is a great question about the young inhabitants of earth which must be answered. Plato and Wordsworth thought that there was a wisdom which a new-born child was near—a wisdom implicit in the meaning of existence, and life, and death. We now talk of babies in terms of responses, blood counts, behavior patterns, nutrition, weight, sense-development, and the like. Beneath these terms there is the problem of self as such. The problem of self is another way of saying: the problem of reality.

And reality can be dealt with in terms of blood counts, nutrition, brain structure, light responses, and so on; but it also must be dealt with in itself. What self and reality are cannot be described simply in nutritional terms, or physiological terms, or even psychological terms in the narrow sense. You cannot describe a child just in terms of behavior, or day-to-day adjustment. There must be a notion of what the behavior as such comes from, and what it is all going towards.

One must answer the question: What is a human self after?—and that involves the question of: What is the existence of a self, and what is it for? Beneath all the eating, sleeping, crying, gurgling of a baby, is the meaning and general aim of the baby—which exists from the day of birth, no matter how unexpressed that meaning and aim is.

As I have said: The first purpose of a self is to be. It therefore has to be asked: What does it mean for a self to be?

Again I must say, this question cannot be answered in nutritional terms, in simply sexual terms, in terms of blood count, brain structure; or with a narrow idea of "adjustment." The question can only be answered—whether doctors, nurses, mothers, psychologists, health-officials like it or no—aesthetically or philosophically.

A self wants to be, has to be, as free as it can; and a self wants to feel, has to feel, all it can. A baby at birth is pushing towards freedom and inclusiveness of perception. By this I mean that a baby wants to feel that *it is;* and at the same time, wants to feel *all that is besides its own life.* In logical terms, a baby wants to feel the utmost particularity and the utmost generality; it aims for uniqueness and it aims for indefinite diversity of response.

When Luella Hargreaves was born, she wanted to feel that *she was*—definitely, unquestionably, really; was one person, untrammeled, unhindered, unsmothered, unannexed by anything or anyone else. At the same time, Luella wanted knowledge; she wanted to affirm her relation with as many things as possible. A human being is simultaneously a free entity and an indefinite assemblage of relations. Luella wanted her mother to see to it that she had a clear notion of what *she was*—as different from any other thing; for after all, a thing or a person is one thing and one person, because *it is* different from anything else.

Luella also wanted her mother to be a means of her feeling a happy relation with as many objects as possible. This going towards freedom and relation, simultaneously, is to be seen in every child. A child wants to have a lucid, intense feeling of *I,* and a lucid, intense feeling of *They.* When Luella's mother told her, when she was twelve months old, that she was the prettiest baby in the world; and that evening put her aside hurriedly when a visitor came in, the mother was making for a disjunction between Luella's feelings for self and her feelings for other things. Lucia hugged Luella fervently while she was flattering the baby, and Luella got a feeling of tremendous snugness and importance. This feeling assisted the attitude of self-affirmation possible in the child; and Luella wanted to affirm herself. But when Luella's mother ceased to caress her when a visitor came in, she accented the competition between the trend in Luella towards the affirmation of herself and the trend in the child towards the affirmation of the existence of other things. Without knowing it, Lucia was helping to bring about the later fidgety state of her daughter.

When Luella was two years old, Lucia said: "You know, brat, you're about the slickest thing in the whole city." The next day Lucia said to Hibbard in Luella's hearing: "I do wish that our infant could have just a little of the control Dan and Helen's children have." When Luella was born she had no inevitable desire to think of herself in competition with other children, though she did wish, deep down, to come to a sense of her own unique being. Her problem was, like the problem of all, to arrive at her own uniqueness by welcoming the uniqueness of other beings. When her mother, at one time, dealt with her as if she were the only important person in the world, and, at another time, as if she were in some infantile war with other persons, a conflict as to herself was encouraged by the unknowingly fickle parent.

A child wants to esteem its parents; but it also wants to have a love for the full world as it may be met. Therefore, it is necessary for parents to bring out in children a love for themselves as parents, which is not disproportionate to a love for other things. Because children can affect their parents in ways that they cannot affect persons outside the family, a disproportion arises between the attitude towards parents (who represent the children) and the world outside the family. This does not help the attainment of freedom and inclusiveness. Luella sometimes heard her parents quarreling with each other; at other times she heard Lucia and Hibbard disparaging others. The situation then in Luella's mind was something like this: Lucia and Hibbard didn't like each other fully; but, at the same time they together could dislike other people, and in doing so seem to approve of each other. Now Luella was a keen child, and this accommodating hypocrisy didn't make her any too tranquil. What Lucia and Hibbard did not see was that Luella wanted to like herself, to like her parents, and to like, at least in a general way, the world beyond parents and self. Existence was presented to the child as a wavering hodgepodge.

Coming back to the basic ideas of freedom and inclusiveness: There is an aspect of freedom equivalent to selfishness in the usual sense. A child wants to be free, because it wants to feel that *it is*. Everything should be done to make the child feel that it can be free, while aware of what is coming to others, and of the possible freedom of others. The child, like the adult, meets the question of: How can I be free and give myself all that is coming to me, and yet give all that is coming to others? Once a decision is made in a child's mind that its own autonomy and happiness can be reached by disregard of outside things, selfishness, in the bad sense, is affirmed; and this selfishness is the ethical phase of that mental split and opposition which, from other points of view, may be neurosis or schizophrenia.

The only reason that an infant mind, or an adult mind, isolates itself or splits itself from other minds and things is because that way seems the only way available for freedom, for self-affirmation. And it is possible to see both neurosis and schizophrenia as having their beginning in the insufficient or corrupt answer to the question: How can one be free, and yet welcome and be affected by other things?

The confusion, for example, that Luella has had to meet has resulted at times in her rushing to her room and refusing to come out when called. She couldn't see how she was able to affirm her own freedom and yet meet the demands expressed and unexpressed of her parents and others. Once Lucia and Hibbard were quite surprised after Luella had gone off to her room in a huff, to see her smilingly come down the stairs later and hear her saying: "I forgive you, Mom, and don't forgive me yet." (Once more I must make it clear that Luella was an unusually keen child.)

Luella once pinched a little girl's leg very hard. The little girl cried. Luella told her mother: "I did an awful thing today, Mom. Could you buy me some candy I could bring Jean tomorrow and maybe some other time?" It should be noticed that the ethical behavior of children, like the ethical behavior of adults, all is concerned with the interaction of self and others. The question beneath the ethical behavior of Luella and everyone else in the world is: How can I be fair to myself, please myself, and at the same time be fair to everyone else?

Joe Johnson, then, and Luella Hargreaves, on the days they were born, faced the same problem that they will face no matter how old they become. Any attitude forced upon them or chosen by them, will affect all later attitudes or choices. For this reason it is clear that any inward decision taken in the earliest years has a great effect on later life. Yet there is nothing final or inevitable as to this later life. If Joe Johnson feels, as a child, that his environment doesn't make sense; that he has to evade; that in order to be free he has to be hostile, he will carry this feeling over to future years. Impressions do not leave one unless stronger impressions take their place. If Joe has a mistaken, wavering, inimical approach to what he meets, that approach will continue, if evidence which his unconscious can accept, invalidating the earlier approach, does not arrive. If Luella, in coming years, doesn't meet with new situations and occurrences strong enough to counterweigh the tremendous effect of the world as she has so far known it, she will carry her present attitudes with her just as she would carry a deep scar, an amputated finger, or a severe burn. These physical injuries, however, are surrounded by variables; and so, early decisions giving a trend to the personality are likewise changeable. The general truth, however, that what we are is what we have been, holds.

There will be a striving on Luella's part for order and diversity in her character. To be pleased deeply is to see the world in some kind of order. The desire of a child to be gratified—despite all that has been written to the seeming contrary—is also a desire for order; for gratification implies a harmony of one's organism with an object. We—children, adults, and aged alike—are pleased when there is a fit blending of ourselves, our feelings, with something else. A fit blending is a harmonious blending; a harmonious blending implies order.

It has been said that children are savages, "amoral," impulsively selfish, because all they are after is gratification (the word *gratification* has taken on a needless quality of psychological and psychoanalytical melodrama). When Luella was born she certainly wanted to be pleased with the world; but she had no unchangeable blueprint towards pleasure. She wasn't insistent on just how the being pleased should occur. She wished to find herself in some interaction with things that would be at once harmonious and alive; orderly, yet not stunting or denying. This desire in itself is definitely a logical one. If this general desire becomes hurtful to people, ugly, distorted, it isn't because there is an unchangeable insistence on gratification that isn't just.

To wish to be pleased is a desire to be fair to oneself; and that desire is both ethical and logical. It is easy to see a drive towards logic in a young child. There are tremendous impediments to that drive; beneath the impediments is the desire itself, akin to beauty and justice. For one of the inherent things in ethics is the desire to please oneself. If one doesn't please oneself deeply and comprehensively, one is not "unselfish," well-behaved, adjusted; one is unethical. It needs to be repeated: To be ethical is to give oneself what is coming to one by giving what is coming to other things. To give oneself what is coming to one, is to enable oneself to grow, to meet objects accurately, to blend with externals fortunately, to meet the world felicitously; that is, to be happy. To be happy, put otherwise, is an ethical obligation. If one is not happy, one cannot be just to other things. Therefore, for a child to aim after gratification is not in itself an indication of undiscipline, inconsiderateness, "amorality."

A child's body is an organization, the principle of which is order. To be alive is to have some order. The relation of brain, heart, liver, blood, bones, and so on, as we find it in every living being, including the diseased, is basically orderly. Where it isn't orderly, there is still a trend within the organism towards order. Where the trend towards order meets opposition, there is pain. To be alive, then, is to be organized; and there is no reason for assuming the existence of a decisive trend within an essential aspect of life—mind

—making for disorder. A child's body depends for its health on its accurate involvement with the world about it; that is, its environment, in the fullest sense. Wherever there is an inaccuracy, deficiency, excess, or confusion in the bodily involvement of an infant with its environment, a condition making for disease has taken place. A diseased body is one which is quantitatively hindered in its full involvement with its environment. A lack of order within a body makes for inaccurate relations with environment. Inaccurate relations with environment make for a lack of order within a body or self. What the child's mind is after is what the other aspect of itself, its body, is after. The mind wishes definition, diversity of response and action; and so does the body. To have diversity and definition or oneness of response, is to possess organization or order. The infant desires this as much as (perhaps more than) a Supreme Court judge or the lady dean of a college.

If a child is frustrated, it is because the fundamental life procedure in it of becoming an integrity, simultaneously with meeting life at more and more points, has met interference: interference which it combats most often murkily or blindly by attack, or withdrawal—or confusion, having in it both attack and withdrawal.

The purpose of education is to bring to the child's desire for order and diversity, fit material through which this desire can operate. A parent or teacher does not bring order to a child as he might bring an apple. It is the duty of a parent or teacher, humbly and respectfully, to see that the desire for full accuracy already existing in a child not be blunted or distorted. For this, an understanding of what mind and self as such are, is necessary. One may say this is hard to know; this is a metaphysical problem. Yet the difficulty of the problem does not destroy the necessity for meeting it.

When Joe Johnson was born, there was something he was after. The force in him that made his heart beat, had purpose to it. His possibilities were his purpose. If we don't know what these possibilities are or what that purpose is, we should honestly say that we are working basically in the dark. We know that Joe wanted to be well. The question is: Well for what? We know that he wanted to have a good metabolism: A good metabolism for what? We know that very likely he wanted to learn the alphabet: The alphabet for what? We know that he wanted to get along with other children and other people: To get along for what? If that deepest purpose, even though he and we do not see it clearly, is deflected or injured, the self of Joe Johnson will not be at ease. If it isn't at ease it will retaliate.

I have said earlier that the principal desire of every human being is to know; that is, to have reality in mind. To know the world is to be at one with it; and this means to be happy. I believe that every activity of the child has something to do with the desire to know. For example, if a child sucks its thumb, there is a desire on its part to know what its self is like. We say that someone enjoyed himself at a theatre or concert; the phrase *enjoyed himself* has in it some kind of new knowledge. We enjoy ourselves when we find something new about ourselves, and can make it continuous, at one, with what we already know.

A child enjoys itself by sucking its thumb. Let us say that there is sex in this. But wherever there is sex, there is also knowledge. Wherever there is enjoyment, there is also knowledge. And so if Josepha Jordan, age thirty, enjoys herself at the theatre and Joe Johnson, age ten months, enjoys himself by sucking his thumb, there is knowledge present in both personal events.

We find that an infant wants to be aware of its own body. It will touch itself, manipulate itself. Why is it necessary to give this procedure all kinds of sinister autoerotic, or sexual meanings, when an injunction present in all history has been: Know thyself? If there are better ways of knowing oneself available to Joe Johnson than sucking his thumb, well, Joe is wrong because a just purpose of his could have been achieved in a more efficient way. Yet the drive behind putting his thumb in his mouth should still be honored. We all have within us a tremendous urge to know who we are, what we are, how we are.

A baby has that urge with great strength. It will use the means available to satisfy itself. If Joe were to disassociate the knowledge of himself which he received by having his thumb in his mouth, from the knowledge he received by hearing new sounds or touching a new toy, this would be bad because the method of self-knowledge employed by him would be incomplete. It could very well be that, disappointed in finding out gracefully and pleasantly what certain external things were, Joe might make up for this lack of knowledge elsewhere by an over-intense interest in himself. This is unfortunate, but the same thing has occurred with persons much older than he. It is important, then, to have a clear notion of personality where it concerns the infant—and, of course, persons other than infants. Personality is how a self takes what it meets. There is power in personality and there is desire; and there is an interaction of power and desire. The infant, like other people, does not know its own desires; that is, what it is going after. Every desire, in so far as it is unknown, is instinctive or unconscious. Yet the fact that the desire is unknown does not lessen its actuality. Infants, like older persons, face the constant job of knowing what they desire. They cannot know their desires unless they know the world these desires come from, and through which these desires will be met—if they are met. Infants, then, *want* to know—as adults do—themselves and everything else at once.

3. MICHAEL HALLERAN AND DANIEL DORMAN

Michael Halleran, infant, like many other persons, does not know what he wants; and his parents and others do not know what he wants. Something profoundly disadvantageous therefore exists for Michael. Michael wants good food because good food is a way of establishing his personality and enabling it to meet with satisfaction the things around it. It is plain, then, that if the right food is not forthcoming, there will be unease within Michael. Yet the purpose of the food is the enabling of the child to be on the right terms with earth. The father of Michael, however, is worse off than the father of Joe and—very definitely—the father of Luella. Michael's father, Edward, feels he doesn't make money enough; and that there are many men in the world who can do things and buy things he cannot. He is bitter, even though that bitterness is not often apparent. And Michael's mother, Lavinia, is also bitter: her bitterness is more often apparent.

Lavinia has nagged Edward. Sometimes her nagging has concerned money directly; at other times other subjects have been used by the vexed wife and mother. Michael has heard the nagging; and he has heard his father complain morosely. He has heard his mother, a Catholic, pray to God; and he has heard her, that same day, scold her husband strongly. Around Christmas, a rather stout priest of the church brought two baskets of food to the Hallerans and said: "These are the blessings of the Lord given to his faithful children." Mrs. Halleran seemed grateful and thanked the priest fervently. But after the priest left, Michael's father, not working at the time, went to another room, sat at a table, and put his head on his arms. Michael saw his father sitting there with his head on the table.

There were visitors, likewise, from a Catholic charity who were interested in the health of the family, particularly

that of Michael and his two older sisters, Vera and Dorothy.
Michael once heard these two sisters quarreling after a visitor from the church had been present. It all was a topsy-
turvy world for the boy. There was a father who drank
and at times sat moodily alone, with his head on the table.
There was a mother who prayed, went piously to church;
and yet nagged her husband. There were two daughters who quarreled and tyrannized singly and together
over the growing male child. God was, in a way, present
in the family; God was present along with little food
and lay-offs and a strike and shoutings and naggings and
weeping.

Michael heard Lavinia say once to Edward: "Lord, Edward, I wish you could be like other men and take care of
your family. I know it's sinful, but I think sometimes maybe
I shouldn't have had any children. Maybe we had no right
to marry." Michael didn't understand all the words; but
there is a way a child has of getting at the meaning of a
grown-up without knowing all the words. The boy Michael, from it all, couldn't see much reason for his being
alive. At about the age of three, Michael began to distress his
mother by wetting his bed nearly every night. At about the
same time he began to show a distressing habit of closing and
opening his eyes with great rapidity.

By now the harassed boy Michael didn't have any reason
clear to him for approving of that world which began with
his parents and his sisters. There are two ways of dealing
with a disliked situation: one can attack it, and one can
withdraw. Both Lavinia and Edward at times, despite all the
counsel of their church, regretted the existence of their boy;
and the child felt that they did. In other words, in Michael's
instance, along with the reasons that may be present for
wealthier parents' opposing the personalities of their children, there was a conspicuous money-reason. The condi-

tions he met, therefore, worked upon Michael to make him withdraw from the world he found.

Lavinia was greatly annoyed by the bed-wetting of Michael; but she felt that he would get over it. She mentioned it once to a visitor from the Catholic charity, and he said: "It is very bad, Mrs. Halleran. Nothing much can be done about it. When he gets older he will stop it. In the meantime see that he gets the best food he can, and doesn't drink anything before bed-time. And as to that other habit he has of closing and opening his eyes, just like that, right in mid-afternoon —well, children are liable to that kind of thing, and he'll get over it, too. It is good that he doesn't break windows and kill cats."

Mrs. Halleran did her own laundering. Though annoyed by the extra work that Michael gave her, she would have endured it had other things been all right. As the boy grew up, he didn't stop the bed-wetting, and he was still given to the habit spasm with his eyes—though less so than earlier. But he became dreamy.

His two sisters, however, were a pair of the leading mischief-makers in the crowded block. No girl or, for that matter, no boy would dare oppose them beyond a certain point. Vera and Dorothy functioned as a team of terrible twins, though there was a twenty months difference of age. They were "those two Halleran kids"; and the block knew them for their activity, their screaming, their daring, and their devotion. Michael was like a quiet, lonely pool to their don't-give-a-damn waterfalls. Vera and Dorothy could say such things as: "Father Donovan is a fine man, but he has too big a behind for any man to have." And once Vera said to Dorothy: "I have a notion the Lord likes you the more money you have"; and Dorothy said: "You know, I think you're right, Sis."

The parents felt that the sisters would take care of themselves—and more, when they grew up. Michael, though, was something else. Lavinia, seeing him quieter and quieter, thought that he would be fit for the priesthood. Even in his eating, there was tranquil method in the boy's motions. He ate as if he were in a quiet land by himself.

At the age of two the child would cry and Lavinia felt occasionally that maybe it was because he hadn't eaten enough. But now at the age of four-and-a-half, whether there was enough food on the table or no, the boy took everything as if it were right. There was a regularity to his voice, and to his walk. It is true he had the strangest dreams. Sometimes he would talk to himself about these dreams, though his mother was there listening. Michael would say: "I was in a green place, and the sky was real beautiful; but nobody was there except me. And I walked and I walked, and I didn't see anybody and the sky was blue all the time. I didn't think anybody else was alive and I said: 'This is hell and I am in it, and under all this green there is a big fire.' But anyway I liked it."

Lavinia once asked Michael how could such a lovely place be hell? "I don't know," Michael said, "but it was, I just felt it was."

Michael is still growing. His mother more and more thinks of him in terms of the priesthood. She has even mentioned it to Father Kern; and he said somewhat approvingly: "Well, we'll see, Mrs. Halleran, we'll see. If the Lord so wills it, so it will be." Whether Michael becomes a priest of the church is yet to be seen. What his mother and Father Kern and his own father do not know, is that the gentle Michael does not love mankind the way a coming shepherd of a human flock should.

Michael is really bitter. But his bitterness, unlike the dissatisfaction of his sisters, has not taken an aggressive form. He is really more bitter than his sisters because his personality-pain has resignation to it; has despair in it. He has been so hard hit by the world that he is fighting by standing aside. His unconscious has not as yet fully accepted the resignation: that is why, despite his gentleness, he still worries his mother by his enuresis. His bed-wetting is a retaliation for his being forced into himself; and is also a release. There are expression and aggression and release in his wetting the bed. That is his way of getting back at the world which has not welcomed the possibilities of his personality. He does not want to annoy his mother by wetting the bedclothes; but the self of Michael Halleran is still active. It still wants to be in a just and felicitous and complete relation with the earth he knows.

The regular eye-twitching is an expression of bewilderment and the symbolic annulling of that bewilderment. Michael does not wish to minister to the souls of humans. He doesn't like humans that much. He sees himself as a choked self which might have been developed. The child has been compelled to be "schizoid." He has, in his dreams, made hell into a place more fitting for him—even while he fears it.

If nothing happens to make Michael justly love the world of God as he can see it, he will leave it whether alive or dead. He is now in process of leaving it. He is, if anything, a quiet, gentle-mannered diabolist, a worshipper of a composed devil of his own choosing. If he reaches an asylum he will be—unless his life and self change—a worshipper of his own devil there, and a walker in his own grassy hell. Michael has withdrawn; and if nothing happens he will withdraw permanently.

There are thousands and thousands of instances of children who, with personalities ready to go, ready to ramify, ready to take the sun and forms and people and sounds and meanings and smells and battles, are forced into a dark evasion and retreat. The evasion and retreat are perhaps not as thorough as that of Michael Halleran. But there is altogether too much of compulsory evading and compulsory retreating.

Sometimes children, hindered from being what they justly want to be, become little Attilas and vexing Genghis Khans and troublesome, fraudulent Napoleons. I do not believe that children are cruel and destructive just so. If they are swerved from the path they deeply wish to take, they will become angry, will revenge themselves wildly, will be cruel.

Daniel Dorman is one of those terrible "problem children" given to destruction. He was born a vigorous child weighing twelve pounds. He did not know, as other children don't, just what was waiting for him outside his mother's womb. But within his vigorous, small body were energies looking for a home.

His mother and father are tired people; people who had a child as a means of bringing something new to their heretofore rather dull married life. Both Edgar Dorman and Olga Dorman are timid persons. They married after a long engagement; and both thought of each other's incomes before they married. They both look upon marriage as everlasting. They are both Episcopalian churchgoers (Olga's mother had called her Olga because she had been reading a great deal about strange Czarist Russia and strange Siberia). Edgar Dorman is a vice-president of a bank in a city of seventy thousand in Missouri; and Olga Dorman, before her marriage, had taught school. They had pretty definite plans for their boy, although they weren't sure they were going to have a child because Olga saw herself as a possible political figure.

The boy Daniel did not know much of the deep intentions of his father and mother; in fact, neither Olga nor Edgar have been too honest about their own feelings with each other. (Edgar's great-grandfather was one of the earliest settlers in Missouri; and he was not beyond killing a white man or black man or Indian who might stop him from doing what he wanted in the undeveloped and promising Missouri Territory.) When the school teacher Olga gave birth to such a vigorous boy as Daniel, she and her relatives and friends were surprised. But heredity has more its own way than the Mississippi.

Though Olga and Edgar saw they had something more than a demure baby on their hands, their plans for their child persisted. He was to have an income; and he was to have respectable culture. Daniel grew up in an air of affluence and secrecy. His parents saw him as a child whose future was in the bag. What worlds were simmering and seething and circling within Daniel were not wondered about by his mother and father. The boy's personality was an administrative area of theirs. What junction of drives and possibilities existed in him was not investigated. Olga and Edgar, like Hibbard and Lucia Hargreaves, had never adequately loved each other. Olga and Edgar, however, did not fight about it. They saw their situation as arising from a world's ordinance; and the ordinance was not to be opposed. The behavior of both was symmetrical and concealing.

Well, Daniel was definitely peevish after six months. At the age of eight months his yelp was mighty. At the age of ten months his behavior was so unruly that a corner room in the third floor of the old large house possessed by the Dormans was made a nursery. A stout, matter-of-fact black woman was his nurse. Daniel's nurse took his frowardness calmly; and the parents felt she was in a casual conspiracy to keep him untamed. Sue, it appeared, didn't mind just how vociferous Daniel was. In a strange way, though, the child seemed to like the unperturbed Sue. Olga had Sue discharged. She did not know that she was jealous of Sue because the child seemed more contented, even though still wildish, with Sue than with his own mother. Sue took her discharge in a matter-of-fact way and went elsewhere.

The boy remained an uncontrolled, small human. He tore the sheet of his crib into strips. He took a picture from the wall and threw it out the window. He found a nail and scratched Edgar's desk with it. He once came downstairs with a peach and started smearing the mirror, while guests were present. He yelled in a tremendous way at four o'clock in the morning so that people in the next house, a hundred or so feet away, could hear. He refused the food offered him and loudly asked for something else. He tore the dress from off a little girl visiting the house. He tried to dislodge a large stone in the yard back of the house in order to throw it. He climbed into a poultry yard and ran after the chickens furiously. He destroyed sheet music lying on the piano played by Olga. He has a habit of rolling himself on the floor when he doesn't like something done or said. This doesn't complete the activities of Daniel.

The boy Daniel, like Joe Johnson and Luella Hargreaves and Michael Halleran, is protesting against the fact that his parents (or the world he knows) have imposed themselves on him—instead of cooperating with him to see that he is entirely what he can be. It appears, then, that the fundamental job of Edgar and Olga was to see Daniel with Edgar and Olga left out for a while. Every person has a right to be seen as an object; to be seen as what he is before he is made to conform to previous notions had by other people of what he should be. If this ethical justice is not given to a baby, if that baby is "arranged" in its parents' minds—there will be trouble.

A question arises: What would Daniel Dorman be if he did not have such parents as Olga and Edgar Dorman? Whatever parents he might have had, it is still necessary and just that he be seen as a person with possibilities, deserving and requiring that these possibilities become embodied in activity. Nothing hereditary in a child can really work out unless there is a situation enabling it to do so. Heredity can be described as environment that occurs before one's birth. Then there is the environment that comes after one's birth. Heredity is *all that* in a person existing before that person is born. Environment is *all that* existing after one's birth. Heredity, therefore, in the fullest sense, would be the whole world seen as existing before the birth of a human. This heredity-world and this environment-world, in a profound sense, can be seen as both the same and different.

In the instances of the children I have chosen, there were no conspicuous hereditary defects. There was no inevitable drive making Joe Johnson divide his world. There was no heredity-drive making Luella Hargreaves have a tantrum and a wide smile, in the same hour. It wasn't heredity which made Michael Halleran decide that the world was not for him. It wasn't heredity, even, which made Daniel Dorman an uncontrolled child in Missouri. When these children were born what confronted them was possibilities. What they wanted was to be true to themselves or their nature, and to get along with what was about them. It was possible at each moment of Joe Johnson's first days to present the organic trend that was in him with a situation which would accord with it. Instead, situations were presented which, it was presumed by others, were satisfactory to him. If something amiss occurs when a child is not presented with what it really needs, a statement saying that it was hereditarily inevitable is certainly out of place. Only when something hereditary has been completed by what is most accurate for it; what is best and most deeply wanted, can it be said that a certain action had an hereditary cause.

No child will clamor for a knowledge of the alphabet. In a certain sense, therefore, ignorance of the alphabet is hereditary. Nevertheless, from another point of view it can be said that a desire to learn the alphabet *is* hereditary. *A person wants to use the deepest powers which he has; and all his powers.* To have a power implies somewhere the desire to use it. There is a power of thought implicit within a child's body or mind. Not to put that power into use means the diverting and injuring of an hereditary trend.

Furthermore, since it is the whole world which is the real mother of a child, there is no reason for believing that the world which created a person did not give that person somehow the means of coming to accurate terms with it. Those who say that a defect in a person, particularly a mental defect, is hereditary, must prove that there was no means within the world capable of effectively diminishing the force making for defect. When, for example, a child is said to break windows because of an hereditary, aggressive disposition, *it must be proved that the child couldn't have come to an equal gratification without breaking windows.* It must be seen that when a child or adult does something amiss, his purpose is not so much to do that particular thing, as to find some means of pleasing expression. The motive of every person —criminal, schizophrenic, missionary, soldier, executioner, aviator, author—is to come to some arrangement with the world by which this person's life seems justified; that is, pleasant. The necessity for being pleased is the one indisputable hereditary drive.

The chief thing in heredity is the fact that one is born. This is simple, but the words *is born* have a tremendously large meaning. For the reason one is born is to go on from there; and each person has to find something justifying the going on from there. All other hereditary drives, authentic or so-called, are subsidiary to the drive implicit in being born itself. All other drives are capable of indefinite alteration, increase and decrease, heightening and muting. But the drive implicit in being born—that is, to live, and to live fully in keeping with the organism—is a constant, essentially immutable.

The sharpest knife in the world will not cut anything if there is nothing for it to cut. If a knife meets only water it will never show what it can do. If it lies in the lower shelf of a store, thickly wrapped, never taken out, it might as well have been a quarter-pound of old cheese. However, this sharp knife also can be used to kill a man. The same sharp knife can be used to cut bread for a hungry man. In each instance of the knife's activity or inactivity, there is a relation of subject and object: every action is made up of subject and object. A subject, from the deepest point of view, is any reality thought of as affecting any other reality. An object is any reality thought of as being affected by any other reality. For a thing to happen, there must be the presence of both subject and object. A person is both subject and object. Heredity and environment are each both subject and object.

When Daniel Dorman was born, his little fists and his definite cry were subjects in so far as they were acting upon the world. They were objects in so far as the world acted on them. The gripping of the little fists of Daniel can be seen as something acted on and something acting. And that is just the way the heredity of Daniel Dorman can be seen.

From the very moment of his birth, his whole past is acting on the world he has met. The world he has met is also acting on his whole past. If an element in his whole past had been different, or an element in the world he met had been different, then the life of Daniel Dorman that much would have been different.

Daniel Dorman was born in a small hospital in a fair-sized city in Missouri. The hospital in which he was born immediately acted on the past which he, when born, represented. Had he been born in an open field, or in an airplane, or in the third story of an old house in Brooklyn, his environment —that is, the world after he was born—would have been acting differently. But in each situation in Daniel's life, there are present and had to be present, both what he had been and what he was meeting.

If we call heredity A, and environment B, then every situation in Daniel's life is A plus B. Let us call, however, a specific situation B-1. There is, then, A plus B-1. The next situation, however, which we shall call C-1, is met by the interaction of A plus B-1. In other words, when Daniel has lived through his first day of life, he meets his second day of life not only with his heredity, but with his heredity plus the events of the first day, the milieu of the first day, the implications of the first day. So Daniel's life goes on. There is a kind of living compound interest which takes place in the history of every person. We never, after a time, meet our environment with only our heredity; we meet our environment with heredity plus the greatly flexible "interest" which is environment. And it must be remembered that if either A or B is changed at any time, what happens when A and B meet is also changed. No one can say just how altering environment can be. Heredity has been looked on as mysterious, unfathomable; but environment is also unfathomable. The sight of a certain leaf at the age of four months may have an effect we cannot chart. It need not be anything as frail as a leaf; it can be something else; but we do not know yet the tremendous impact of events the first twenty-four months on that puzzling, yes—but indefinitely alterable thing called heredity.

The blood cells of a child meet a situation at the age of ten months (the blood cells have already been affected by environmental occurrences). The blood cells are now not only what they were, but blood cells plus a new situation. For example, hunger is environmental; accidents are environmental; shocks are environmental: all of these have a profound effect on the world as it is in a person when born; that is, heredity. These environmental facts definitely, profoundly alter heredity. Five days of environmental hunger can revolutionize the most fortunate, haughty heredity in the world. But environmental effects need not be so obvious; and *hereditary possibility may never meet fulfillment because of some environmental failure or environmental excess.*

In dealing with environment, we are up against a tremendous aggregation of important, but hardly seen, variables. All that we can say definitely is that the heredity of each child deserves the environment that will *complete it.* If the child does not get that environment, that exact and felicitous environment which it deserves, we are not justified in saying that a defect possessed by that child was an inevitable hereditary manifestation. If environment can affect heredity for the worse in terms of hunger, shock, accident, how far can environment affect (that is, complete) heredity for the better? That is one question which persons disposed to accent the fearsome and powerful effects of heredity have not met.

When a child grasps objects, it is trying to bring out the hereditary possibility of grasping. The child does all it can to have the world that it meets fulfill the world that it began with. But choices are imposed upon the child—choices which take the place of those which somewhere the child can and should make. It certainly is unwise to say, if evil occurs, that this evil was an outgrowth of an hereditary situation. We do not know just how subtle and pervasive and deep may be the effect of family conditions on an infant. We don't know—despite all the studies and investigations made—just what the infant feels; because feeling is a much bigger thing, a much subtler and more wonderful thing than biologists, psychologists, or psychoanalysts most often think it is.

All medicine is environmental; all education is environmental; every happening in the life of child or adult is environmental. For anything which can either hurt, or cause to swerve, or complete hereditary possibility, is environmental. In the fullest sense, there is no limit to environmental power. Everything, including the past, once it is seen as affecting a person's life, is environmental. If a person can say of anything: "This now can affect me"—and this thing is of the world that he knows after he is born, he is talking of environment. Put otherwise, environment is the possible world affecting a person all through his life. In keeping with this idea, heredity can be defined as the environment that occurred before one's birth.

Bad heredity, therefore, is the past in a human organism working to make that organism meet environment disadvantageously. Health is that situation in an organism enabling the organism to come to its fullest meaning by dealing with what is about it—or its environment—justly; so that what the organism is can fully be brought out. If a baby were born with hereditary defect, the meaning of hereditary defect here is: The presence of something, or the lack of something, causing the baby to be at odds with its environment.

The quality of heredity can be defined only in terms of environmental accuracy or inaccuracy, completeness or incompleteness, happiness or unhappiness. If bad heredity occurs, even so it is not fanciful to suppose that there is a force within, or at least concerned with the organism, *against* that bad heredity. By this I mean that since every organism, or person, or self, for its own preservation, has to come to accurate terms with the world in which it has life, beneath an inability to do so is a trend to destroy that inability.

Heredity has been too much regarded as some force opposed to everyday existence. If a child is born blind we must see that the child's heredity—that is, its *past* environment—has not "wished" that the child be blind; for blindness is an inability to deal with the outside world accurately or completely. The supposition here on the part of many who have seen heredity disproportionately, is that the world as making a child's past is opposed essentially to the child's present or future being successful. If a child is born blind, we must see that despite the blindness, *there was a force* which was against blindness—even if that force lost. For when nature came to eyes, these eyes were "meant" to function. The syphilis, for example, that a child is said to inherit, was environmental in the father or mother: this means that a happening involving basic infection occurred after birth. What, therefore, could have been prevented in one organism's environment has taken a congenital form in another's. Past environment here has affected heredity.

Every organism's life or every self's life is made up of two worlds, or rather two forms of one world. The first of these forms is the world seen as past. A child born today has as its heredity the world that existed before it was born. That heredity culminated with great-grandfathers and great-grandmothers, and grandfathers and grandmothers, and father and mother; but it is still true that in the most complete and most correct signification, the heredity of a child is the whole world narrowing to a point in itself at the time of its birth.

The world can be seen as something endlessly wide, endlessly diverse, reaching particularity with the birth of a specific self. Heredity, in other words, takes in all of biology, all of anthropology, all of sociology, all of geology, and so on, as these are accumulated and intensified in a specific, living human organism. The whole world has worked for the creation of each living person. What, however, is hereditary for one person is environmental for others. That environment might have been changed; and this means that the heredity of a person born lately, also might have been changed.

Heredity, at its largest, has a meaning that goes beyond germ cells, and chromosomes, and nuclei. The past, which is the heredity of every person, took biological shape in terms like these; but in order to understand the meaning of the biological situation, the reality which biology represents must also be understood. After all, the purpose of heredity is to meet environment; and so to presume that the environment which heredity is to meet is antagonistic to that heredity, does seem, offhand, to be unwise.

All hereditary defects, all hereditary assets, are caused by environment in its fullest meaning. For, as I have mentioned, heredity is environment, as past, working now. But the world is constantly fresh; the future has an unlimited strength to change the past; and also to change that momentary aspect of the past and future, which is the present. And the past can be used to make the future sensible.

All this means that when a Joe Johnson is born, or a Luella Hargreaves, or a Michael Halleran, or a Daniel Dorman, we shouldn't say that their fates are in the bag. Their past as heredity comes from the world they meet as they go on living. If there is a oneness between the drive of the past, as heredity; and the possibilities of the future, as environment, these children can get along with that whole world which, really, doesn't mind getting along with them.

10

Psychiatry, Economics, Aesthetics

Aesthetic Realism: A Summary

Aesthetic Realism is based on the fact that (despite what many people believe) aesthetics is the deepest good sense and stands for what everybody deeply and unconsciously is after.

For instance, everybody is after freedom and security. You can't play off one against the other as many people try to do. So you have to have both. In aesthetics (which is the real dialectics of the world), and only there, do you have both at once. In a Beethoven symphony, for example, there is a feeling of freedom but also a feeling of accuracy, of security. There isn't freedom at one time and security at another. The symphony is freedom and security, abandon and logic, *simultaneously.*

What does this mean? The "neurotic," or for that matter, the worried "normal" person wants to be orderly at one time and unrestrained at another. There is a fight in him of the desire to be gay, undisciplined, free, and the desire to be factual, rigid, precise. The self really wants to be factual and gay, precise and unrestrained, at once. A good comedy, a solid poem, a true painting, a fine dance, can be gay and precise at the same moment.

Of course all this implies a different approach to aesthetics from that of the ordinary professor; from that of the "man on the street." Aesthetics, we believe, is in baseball just as it is in architecture and is in a Polish woman's colored apron as well as in a Mozart concerto.

Aesthetics is in everyday ethical situations. People want to be selfish; and yet give what is coming to the other fellow. Well, they have to be both selfish and fair at once. They have to think outside and inside. Take Beethoven again. When you hear the *Emperor Concerto* you feel that Beethoven is entirely himself, that he is giving his ego a grand time; but you also feel that Beethoven is standing for other people, for reality, for you and me. A "neurotic" can be jestingly defined as "a person who makes a loud outcry over losing something he doesn't want to find." When we feel "strange" or "low," a hidden part of us may be colliding with ourselves as conscious.

The one thing Aesthetic Realism has in common with Freudian psychoanalysis is a belief in the existence—the full existence—of the unconscious. (The way Aesthetic Realism sees the unconscious is, however, profoundly different from the psychoanalytic way.) When we unconsciously want to please our ego, or what Aesthetic Realism calls the ego as center, this drive may collide with a wish to have outer things please us. We then play off ego as "center" against ego as "circumference" or as "area."

This sounds, and we regret it, a little portentous, but it is what goes on. We are trying all the time to please a self under our skin and a self that begins where our finger tips end. So we have vanity; and pride. Vanity, or 2-A, is when the ego wants to please itself and doesn't want to see the outside facts, or the world as not oneself. Pride, or 1-A, is when the ego, or self, wants to be pleased just as much as in vanity but not as against the facts, or the world.

Here a story may be told to illustrate this matter of pride, or 1-A, and vanity, or 2-A. One of the maxims of Aesthetic

Realism is: "If you like yourself for the wrong reason, you will dislike yourself for the right reason."

The story mentioned goes as follows:

A painter of the Middle Ages was going to be put out of his lodgings by his landlady for not paying rent. The night before the eviction the devil comes to him and says: "My friend, between you and me, I know you're in a tough spot. Now I've a good idea. I know you're a good painter, I know that all right. But nobody knows you're a good painter, and maybe nobody will. My idea is this: I can make you the best known painter in this town, province, maybe in all Germany. But you're going to be a bad painter. However, no one will know about it in your lifetime, so you don't have to worry about that. Now what do you say?—Do you want to be a good painter and have no one know about it, or do you want to be the best known painter in Germany?—Oh, I know all right, there's something about this you don't like. Anyway, think about it and any time you make up your mind I'll be around again."

The painter had a hard time of it making up his mind. The next morning the landlady's child saw the paintings of the to-be-evicted artist and said: "Ooh, I like that." So the artist was encouraged not to take the devil's offer.

The story illustrates the fight that goes on in everyone. We want to be praised, to have power, but we also want to deserve this. There is such a thing as the *ethical unconscious.* Well, if we praise ourselves and we know we have been unfair to outside reality in doing so, there is a troubling conflict in us. This conflict shows itself *in* sex: as it does in other things. We can't really think another person loves us unless *we* really *like ourselves* with the facts present, that is, have the 1-A feeling.

To love ourselves really, we have to love and want to

know outside reality; that is, the outside form of ourselves, or the world. All this is abstract. There is evidence showing that the collison between "I" and "What Isn't I" makes for such things as sleeplessness, headache, stuttering, "fears," digestive aberrations, and so on. These disturbances are not the province of Aesthetic Realism. Aesthetic Realism deals with the *self as such,* philosophically, deeply, directly—that is, aesthetically.

Aesthetic Realism sees the self as the individual form of the universe, or God. (In Aesthetic Realism, God is reality seen as personal, or the universe as having purpose or meaning.) Aesthetic Realism is, therefore, religious, once religion is seen as our attitude to the most powerful or beautiful thing we know in existence; not as something institutional, narrow, and "out of this world."

In its presentation of how the self against itself makes for unhappiness, trouble and disorder, Aesthetic Realism keeps, we believe, a just distance away not only from Sigmund Freud but also from Mary Baker Eddy. Sex itself, when sensible, is like aesthetics. Even a councilman, or a salesgirl, or a radio announcer, or a race-track tout, in the depths of his active soul or organism, is going after that dynamic tranquillity which is happiness or aesthetics. We all want what aesthetics represents: rest in motion, order in freedom, organization in strangeness.

Preface

—So I says to him, "Jake, don't be a dope."
—So he says to me, "Looie, I don't take orders
from anybody."

The whole world reaches everyone, and this means it reaches the unconscious of everyone. Economics has something to do with the unconscious. The unconscious, in turn, has something to do with everything, including economics.

In this publication of Aesthetic Realism, the purpose is to show that economics is not only a political or "sociological" matter. Our attitude to economics has a large effect on our very selves, on where our selves begin; on our physiological well-being, our psychological fate.

The general aim of Aesthetic Realism is to integrate the various ways the world can be seen by any one person. Our selves are simultaneously biological, historical, psychological, sociological, religious, political, ethical and mathematical—nor, it can be said, is this all. We see aesthetics as a means of maintaining unity in difference, and oneness in opposition. There is nothing really with which aesthetics in this meaning has not to do. Aesthetics even can be concerned with a corrupt, silly, and misbehaved congress. *The organization of a trade union is akin to organization in aesthetics.* The motto of America, *E Pluribus Unum*, "From Many One," is aesthetic essentially. What America needs, along with good food, is a true, earthy, complete understanding of the organization of reality, so that reality is seen and felt more. This organization can be called aesthetics.

Organization is primal in the meaning of aesthetics. Our present world and our present America need to be organized so that they be efficient and ethical at once—and if they are that, they will be delightful and healthy and free. A particular self, our present publication states, cannot be healthy unless it truly aims for a healthy world which is not itself, and yet includes itself. Right economics and true politics are a psychological necessity, not an elegant alternative or an "incidental."

It follows that the world should be owned by the people living in it. Every person should be seen as living in a world truly his. All persons should be seen as living in a world truly theirs. In the same way as 10,000 persons can be listening to an exciting composition of music, each feeling that *he* is listening to it, while others are listening—so each person can see the wonder and delicacy and largeness of the universe as his, while knowing that other selves are apprehending pleasantly this universe.

The purpose of economics or politics is to maintain the collective while intensifying the individual, to support gloriously the universal while heightening properly a specific person. When this is done, we shall have aesthetic economics and artistic politics. This would be good and accurate; and the meaning of it is so large we can hardly realize it now.

Is not an honest world a beautiful world? Would not a beautiful world be got by honest economics, good politics? If this is so, why can't we say, aesthetics belongs to politics, too? *Aesthetics is reality truly organized.*

Well, it is said in the following pages that a person *has* to see it this way. If he doesn't, he so much invites for himself the repertoire of the psychologically undesirable—all those

things in the text books coming under the heads of nervousness or neuroticism and psychosis. Does he have to? This
pamphlet shows that he doesn't; and that he should and can
organize psychiatry, economics, aesthetics.

ELI SIEGEL

The names of the persons in this work are imaginary.
The persons are real.

Psychiatry, Economics, Aesthetics

THE BASIC object of psychiatry is to enable a human organism to use all its energies without needless conflict. There are two reasons why a human organism, or person, can fail to be entirely himself; that is, not be completely "sane." One of these reasons is in the person himself; the other is in what's around him. A third reason, of course, may be considered as the separate person and the world around him taken together. It is the duty of a psychiatrist to consider all the factors that may have worked towards bringing about painful incompleteness in a human being. A specific practitioner, to be sure, cannot alter the milieu in which a patient functions, but he can be a means of affecting the attitude of a patient towards his milieu; and this implies a consideration of that milieu itself.

Something like struggle is needed by the human being. Something even like discontent is needed by the human being. The satisfaction of desire implies some opposition to the desire. One cannot think of a world made up of smooth roads strewn with roses and bordered by exceedingly accessible marshmallows. The world, like the human body, is a compound of resistance and ease, obstruction and going forward, obstacle and companion. The struggle, however, that a human being must welcome should be a struggle which does not obscure a deeper struggle; which does not make him think that in its successfully being met the large problems of self have also been met. It must be, in other words, a healthful struggle; a necessary struggle, a beautiful struggle.

It is important that a human being see other human beings as different from himself. It is also important that conditions be such he does not feel that the misery or deficiency of other human beings is his victory. For a self does not really want that. The self does not want to be strong by the weakness of others. It wants to be strong by what *it is*, rather than by what others are not. Wrongfully to be contemptuous of other human beings is inviting mental unhealth for oneself.

The fundamental, unremitting drive of every person is to be at one with things as a whole. To be at one with things as a whole carries with it some idea of power. And power is not just the ability to affect or change others; it is likewise the ability to be affected or changed by others. If a person's power is only of the first kind, his unconscious will be in distress. He must see that the existence of others is not in competition with his own. He must see that his own well-being depends on a simultaneous giving of himself to things and acting on things.

Psychiatrically speaking, is a self fully expressed by possession? If it is, then there is no question but that possession should be encouraged. If the self is not fully expressed by possession, then, not only from an economic point of view, but from the point of view of therapy, and not only sentimentally, but with strictness, a human being aiming for deep health should be told that possession—at least as it has been historically—is bad for him; it is bad for him in the same sense as bad air is, or bad eggs are, or a broken foot is.

The question then is just where owning is hurtful—if it is hurtful. In abstract terms, owning or having is hurtful where it stops one from being. It can hardly be shown, just so, that when a baby is born its deepest purpose is to acquire six hundred shares of a certain steel, or eight hundred acres of a certain land, or a factory employing twelve hundred persons. If such shares, or acres, or factory by being possessed enable a person to be what he wants to be, superficially and deeply, consciously and unconsciously, then it should even be a psychiatric monition to persons that they acquire shares or land or factories. Anyway, I do not see where psychiatry, in the largest sense, can honestly pass by the question.

Related to the question presented in the preceding paragraph is this one: Does the possession by one person of so many shares of steel, so much land, or such a factory, make for the mental health of persons not possessing these? If it does not make for the mental health of persons other than possessors, then it is likewise the duty of psychiatry, with a large point of view, to amend the situation. A psychiatrist cannot, self-respectingly, work for mental health in America or elsewhere and disregardingly permit or approve the existence of public conditions likely to cause mental unhealth. Economic situations, therefore, which either make for emotional accuracy and soundness or inaccuracy and unsoundness, are rightly the field of a person studying the procedures, purposes, and possibilities of mental therapy.

Lately, there has been a disposition on the part of many, who on the whole agree with Freud, to part from him in the matter of ascribing functional mental ailment chiefly to sex. These partial dissidents from Freud have accented the factor of insecurity in the causation of mental instability. Insecurity, obviously, is a large term; there are many kinds of insecurity but the word cannot be disjoined from such things as jobs, wages, costs, competition. If insecurity makes for mental mishap, surely what makes for insecurity needs to be studied. And this should be studied, not as a matter of politics alone or of economics, but as a matter of psychiatry in a comprehensive and exact meaning.

Psychiatry differs from current academic economics in that while the purport of mental therapy is that an individual needs to see himself in relation to objects, other people, reality in the wide sense; accepted economics tends to assert the centripetal, separating needs of individuals. Psychiatry says: see them; the economics of the moment says: get yours. It is hard to see how a deeply tranquil attitude towards other people can arise and be maintained while a person is driven to be in constant economic combat with those people. To say to the same person: Like your fellow beings, adjust yourself to society, get out of yourself; and at the same time to force him to dispute, virulently perhaps, the possession of a job with another, the acquirement of shares, and the value of a house, already makes for imminent neurotic possibilities. We can't have human beings caressing others terminologically and kicking them financially.

The basis of present day economics; that is, the general way of making a living, can be justly given as the private ownership of industry. In psychiatric terms, this is equivalent to ownership of that which concerns many egos by one ego. If this one ego were mentally benefited, the aim of psychiatry would so far be achieved. Even if the other egos concerned were hindered from completion, we should at least have spiritual goodness for one. It is rather one-sided, but there is some good. Psychiatry points out, however, that the aggressive domination or control of other personalities by one personality is bad, even for the personality controlling. It should be asked, therefore, not only by economists, or politicians, but by psychiatrists, whether ownership by one self of the means by which the organic needs of many selves are supplied, is healthful. This question has—if asked at all—been asked in a remote, gingerly manner. I propose to ask it lucidly, squarely.

Altruism has been looked on, most often, as a sentimental, soft word. But the real meaning of altruism, psychiatrically speaking, is hard and inevitable and big. Insanity is principally caused by a lack of otherness; this lack makes for incompleteness of self. When the self accepts its incompleteness, it has accepted insanity. It therefore follows that if an inherent aspect of selfness is otherness, for that otherness to be lessened is dangerous to the welfare of the self. We cannot be whole beings if we are not fair to what is not ourselves. It is incumbent on ourselves, therefore, to be fair; that is, to be altruistic. Altruism here is the same as selfishness in the largest and strictest sense. For when a self is not other, it is not entirely what it is as such. To be selfish is to be the whole self; to be the whole self is to have a sense of otherness. Consequently, as I have stated, to be selfish is to be altruistic.

I do not in the least intend these last words to be taken as logical virtuosity. I see them as plainly practical. If private ownership of industry also gives rise to incompleteness of self, then private ownership of industry also gives rise to neurosis. One does not come to terms with the world by owning certain phases of it. Owning does not satisfy the unconscious drives of the self. We can own the world only by knowing it. We can possess the world only by having it in our minds; that is, by having knowledge of it. All other possession, both in love and economics, is false and hurtful. It is seen by the possessor as a substitute for real possession, but it will never do. The unconscious will never be at ease. The world was meant to be known, to be felt, not to be parcelled out into huge segments or lesser segments for the complacent but deleterious delectation of some and the domination and manipulation of others.

The word aesthetics is part of my title for this work. To me, aesthetics stands for mental health. It also stands for economic health. Before contemporary political movements which, in one way or another, have been against private ownership of the means by which all people live and sustain themselves, aesthetics was the chief opponent to that way of dealing with common human resources which, accenting privateness, ego-domination, I see as psychiatrically unsound. The artist has felt, in so far as he *was* an artist, that the world was most properly used by being known and felt, and that activities arising from knowing were the correct activities.

There have been limitations to art and aesthetics in terms of actual human beings. Yet the profound trend in art or aesthetics has been the completing of the self by the merging with, yet independence of, reality other than the self. Through merging with things, the artist has become deeply independent. In feeling things he has controlled them and been controlled by them. He has come to power by undergoing the might of things and giving them form through his personality.

As artist he has seen the world as different, but himself as free in accepting and merging with that difference. He has not imposed his self on objects; he has let objects become himself. All this was contrary to the idea of possession as such. The possessor has felt it was more important to feel that a tree was owned by him than to feel that he knew what the tree was and what it could mean. And he has let the ownership of a tree, or grass, or a field, take the place of being fully affected by these things in nature. The artist has been forced to possess, forced to acquire, forced to compete, but as artist he was not after possession, or acquisition, or competition. He did not feel that his own strength and development depended on his having what he did not want other people to have, or in doing what he did not want other people to do. His strength did not have a basis in his fellow-beings' weakness.

The artist created; the owner possessed. Creation is being and doing; ownership is having. Psychiatrists, at the present time, accent the importance of a creative attitude to the world. It is, however, unwise to extol creation and to disregard those conditions which make creation hard or prevent it. Many persons want to be creative, but the conscious, fierce current of their lives is acquisitive. One cannot be creative with one hemisphere of oneself and acquisitive with the other. The hemispheres will collide and make for neurosis.

The only way to avoid neurotic factors is to decide that if a showdown arrives—and there should be a showdown—between creation and acquisition, acquisition should lose, should become subsidiary to creation. It is true that man wishes to be creative. It is also true that a phase of him wishes to be acquisitive. The psychiatrist should decide which phase ought to control the self. If he decides that the creative side most truly represents the healthy man, he has decided that the aesthetic attitude to life is a healthy one. Psychiatrist and artist are here one. Possessions, capital, investments, are what one has; labor and creation are what one does.

All creation is labor. Labor is the changing of the world so that the purpose of individuals is reached. It is the giving of ourselves to the world so that the world gives itself to us. Creation is a high quality of labor but it is still labor; it is still what one does, not what one has. A healthy mind has to reach an exact relation between having and doing. If a person does not, despite all his desire to be creative, he will not be. He will be false to the foundations of what he is.

Creation always involves three things. It means that A has accurately given himself to B so that a new thing, C, occurs, which is neither A nor B, but both. A workman makes a table. The table has himself in it, has the wood with which he began, but as a completed table is neither workman nor wood, but both. An artist embodies an idea. The embodiment of that idea is himself and what he wrote about, but is neither taken alone; it is both. In creation by giving oneself to something, that thing becomes the giver. It is the healthiest process in the world: it is what man is after; it is the most intense kind of growth; it is against possession as such.

In possession there is the feeling that one has justified oneself by making something subservient to oneself. The feeling is that this object is an appendage of me, I control it, I can do with it what I wish. But there is no springing of the self to merge with the object; there is no desire to belong to the object. To wish to possess an object without having the object possess us—no matter how abstract this may sound—is, strictly speaking, unhealthy, neurotic.

Any situation where the idea of usefulness to others is at war with usefulness to oneself is unhealthful. If a person cannot take care of himself without being hostile or doing injustice to the selves of others he is, mentally speaking, unlucky. The question is not whether "altruism" is desirable, but whether one can be fundamentally well without it. There is an instinct in a human being to express himself accurately as to others, and accurately here means justly, fairly, ethically. We cannot be accurate with ourselves, certainly, if we are not accurate with what is not ourselves. Accuracy and ethics go quite together; consequently if it is desirable to be accurate as to oneself, it is desirable to be accurate as to what is not oneself. Successful ethics cannot be single, one-track, or unilateral. It always implies a proportionate interaction and togetherness of organism and surroundings of organism. If ethics were seen as a phase of universal accuracy, the word ethics would not have the soft sound that it has.

We are acquisitive because we want to take care of ourselves, to do right by ourselves, to give ourselves what is coming to us. Were acquisition a means of getting for ourselves what we deserve, what is coming to us, acquisition would be beautiful; for everyone is obligated to give himself what he deserves, what is coming to him; if he doesn't give himself what he deserves, then he is not giving to other things what they deserve, either. A conflict between altruism and selfishness is the basis of a nervous conflict. We acquire with one phase of our being and we repent, seemingly generously, with another. Our grudging activities are not integrated with our expansive, granting, or charitable activities. To clutch with one hand and to shower with the other hand is a phase of nervousness.

The dilemma between acquisition and creation, clutching and granting, self-contraction and self-expansion, is common in our present world. We meet it in all the professions, all the trades, all businesses, and even all laboring activities. Dr. Frederick Major, for example, a practitioner of orthodox medicine, is quite nervous. Sometimes he sleeps badly even though he is versed richly and subtly in the properties of sedatives. To be sure there are other aspects of his nervousness, because the forms of nervousness and their causes go together. In this place, however, I propose to deal chiefly with one aspect.

Dr. Major, twenty years ago at medical school, went at medicine enthusiastically and grandly. He did not see medicine as but a superior means of getting fees from the citizenry. Certainly he wanted to live well and he had a right to do that; yet he saw medicine as a mighty manifestation of the beauty and power and depth and fineness and tenderness of man's mind. He saw Hippocrates as akin to Christ, Galen as akin to Dante, Vesalius as akin to Shakespeare. It is right to live well, it is right to see medicine, like spring and rivers and food and music, as useful and great. But when Dr. Major began to practice there were two confluents in his mind: one flowed towards fees and position and conspicuous respectability; the other towards greater and greater knowledge, research, pervasive and deep usefulness. For Dr. Major was not a run-of-the-mill tester of pulses, examiner of urine, and prescriber of pharmacal products.

For a few years he read and pondered and collected fees. He tried to see medicine in relation to thought as a whole and, at the same time, to make his practice more and more lucrative. Soon there was friction between his motives and activities arising from these motives. Were he perhaps like others, he could have become smoothly the businesslike, suave, seemingly unilateral man of medicine and fees. This he did become to a point, but the other Dr. Major was still around. That Dr. Major did not like the executive Dr. Major, the ingratiating Dr. Major.

Our doctor's desire to help himself was subterraneously fighting his desire to be of use to others. For there was a desire to be of use to others in him, just as definitely as there was a desire to drink wine, or to read a paper to his county medical society, or to be the professional medical advisor of the governor of the state. The expansive feelings of the Frederick Major at twenty when contemplating medical school, were still in him; they had not been banished; they had simply been put on the shelf of the unconscious.

The process making for the most respectable pampering of the ego of Dr. Major is sharply, continuously, and most powerfully at odds with the Dr. Major who wishes his skill to be abroad and to be of as great use to the world in general as it can be. Not that in the world of Frederick Major can he just go ahead and be useful and learned and creative; there are hindrances, great hindrances. But Dr. Major, for purposes of his own comfort, has wanted to see these hindrances as inherent in the nature of the universe; and *that* his unconscious cannot accept.

Therefore, our practitioner is deeply frustrated. Were he to see these hindrances as not inevitable, as transformable, his desire to be useful and his desire for fees could be in some kind of efficient partnership. But he has used a situation of the world to *suppress* a basic trend or desire or attitude in him. This basic attitude or desire comes splinteringly forth in a charitable gesture or a semi-hypocritical statement about the perils of commercialism—a statement made at his medical society meeting. Chiefly, however, his profound wish to be free and useful rather than narrow, gives rise to a nervousness of procedure, a touchiness, depression, and, constantly, an organic self-criticism. For Dr. Major has accepted one part of him as standing for the whole; he has divided himself; he cannot be free and his being cannot approve of what it is. The disapproval by his being of what it is, has made him nervous.

The conflict that a doctor faces can be put somewhat crudely in this form: as a human being he wants people to be well; as a professional man he wants them to be other than well. This can be denied, for it can be said that even if a doctor did not desire sickness, there would be sickness. That may be, in a fashion, true, yet what I am talking of is not the outward smoothing over of a difficulty, but the difficulty *where it begins.* Unless a desire to collect fees is *entirely* at one with the desire to see people well, a doctor *cannot be basically comfortable.* If, at any time, the businesslike propensities of a medical man affect disproportionately himself as scientist, there is not only a so-called ethical or cognitive dilemma; there is a conflict involving the well-being, the nervous or emotional or human status of the physician himself; for physicians, like other people, must be integrated. One cannot have a running battle between fees and science going on for years without that battle affecting the person in whom it takes place. That battle has existed. The desire for personal acquisition and comfort has fought with the desire to be more and more useful. Doctors have chosen to be the advisors of the monetarily endowed rather than the helpers of men.

Doctors, like other people, want to like themselves for the right reasons. A right reason is the feeling that one is useful. The feeling of usefulness is basically this: by the existence of oneself other things are larger, more beautiful, happier; take on new value. The deep belief that one is useful is equivalent to pride. After all, when we like ourselves there are various inevitable criteria. We cannot like ourselves if the relation we have to other realities is not acceptable. A doctor, then, is impelled by the motives of all: the motive to be comfortable, the motive to be pleased with oneself accurately. Where Dr. Major's fee-acquiring activities pleased his self, taken in its entirety, he was wise; where they didn't, he wasn't being truly practical. The whole question of commerce and professions and science needs to be seen from the point of view of effect on the self where it begins and where it has to become manifest.

Physicians are unusually subject to concomitants of the dilemma between usefulness and comfort; for they are impelled to consider the woes and the sufferings and the worryings and the critical well-being of humans. However, since all activity of a professional kind, or commercial kind, or craft kind, has in it the interaction between usefulness and self-comfort, every person in the present day world is affected by the conflict implied.

Lawyers, for example, for quite a few centuries, have been suspected and satirized in so far as they were likely to want human beings to quarrel, go to court and continue doing so; since lawyers live by the public disagreements within civilization. It is very well to say that a lawyer doesn't have to wish that people disagree. It is easy to say that lawyers in their organizations have established rigid ethical codes of procedure; it is also most presentable to say that lawyers bring justice out of an ugly and tangled and unjust situation. A more accurate judge, however, of the problem that men of law face than bar associations, is the unconscious of lawyers.

A lawyer has to make a living, he has to wish that he make as good a living as possible; and the impetus of this wish can set going all kinds of thoughts harmful to an integrated self. He can act ethically in keeping with present day requirements, but his personality may yet be tangled and asunder. The desire on his part to be useful comes deviously, and sometimes head-on, against the desire to be comfortable. If he chooses the comfortable there will be protest within him. If he chooses the useful in the largest sense, he may feel he is unworthy, naive and innocent, a little boy blue, and so on. He desires to be comfortable most often and will present an ethical picture of himself to his perceptions. The question is how sound that ethical picture is.

Luke Harlow is a lawyer in a midwestern city. He has found himself wishing that people of his acquaintance living in the married state meet trouble. When he recognizes this wish, he chides himself, with a twinge. He has caught himself also wishing that an accident occurring to a friend be really severe so that the amount Harlow can claim as damages be large, and his own emoluments considerable. He has likewise, somewhat dimly, recognized a wish on his part that owners of real estate engage in litigation; and a wish that business houses be sued so that he might be retained as counsel. Harlow is a comparatively sensitive lawyer. He recognizes that his personality does not have smooth sailing in his profession. How good a job has he done in the appraising of what his whole being has to meet?

Well, in proportion to his sensitivity he tries consciously to allay the pains his sensitivity causes. For some years his life within has consisted considerably of the raising of painful sensitivities and their fairly efficient smothering. He has not let his sensitivity go the whole way; he has not been willing that the source of his sensitivity win out, so that he can take a clear and healthful stand. A quivering pendulum of attitude has gone on for some time. Sensitivities have risen to be darkened or removed by: "After all, if I don't—"; "That's the way the world is and who am I to change it?" —"I do all that I can, considering, and more. . . ." In all these self-reprovings and approvings, the basic things in Harlow's personality do not come forth clearly, freely; they are checked by a "there, there."

To be sure, lawyer Harlow has other troubles; connected, however, as to their source, with these. Some years ago Luke Harlow took two months off to go to a sanatorium in a Cleveland suburb. He left all his affairs, philosophically, to be taken care of by an assistant. He called it overwork, and, in a sense, it was; because he had overworked an ethical repelling possibility and his ethical recommending possibilities. There was an aspect of self which he brought to his daily work that didn't belong there. He went to his work with an unconscious slant. He got by, he gets by. He does not know where his constipation comes from, his peevishness, his wakings in the night, with the thought he has experienced something terrible. These things may not be owing only to the unconscious misgivings and friction he has about his work, but they help. Without knowing it, Harlow is an enemy, to a large extent, of men and things. He has associated trouble in society with satisfaction to himself. He has found triumph in the bickerings and frailties and civic wretchedness of others. He would deny this, certainly; but it is true.

Now one fundamental position of Aesthetic Realism is that one cannot be, no matter to what extent, an enemy of mankind or reality and get by—at least as a healthy self. It is difficult to have mankind completely sensible, completely free, completely just. Yet when one does not *go after* wholly this tremendous and difficult, yet thinkable objective, there is noxious tumult in that person. You cannot make a situation completely but you can accept a process completely. Surely it is most hard to have men just and wise and amiable —most hard; but the process can be accepted one hundred-hundredths right now. It is difficult to build an intricate, massive cathedral, but one can accept the idea of building it forthwith.

It is attitude, approach, process that are important here. When a person consents to wish that man not be as fine and happy as he can, there is trouble. The most awful compulsion of the present day world, causing men to find their comfort in the defects and mishaps and uncomeliness of others, likewise causes, or helps to cause, persons not to function wholly.

We have, then, lawyer Luke Harlow wishing well for his fellow men as a Christian, a neighbor, a citizen of good deportment; and wishing ill for them unconsciously and sometimes, though obscurely, consciously. This condition, as I have intimated, should be seen in terms of public health and of individual well-being. Utopia is clearly not on the next block, but it is imperative that one not *wish* in any fashion that it be far away. We cannot let our unconscious exploit, for our contemporary comfort, the insufficiencies of human history.

Lawyer Harlow is living by the quarreling of others. That he has to is clear, but that he has the right to abstain from doing anything which may destroy this condition is not clear. What Harlow has to do is to take and use this condition without in any way compromising with the constant necessity of destroying it. A woman who "loving" her husband feels weaknesses in him and consents to them (as many do for these weaknesses give satisfaction to their own desire for self-importance) is subjected to interior discord. A man who lives by the weaknesses of mankind and does not do all he can to destroy the necessity for doing so, is likewise subject to interior discord. These situations are akin.

There is no way of charting just how much injury to the selves of Dr. Major and Mr. Harlow has been incurred by their acceptance of a life and livelihood too much bound with, and too favorable to, a disorderly world. They both have been interested in bringing about order in the lives of men, but in doing so they have come to terms with a larger disorder. Dr. Major is interested in the alleviation of disease, but he has consented to combat disease within a diseased framework. Lawyer Harlow has sought justice, while parleying sweetly with injustices in his own being. The concept of disorder is large; it concerns the bones of man and the blood of man; but there can be no full order in these while men themselves are unsymmetrical as to each other. There can be no justice as to a suit or a deed while the very field in which justice is sought does not jibe with the deepest wishes of the men seeking justice. Civic order is inseparable from order in the unconscious. The unconscious extends to city, and hospital, and room, and government.

Hal Stearns teaches in a California college. He is a graduate of Columbia and received his Ph.D. there. At college he
was competitive; could not abide the idea of anyone receiving higher scholastic grades or honors. Nonetheless, he felt
a decided impulsion towards learning. He has given severe
nights to the study of Anglo-Saxon and is a rising authority
on the literature between Chaucer and Spenser. He wrote
his Ph.D. thesis on *Social Problems in Tudor Poetry.* His wife,
Grace, is an M.A. and she has set for herself a career as a
writer of books for children. It is likely that Hal Stearns'
wife will become much better known than he, for learned
writings on Tudor literature and such matters, as things go,
do not bring wide acclaim. Hal Stearns' personality harbors
competitiveness of all sorts; still it is in the employ of a desire
for documented learning.

Stearns often broods bitterly over his college prospects.
He cannot look blithely at his future in California. He frequently has visions of being supplanted, neglected, de-
graded. He once wrote a review in a learned journal of a
book on John Skelton—a review which swarmed with precise, learned arrows. It surprised readers by its virulence;
they were impressed by learning in the review—there was
no doubt of that—but the tone was waspish, bristly. Stearns
could consciously avow, if he pressed himself, that he was
jealous of a rival in a chosen field. He was not aware, however, that in his review there was an adroit and most vigilant
setting forth of the reviewed author's insufficiencies and
missteps, and an astute obscuring of his qualities.

Stearns is learned, but he sees learned people, deeply, not
as comrades but as adversaries. The charming and wide and
subtle field of learning is for him a battlefield of egos. There
is an impressive formality in his behavior. There is no question that he is distinguished. Learning in him has taken an
appearance both military and bland. He sees learning rightly

as unlimited in breadth and as multitudinous; but without knowing it, he has taken a pedantic, gangsterish point of view. Simultaneously with being impelled to ascertain a new fact about Stephen Hawes or to arrive at a new approach to Thomas Tusser, his ego contracts and attacks.

There are, likewise, salary troubles. Two months after Stearns' taking the California post he began contemplating a change meaning a higher salary. He does not know that a good deal of his restlessness about salary, the feeling that he is underpaid, arises from a general dissatisfaction with the unintegrity of his basic attitudes.

Stearns has arrived at a belief which he has somewhat jestingly described as "democratic toryism." He talks democracy; but he feels that learning in itself has set apart the group having it. At the age of thirty-four he has cultivated a severe pomp and a symmetrical haughtiness. One student has called him "Pharaoh." A fellow instructor, at one time, quite suddenly, called him "Major." Hal Stearns is solving his self's difficulties by attempting to "militarize" them, by giving them a metallic outwardness.

But he isn't happy. He hasn't seen that he can't love learning without loving what learning means and what learning is for. He has not seen the import of expression in learning. He has not perceived that there can be no joy in communication without a love for those towards whom the communication is aimed. He has not realized that, when ranging in the field of Tudor literature or elsewhere, if his whole self does not range, there will be the tension and the tug of divided process; nor has he realized that the disposition to consider his students barbarians (though he conceals this) does not make for his own felicity.

Of late Stearns has become interested in college politics. He still wants a higher and higher salary, but he is after more than that now. He has talked of the "learned as the legislating" and he intends doing something about it. "Perhaps," he has thought, "I can stay here in California. There is no reason why I cannot get a full professorship. This college is a big one. I am more learned, have more insight than President Emerton. I will make it clear that there are other fields than Tudor literature in which I can be supreme."

Recently he has been quite gracious, subtly affable, trimly complaisant to President Emerton and other dignitaries of the college. He wrote an article on "California in English and American Poetry to 1870." He sent an abstract of the article to a San Francisco newspaper. He has even decided to use his undoubted powers of research and documentation, not so much for sixteenth-century concerns, but in behalf of California and the twentieth century. His contracted self of the past is planning a jump of large scope.

Stearns' ambitions go on, so does his unhappiness. As a child he possessed a habit spasm involving a strange twirling of his left hand. Recently there has been a spasmodic, uncontrolled slight shudder of the left side of his neck involving the shoulder and, quite faintly, his left arm. This motion is, in a strange way, somewhat becoming. It adds an impressive military intensity to his demeanor. Also, however, there have been outbursts against his wife. Only a month ago he glared at her in a way that frightened her, when she came home late from a visit. There likewise have been bad headaches.

From the foregoing it is plain that the personality of Hal Stearns has had adventures. These adventures have involved fierce competition for honors at college, unremitting study of a scholastic subject, intense attempts towards greater emoluments, energetic depreciation of esteemed rivals. There is now the plan to reach great political and financial goals. The one adventure in which Stearns' personality has not fully participated is the adventure of binding his attitudes or drives together. That would involve a conscious contemplation and appraisal of what he is; and this contemplation and appraisal has neither been inviting nor available. But Stearns suffers from its lack.

For learning, even in the field of *belles lettres,* is an activity of an organism with desires, with tendencies. These desires or tendencies must find integration where they begin. The desire, on the one hand, simply to excel another student and, on the other, to ascertain a truth of the past, have not been teamed by their possessor. These desires have proceeded in parallel paths consciously, but in paths that ran into each other, unconsciously.

So it has been with other desires of Hal Stearns as a man of research and academic prowess. A desire for learning as much involves the psychological concomitants of physiology as a desire for skiing or eating or making love. The body, the self, work in the matter of footnotes as much as they do in serving a meal, greeting a visitor, or scolding a child. Our body is everywhere, and that means our self is.

The acquisition of knowledge is a happy exposure of oneself to facts. That exposure should be electric, and accurate, and loving; it should give and embrace. There should be no reservations of a pampering or aggressive or contracting kind. Otherwise, the acquisition of knowledge is just acquisition; it is just profit; it is just possession in the same sense as the acquisition of shares, or real estate might be. The question is: How well does the self like it? The self of Hal Stearns does not like it altogether. Nervousness, if not on the march in him, is at least creeping. The signs are obscure; however, they definitely exist.

In Boston, George Hall is a policeman of fifteen years' service. His job has been to apprehend the law-defying; and he has done so. He has searched for the manifestations of crime, with zeal. He is now a lieutenant. He is respected in the force. He has done such things as apprehend a boy of seventeen breaking into a pawnbroker's shop, and take into custody a man beating his wife openly in the street. He has gone into another state to bring back a bank embezzler; and has seen to it that pickets do not molest passers-by near a department store. He is proud of his record. Once a bullet scarred his shoulder and he has shown that shoulder to intimate friends. George Hall, likewise, is religious. He attends mass often.

Hall can still remember how, fourteen years ago, after "nabbing" a shoplifter and bringing her to the police station, he felt very uncomfortable when he reached home. There was a nausea around his stomach; he sweated; he felt weak. There was a diarrhea of three days. He felt that the shoplifter looked a little like his mother, but he didn't see why that should bother him. That woman had no right to be taking a shawl and a fountain pen from one of Boston's most noted department stores. He didn't like the idea of running after a woman in just that fashion; particularly he didn't like the idea of having to seize her when she slipped near a curb. The city of Boston, however, was paying him for just that.

Policeman Hall dreamed of the shoplifter. He dreamed that he was pursuing her but that, strangely enough, he had three bananas in his hand. These bananas he did not know (or did not think about) were bananas which, at the age of nine, he had taken from a fruit stand and brought to his mother. One she had eaten, another he ate himself, the third was presented to a visitor who came in shortly. Policeman Hall does not yet know that what troubled him was the idea of chasing after other people while thinking somewhere he ought to be chased after himself. George Hall had been a harum-scarum boy and his mother had liked the idea of his becoming a policeman and being sensible. At the age of twenty-two he had attained the security of a servant of a mighty municipality. Putting the law into action was seen as a fine thing by the young George Hall. His mass-attending and his protecting people of Boston seemed a most desirable and respectable combination. Yet Hall, like other servants of the law, protected civic virtue while not deeply sure of his own virtue. That is not a good situation. Civic virtue should be protected, but not because there is position in it and a stipend and conscious ethical satisfactions. We cannot remedy the evils within a city while the evils we have are not seen by us. At least, we cannot do this without some kind of protest or obstruction.

George Hall, for reasons unnecessary to describe here, did not marry. When his father and mother died, he set up house with an aunt and her children. Last year there came to him a stronger desire to drink than he had noticed previously (his father had drunk a good deal). He got into a somewhat unrestrained argument with an inspector. The department took the side of the inspector. That was six months ago. A few days ago, with the memory of this humiliation, as he saw it, still in him, Hall found himself, weirdly enough, placing his pistol against his temple. He said: "Jesus Father, what am I doing this for?" He hurriedly put his pistol in the drawer. The family he lives with knows nothing about it, nor does anyone.

There have been suicides among policemen, and the causes, as the newspaper stories about these suicides indicate, are hard to establish. There is no doubt, however, that a person paid to maintain virtue, finding his satisfaction in hindering others from attacking the interests of society, and still not at rest deeply as to the virtue and beauty and order of his own self, can undergo great internal discord. We cannot correct others, we cannot get our livelihood by the halting of others, when good and evil are not at ease in ourselves. Policemen will kill themselves as other people do if they don't like themselves.

The causation of the desire in the policeman to kill himself cannot, I think, be understood if one dismisses the dilemma within him arising from an inaccurate relationship among himself, what he does, who employs him, and the people he must watch and, if need be, arrest and have punished. Virtue cannot be departmentalized. It can be organized, but there must be no tremendous constricting impediment in that organization. There is that constricting impediment in the mind of George Hall, a policeman who has dallied with suicide.

Emotions should be considered in terms of their effect on persons. Here it is proper to consider the practical and physiological meaning of two emotions, or two aspects of one emotion: envy and resentment. It has always been held that envy is not a beautiful emotion, a proper one, an ethical one; and not much eulogistic has been said readily of resentment, either. However, were these emotions only unseemly, "unethical," yet permitting human beings to go through their lives unimpeded, unhurt, strong; the unseemliness and the ethical inappropriateness could be put aside. The problem for the while is what psychological or physiological change in a specific human being, envy or resentment makes. If the change is bad then envy and resentment are practical menaces.

A "bad" emotion like envy has next to it certain quite praiseworthy states like emulation, ambition, self-criticism. It needs to be seen, then, in any instance of envy what the envy is about, from what it arises. A human being should criticize another; should, if another human being has something good or powerful or beautiful about him, try to have it too. The zeal to attain a good or beauty possessed by another need not be bad in itself. The particular state of envy must be seen in terms of its source and its relations.—Well, envy is bad only when the whole being is not behind it; it can, strangely enough, be said that envy is bad when it isn't completely envy. When "envy" is courageous and complete it changes into thorough, useful self-criticism. As it is, self-criticism is always present in envy—but obscured.

As I have stated, the contemporary way of life brings about in people a desire to be something and to do something, not so much because these people want to do this thing and be this something, because they are good in themselves, but because other people are doing something or being something. We all have a desire for self-justification and if we cannot make or fulfill that desire for self-justification by knowing and articulating our deepest states, we shall justify ourselves in terms of a self-hurting competition. The present world makes it seem right that we go after objectives in terms of "showing" other people, excelling them, and degrading them. In attaining these objectives the deeper desires of the self are disregarded or deflected.

Close to envy, envy in the bad sense, is unhappiness because someone else has a means of happiness which, if we had, would make us happy. This, simplified, comes to being unhappy because another person is happy. Out of this feeling comes a related one that another's unhappiness is our happiness. The most dangerous and ugly thing about competition as we have it today is that it works to nourish and maintain the neurological belief that unhappiness in someone else is happiness for us.

Resentment is close to envy. We feel ourselves at war with others. Somebody wins a point over us. If we could we would make things even or get revenge. While we can't, we resent. Again, the resentment must be seen in terms of its sources. To resent a thing because it is strictly ugly, hurtful, unjust, will not make for nervousness, or ulcers, or dyspepsia, or fidgety sleep. As far as I can see, the directions and objectives presented alluringly by present day economics are on the side of resentments, deleterious to the organism, distorting to the self, and outrageous to the unconscious.

Nathaniel Dresser is an energetic purveyor of real estate in Milwaukee. He is constantly making deals of one kind or another. He is buying property and selling property. He has become interested in the building of houses and has employed labor. He married a girl better educated than he and now has a son and a daughter on their way to college. He is a member of the Chamber of Commerce.

At one time Mr. Dresser was a carpenter. He felt then that his employers were getting the better of him and he resolved he would show them. He was aware of unusual energies in himself and though he was a member of a union felt that the other persons in the union were 'way below him and when it came, as he said to himself, to: "real guts, the real something, you got it here or you don't have it." Anyway, Dresser felt there was no reason he should do carpentering all his life; he could employ carpenters and other people. He rented a rooming house and put it in the charge of his sister, Vivian. Vivian made a go of it; she got her share and Nathaniel got his. He picked up, in one way or another, a knowledge of real estate and its possibilities. He bought a house on mortgage and sold it outright a year later at a profit of $2,800. He had chosen wisely, his advisor had been his sister, and though he quarreled with her, still in so far as they had the same objective they got along. Later, he bought two other houses one of which he changed into a rooming house and the other he rented. Profits were steady.

Dresser was Jewish. His father had been learned in the Talmud and was a very religious Jew. He died three years after the family had reached Milwaukee from New York.

His mother likewise was very orthodox and, affected by her husband, had in her mind the ethical and religious principles of Judaism. Nathaniel himself, fond of his mother, had studied Hebrew. When she died, when he was twenty and an apprentice to a carpenter, he still remembered her attitudes, her words; was still somewhat impregnated with the teachings of the rabbis. His father and mother had been poor and he resolved not to be poor. He would show them there in heaven that their son could conquer the disadvantages and the tribulations they had met. So the young man, who knew the Ten Commandments in their original tongue, and that grand miscellany of ethics and allegory and practical wisdom—the Talmud—and the sharp and very often mighty spiritual counsel of the rabbis, resolved to conquer Milwaukee.

Dresser was involved in a deal. The person he was dealing with was likewise sharp, and Dresser felt that he was either to outsmart or to be outsmarted. He had his sensitivities then, and it wasn't with too much gusto that he tried to get the better of Hugh Robinson. Robinson, he found out, could do a good job of getting his and leaving others without theirs, and Dresser resolved that he would not be holding the bag while Robinson took a happy, profitable trip. Through an adroit use of lawyers, business sense, and timing, Dresser was successful. The feeling of commercial battle grew in him. He made of selfishness a crusade.

Dresser bought property, sold it, built houses. He talked to union chiefs, got the best prices from contractors, manufacturers, plasterers, plumbing companies, and didn't let anybody get away with anything worth retaining by himself. At the age of thirty-five he married. A year later he seemed to be touchier than ever to his business associates. He exploded once when his wife insisted on getting a certain kind of fur coat and no other. Yet Dresser, when he married Isabel, had thought of presenting her as the best dressed woman in Milwaukee; for he had his ideas of magnificence. He quarreled more bitterly with business contacts and with relatives. His sister, Vivian, and he had a virulent battle over money. He once sent a union delegate out of his office, but had to repent later. He would hire a strike-breaking agency to keep things quiet while certain buildings in which he was interested were being constructed.

At the age of thirty-nine Nathaniel Dresser, visiting his doctor, was told he had stomach ulcers. At this time his wife was giving him difficulty; so were his little boy of two and a half, his partners (these partners were mostly temporary), his lawyer, his chauffeur, his stenographer—and it may be said, people in general. At this time Dresser was engaged in combat, but no longer so sure of the grandeur of the objective. He wanted to beat Mr. Smith and Mrs. Levy and Mr. Montgomery and Mrs. Templeton but he didn't know that his whole being wasn't going towards victory. When these misgivings reached him, however faintly, he could not welcome them. Instead of criticizing himself as he really wanted to do, he became more morose, more virulent, more bellicose as to others. As his morosity, his virulence, his bellicosity increased, the feeling somewhere in him that his fundamental direction, primary goal, was being side-stepped by him, became unconsciously stronger. The heightened going forward and the lessened belief in the activity of going forward showed itself physically. There was constipation, there was bad sleep; and then one morning Dr. Elmer Francis told one of his most respected patients, Nathaniel Dresser, that it looked like ulcers and he needed a diet. He was also told to cut out the worry, it would all be the same a hundred years from now.

But the self-machine of Mr. Dresser was all wound up, in fighting trim, raring to go, and yet not sure of where it was going and why. Unfortunately, Mr. Dresser really didn't want to know why. He could not at this time, very well, put into action clearly the principles he had heard from his father, from his mother and the Hebrew school. He remembered them all right but he remembered them through the haze of Milwaukee activity. Besides they belonged to culture; and culture was something you went to when you were through with business.

Yes, Mr. Dresser was resenting things. If he could really feel that his wife was unjust to him when she wanted to take an expensive trip just while he was deep in a great commercial project and couldn't get away, it would not have been so bad. If he could have really felt that the lawyer of a rival of his who had got the better of his own lawyer and of himself—if he could have felt that this lawyer was really unjust, he would have resented in a clear sky, directly, cleanly; but the direction of his resentment was not straight, it could not go on unimpeded, it was not based on a certainty within the self of Mr. Dresser. That is why he resented the opposing lawyer, Harry Land, and, at the same time, resented himself; because he could not wholly feel that he had a right to resent a lawyer or a rival doing fundamentally what he was trying to do. Nor was he sure by this time, if he could get revenge on Harry Land, that he would have got what he wanted, since revenge, again, would have made him resent himself.

Resentment which did not terminate in guilt, or organic dislike of oneself, would not make for stomach ulcers. The resentment that gets twisted, that goes back on itself, that works like a coil of wire of which the middle gets tangled with the ends—that kind of resentment is no good psychologically. As I intimated when I said that the mischief with envy today is that it is not complete, so the mischief with resentment is that it is not complete. When envy reaches a certain point, instead of being a source of essential satisfaction to the possessor (because it cannot truly go further) it is something making for unhealthy ferment in a person. So with resentment: if it had a clear road, resentment would be accurate discontent, a healthy sense of injustice, a desire for praiseworthy revenge. But since the civilization of the moment does not provide most often a channel for accurate, complete, unobstructed resentment and envy, these emotions do not complete themselves by becoming an anger at injustice or a healthy desire to criticize oneself by means of what another does or has. Nathaniel Dresser has been caught in a tangle of combat, resentment, and disbelief in his own deepest motives and objectives. For this reason, although his wealth has been increasing, he is looked on by his latest partner as a fellow whom he has to do business with but, "Oh, what a bird."

He is tolerated by his wife because she has means of diversion apart from him, or at least means of interior solace; and his son and daughter both hate him, both irritate him, and both use him. They do all they can to alleviate his digestive troubles. When he is in a bad mood they have all come to a technique of dealing with it. Harold, the boy, knows that he can defeat his father by appealing to his fatherly possessive drives; and Ruth, the girl, can likewise get her way. Sometimes, however, the family irritations cannot be anticipated and there are scenes.

There are scenes with Mr. Dresser elsewhere. He discharged his stenographer at one time because she had misplaced an address and called her back that evening. He once left a business meeting in a tremendous anger and he was found later in the bathroom, panting. At the present time a heart condition seems to be appearing along with the ulcers. It is worrying Mr. Dresser. A few nights ago he was looking at a picture of his mother and saying to himself: "I wish,

Mom, you were here, I wish you were here." But his business interests go on, he is a director of various charitable and semi-charitable institutions, and he is seen as a man who has won out. He, himself, at times, doesn't know whether he has.

Henry Jones has the position of assistant editor in a publishing house. The house has its ups and downs and the tenure of the personnel is uncertain. The chief editor, John Simcoe, is erratic though undoubtedly he knows books, has insight, can pick a good-seller, and knows how it should appear before the public. It was through a friend of Simcoe's that Henry Jones got his present position. There has been talk of the firm's merging with another and there has been talk likewise of making its annual publishing list smaller. Simcoe has wanted to quit his job at times, and once, in an altercation with the owner, David Lang, said sharply: "You may expect my resignation in a few days." However, both Simcoe and Jones are still working members of the staff.

Jones has a wife and two children. He has definite ambitions. He feels often that the firm does not need both himself and Simcoe. He is worried about his job. He has tried to find a place elsewhere but he hasn't been able to be successfully energetic about it. Once, when Simcoe was away from the office for two days, Jones became aware that he was hoping the chief editor would be so drunk, or so sick, that he could not come back at all. Jones has sensibilities and he felt, even while having these feelings of an anti-Simcoe nature, they were not the most noble in the world.

Jones' wife, Rita, prods him and constantly brings up the necessity for a larger income in the family. Henry had been an outstanding student in his college and Rita had married him largely because of his conspicuous endowments. He had always wanted to be connected with publishing and literature and Rita had seen the desirability of this likewise. Rita has a power for subterranean, gentle, but unmistakable sarcasm; the sarcasm, as it shows itself, has some of the quality of a monitory caress. So Henry is being impelled towards the heights by his critical wife and concurrently is surrounded by doubts, fears, and incitements that cannot go the whole way.

Sometimes he does not like the publishing business at all. He would much rather that he were strictly a literary man. He has thought of writing a novel but hasn't gone very far. He has said to himself: "I'm no Dumas, or Thomas Wolfe, nor even an Edgar Wallace"; and he doesn't know it, but there is a desire on his part to foil his wife—along with the desire to show her that he can do all the things she expects of him and more.

Simcoe has said to him: "Jones, you are one of those persons who gets things done. You're one of the chaps without whom pyramids could not exist." Jones has remembered this statement. He dreamt of pyramids once, but he didn't like what Simcoe said because Simcoe apparently had arrogated to himself the dash, the élan of creativeness, of originality; while to Jones had been given the comparatively workaday ability for sober construction.

Jones dreamt once of John Simcoe and his wife Rita, talking to each other and pointing their fingers at each other from opposite sides of the street. He hates, to a substantial degree, both his wife and his chief editor; he is in competition with both. But when he is more than customarily displeased with his immediate superior, his affection for Rita enlarges. Then there are his children. They, to his harassed, ambitious mind, seem to ask of him too: "What are you going to do next, daddy?"

Jones was put in charge of a rather shapeless manuscript containing original material about the war. He put it into order, suggested a new title which was accepted, and the book had a good sale. He was smiled at in the office by Mr. Lang and felicitated on his editorial achievement. Still, elsewhere, though the firm made a profit, there were disappointments. Jones could not feel that his position was certain, was lucid. He still imagined jibes from his editor and from his wife. He still felt that the mental endowments his wife had seen in him had not come to fruition. He still hoped, sometimes consciously, that Simcoe would become so erratic he could displace him. Yet that would please Rita, and without knowing it, Henry was not entirely for pleasing his sharptongued wife.

Henry Jones is in the position of many. At present, in America, there is a hankering for jobs, a desire to displace others, a wish to advance oneself—and the hankering and the desire and the wish do not have a calm basis, an orderly basis, a beautiful basis in the mind of the person possessing them. In the lives of hundreds of thousands is a hurtful tie-up of economics and competition and love, and competition within love—a tie-up that, looked at, is hardly useful, hardly healthy, and in human terms, hardly tolerable. Emotions must have a basis acceptable to the unconscious, and a procedure likewise acceptable. The network of our emotions must have a certain orchestration, not a murky, disorderly, detrimental tangle.

When Henry Jones desires the job of John Simcoe his unconscious does not desire to have this desire in just that way. Whenever one has a desire and one does not *desire to have this desire,* in terms of the self where it begins, there is living trouble. It is very hard for Henry Jones to arrive at some useful, healthful coordination in his mind of job, Rita, Simcoe, ambition, and literature. Since the honest attempt to make such a coordination would imply a critical overhauling and unhindered appraisal of Henry Jones' situation as to the world and his particular world, the attempt is not really made. While it isn't made, Jones is responding excessively, yet incompletely, to the data of his life. He often sleeps ill. He has slapped his daughter, age eight, with such fury that the child did not wish to talk to him for four days. Once he left Rita and his children for two days. He went to a roadhouse with a college acquaintance and came back in a taxi and had to be carried by the taxi driver and his wife into the house. This particular incident he does not wish to recollect at all. There is, at times, an excessive desire to urinate. He is troubled by hemorrhoids and he becomes so moody that the only words he wishes to utter are those of a strictly "business" kind.

It is not necessary at this time to relate the distresses of Henry Jones to his life as a child. What is necessary to be seen at this time is that the pitting of himself against others which he has done, which he has had to do, is a factor in the uncertainty and disproportion of his deepest nervous responses. The psychological, or, if one wishes, physiological derangements within his body are largely owing to the fact that he has accepted a world which is not the world he truly and deeply desires. But he has not articulated his deepest, most comprehensive desires and therefore his body, his nervous system, his self has "articulated" in pain what he has not expressed lucidly, forthrightly, completely.

The question, then, about economics is how far it accords with what man fundamentally wants. The unconscious, unlike various parliamentary bodies, will not really stand for compromise. Compromise in psychological terms is unhealth. Compromise is neuroticism, because the factors within a compromise are simply placed as reapportionment in opposite camps, not either destroyed or merged. There is no such thing as a healthy compromise in terms of the basis of our nervous system. There is integration, but integration is thorough; compromise in the ordinary sense is business as usual and business not as usual, until one is aware of trouble. The self will insist in one way or another on getting wholly what it wants; and if it gets part of what it wants it will use the strength of part of what it wants to get the rest. This is what life means. The unconscious does not retire, it does not let well enough alone. In its very nature it is dynamic, ethical, and tremendously demanding. It would be just as foolish to say that the unconscious can go so far and no further as to say that a child who, biologically, could grow to five feet ten could stop growing when he reached five feet.

Sometimes there is an attempt to make the best of both worlds in a liberal or radical political fashion. By this I mean that persons will, quite often, take a political point of view which is collective, has otherness in it, seems sacrificial and altruistic, and yet have within them a preponderant belief in the self not as other, not as related, but as a point and as apart from reality as a whole. Since the self is basically after integration in duality and variation, a cleavage or lopsidedness of this kind is likewise harmful. In everyday terms it has resulted in persons being noble, self-denying publicly; nervous, narrow, nagging, reclusive, and unjust privately.

Stella Winn is a member of a very active left group. In college she majored in sociology and German. She married, six months after graduation, a young man as intense as herself and likewise given to questioning society as it is. When Stella married Edward Hale she felt she could find happiness in a profound domestic life. She had a child and gave that child all the emotional energy and care she could. Despite the presence of the child and the iconoclastic attitudes of both Stella and Edward, they disagreed between themselves.

Stella decided to combat the narrow, self-regarding tendencies within her by giving herself to work for others—work held in disesteem, work somewhat dangerous, work that was exacting and disciplined. She joined a left group looked on with disfavor, suspicion, and hate by many people; chiefly so by the class of people from which her father and mother came and most of her relatives. She was swept by a glow of self-effacement the first months of her joining the radical group, and felt that her dissatisfaction with herself would be done away with. After a few months she persuaded Edward, who had been somewhat skeptical, likewise to join the organization. He did, and sometimes they would find themselves at the same meeting. She was a social worker and he was on a newspaper and therefore they could not engage in the same activities, but often they met at the larger demonstrations against fascism or for the remedying of some injustice or in the celebration of some holiday.

For a year or so Stella and Edward thought they were not the egoistic, irritable beings they had been too often. They decided that their boy, now four, would be rid of the pretense and misconception and general falsity prevalent in a competitive, profit-seeking world. But Stella, though she took on assignments, organized, acted as an inciter of many —and an efficient one—could still arise in the middle of the night with a strange, throbbing fear. She could talk back to a policeman if need be, but this shapeless fear was still hers. She could feel that things were black suddenly and that she was a wretched, undeserving being. There was sleeplessness and there was digestive trouble.

One evening, about eight, just before she went off to a meeting, Stella found herself bitterly quarreling with Edward; she slapped his face and then went off to her room, lay down on the bed sobbing. For some reason the meeting seemed unimportant and she did not go. Edward went out, came back, there was a reconcilement and things went on smoothly for a while. But another quarrel occurred; there was more dejection in Stella; she became acutely suspicious of Edward's feelings for another woman (even though jealousy was to her a hardly respectable emotion). She stopped sleeping with her husband for weeks at a time. There is now an accepted semi-formality in their behavior. Stella has thought of leaving her husband and going off with a man in her group a year and a half younger than herself. At times she has become too irritated with her boy Tom, and has later been ashamed of her irritation. Her organizing work, however, her fulfilling of assignments, her holding of elective positions have gone on.

The profound trouble with Stella Winn is that she has become altruistic, collective, not as a completion of egoism or narrow individualism, but as a set-off to these, an atonement for these. Collectivism and altruism are not atonements for individuality, they are completions of it.

Whenever the collective fulfilment of ourselves is not joyous wholly, it is also faulty, insincere. Stella joined a left group not so much—though she would deny this—because it was a beautiful thing to do in itself, but because there were worries she wanted to destroy. Without knowing it, likewise, she used the fulfilment of her collective assignments as the go-ahead signal for the luxuriating in of her concealed "point" self. She really did not see her political work as a continuation, extension, flowing from herself where it began. She denied herself in order to have permission to enjoy herself spuriously. It was as if a child had got itself whipped on purpose in order the better to enjoy some sweets it had stolen and concealed. Unfortunately a good deal of sacrificial public political activity in America and elsewhere is of this kind.

We often don't go with our whole selves towards remedying the ugly economic conditions of the world; we don't join a beautiful, just cause because we entirely, comprehensively, deeply see it as beautiful, but because we see it as making up for, atoning for, defects in ourselves. We are ready to suffer for our defects but we are not ready to give up those defects sharply, cleanly, wholly. We can't really—unless we see much more than most people want to.

This is why persons advocating just, necessary political purposes can be narrow, smug, irritable. It is not the purpose they are working for, nor the group as such to which they belong which is at fault; it is the reason that persons like Stella Winn have come to advocate this purpose or to join this group. No matter how beautiful a thing is, if it is approached, welcomed, as an offset to something else, with that something else still yearned for unconsciously in opposition to the new thing—there will be mix-up, insincerity, narrowness. In the same way as a fine thing like poetry or painting can be misused, so can left politics be misused.

Stella could advocate discipline with such an insistence that to a sharp outsider there was something even greasy about the advocacy. She could appear noble, but she could be unbearably smug without knowing it. She did not see that now and then, even in a left cause of great rightness, of tremendous truth, there could be an association of "inaccuracy," lightness, humor. Since Stella was using left doctrine as an atonement, she could not be flexible with this left doctrine. She saw it as a kind of granite to be altered only in a disciplined manner by the formal statement of an authoritative, clearly accepted, disciplined decision. She wore her virtue too much like a stone around her neck. She rejoiced in the restriction because the restriction reminded her that she was suffering and therefore she could have that inner life about which she felt deeply guilty.

For Stella, despite all her external courageous activities, unconsciously had an internal life apart from the "masses," apart from her organization, apart from Edward, and even apart from her boy. She would deny this hotly, but she really saw people not as completing herself, but as suspicious objects she could try to change.

Once Stella had a dream about enjoying ice cream. There was a table full of ice cream cones and she was sucking one cone. There was a clatter on the ceiling above and there was a motion downstairs. She rushed into another room, hurriedly, and somehow the cone she was eating dropped to the floor. She felt there was nothing but dark in the next room. —Stella liked ice cream cones a great deal. As a child she liked to buy ice cream cones and enjoy them away from other children. This particular dream, the like of which she had recurrently, pointed to Stella's liking to enjoy herself without anybody else having to be thought of at all. This dream went on even after Stella was known in her city as a bold person who would work for what she believed steadily, without intimidation.

Once Stella was rather drunk at a party of left persons— all active—in New York. There was gaiety there and there was sophisticated talk. The people drinking had been south and fought for the Negro, had taken part in union struggles; one or two had fought in Spain. Stella, about two A.M., found herself asking: "What are people? Am I people?" And John Studley said: "Stella, old dear, you certainly are. We're the people, though at times they don't know, the poor dears, that we are." Stella, the next morning, remembered the phrase: "Am I people?" She didn't know why she had asked it but she felt it was amusingly significant that she had.

Stella is tormented by the fact that despite her collectivism, there is a bridge between self and otherness she hasn't yet crossed. The fact that she wants to cross it, that she has suffered in not being able to cross it, is all in her honor. The difficulty she faces is certainly faced by those who have not consciously tried to make the world more organized in terms of permanent and everyday justice. But because Stella has these collective trends, the feeling that her self can be apart is more than otherwise painful. She is really displeased with herself. She does not know that she has used sleeping as a contrast to, a reward for her outward activities, not as a culmination in tranquillity of them.

As she did, when she was a child, Stella still associates her being alone in the bathroom and biological procedures there with a sense of self-triumph arising in a different way from the triumph of altruistic activity. She wants people to be free but she cannot see her husband, Edward, as loved and yet not herself. She cannot look upon her child, Tom, as dear to her and yet a being just as much not herself as the President of the United States. She still has the profound tendency to see her greatest triumph as consisting of her being able to dismiss the world when she chooses. She knows that this is wrong, in her fashion. She disapproves of herself in terms of her body. She has had headaches and nausea, but she cannot make a clean break from her earlier lonely triumphs to her later chosen activities. She cannot definitely merge the pleasure in being different from everybody else with the sense of completion which occurs when she feels or can feel she is related to everyone and everything else. There is war in her; the war is sporadic and it comes from the fact that political justice is looked upon by her not as a completion of justice to herself but as an atonement for the unconscious pampering of herself.

Politics, like other phases of general thought, is often an embodiment of, and often a contrast to, the inner situation of persons. A senator can be mean and fearful and narrow and oilily egoistic in his public behavior and make up for this wrongness by a show of overbrimming generosity privately. We can show our hate to the world in a political or economic way, and try to make up for it by a lavishness to an individual whom we can see symbolizing a world. It has happened that egoism taking an industrial form can atone for itself by a seeming abundant altruism towards a child, a chorus girl, or even a stranger. Our contracting tendencies are not seen, inwardly, as one with our generous tendencies. We use contraction to make up for expansion and we use overflowing of self to make up for niggardliness.

Nervousness has a constant relation to our sense of values. We are either seeing outside things as liked, or something identified with ourselves as liked. There is a shuttling between the self as center and the self as circumference-and-area. This can take form in such matters as paying a check, or a salary, receiving and giving presents, borrowing and lending, financial envy and financial pity. In every human relation, the final rightness is always aesthetic; because that which stands for the self must be satisfied simultaneously with that which stands for other than self; and whenever that is done the equivalent of the aesthetic process has been welcomed and used.

11

An Approach to a Philosophy
of Self and Disease

An Approach to a Philosophy
of Self and Disease

NOTE. Aesthetic Realism is a philosophy which, if learned with respect, steadiness, and lack of petulance, can be of great use to those professional people who, in one way or another, are trying to make the people of America less unhappy. It should be clear that Aesthetic Realism, in discussing "physiology" from a philosophic point of view, is trying to inform the contemporary colleague of Sir Thomas Browne (1605–1682), not trying to be in unnecessary competition with him. Further, in reading what follows, it is well to remember the original meaning of the word disease: lack of ease.

1. GENERAL BASIS

AESTHETIC REALISM sees the cause of mental disturbance as the wrong opposition of self to reality—which opposition may show itself in the sexual field. Here, not the general opposition of self to reality, or the way this opposition shows itself in sex will be considered: rather the way this opposition includes the physiological. For to say that the self is opposed to reality is to say that the self, or organism, is at odds with its environment. Now there are two basic conditions in every instance of disease:

1. A discord within the organism, or self;
2. A discord of the self, or organism, with outward conditions.

From the psychosomatic point of view it is fairly clear that if the self *hates* reality, one of the components of the very basis of disease is accepted by it.

It follows then, that to be opposed to reality or environment, to fear it, to hate it, even to be contemptuous of it, is accepting a situation making for that general state called disease, illness, sickness, maladjustment, unhappiness, and the like. The tie-up between physical malady and psychical malady is to be found in the opposition present, in both, to outward conditions. The liver, for example, in refusing to function, is stating that it is getting along ill with whatever may come from the outside world to the liver or body; in this instance, food or drink. A respiratory ailment implies a difficulty of the organism in meeting the outside world or environment, as it takes the form of air. A digestive ailment likewise implies a discoordination between the organs or phases of the body or self; and also a discoordination between the body as a whole, or part of it, and the environment as a whole. In other words, all disease, psychically or somatically, is a difficulty of the organism "intra-murally" or "extra-murally"; and this means a division, a disjunction of part against another part or whole of an organism, or between the organism and reality or environment as a whole.

In psychical ailment a person looks upon reality as an enemy and so does not get along well with it. In ailment of a seemingly physical kind, the body does not get along with reality even though there is no apparent enmity. In stomach trouble a stomach is not functioning well in terms of what it meets from the outside world; in mental trouble a mind is not functioning well in terms of what it meets from the outside world. In stomach trouble there is a discord between the stomach and its contents; in mental trouble there is a discord between the self and the contents or components of that self.

A self can be described as the particular way, seen as a whole, which an organism has of meeting the world and feeling its own existence. In every action of the self, there is an apprehension of the world and some response to its own state after that apprehension. The self can likewise be seen as every aspect of an organism taken simultaneously together. In the same way as an action of the United States as a whole would affect, however imperceptibly, life in Syracuse or Seattle or Santa Fé, so the state of the self as a whole, would affect every phase or component of what it is, including physical divisions: that is, heart, stomach, lungs, blood, cells, feet, eyes, brain. It is also true that just as a flood near Memphis, Tennessee, or a fire in Syracuse, or an earthquake in San Francisco, or an invasion of the East Coast, would affect all of America, so a happening to any phase or component of the organism would affect the organism as a whole, that is, the self. There is an indefinite interaction going on in the life of every person: Of phase or component of the organism and the organism as a whole; of the organism as a whole on phase or component; and of the outside world on the organism as a whole and phase or component. This interaction, which can be seen as triple, or quadruple, or quintuple and even more, is simultaneous. At any one moment in the life of any person, the world is affecting every part of that person's body and the self as a whole; every part of a person's body is affecting every other part; and every part is affecting the self as a whole. All this occurs while the outside world, or environment, or reality, is affecting the organism and every phase of it. Where the organism undergoing this interaction finds growth and freedom in it, that much disease is not present; where there are slip-ups, discord, enmity, disproportion, there is disease. A malformed or an enlarged stomach is a phase of disease. A concept of reality which is malformed or excessive, is likewise a phase of disease. An excess of blood cells is disease; a paucity of blood cells is disease. An excessive response to objects is a phase of disease; an insufficient response to objects is a phase of disease. These statements, I believe, point to where bodily disease is akin to psychical infelicity, or bothersome imperfection.

It is my opinion that an adequate notion of disease can be had only where the interaction of self on part of body and part of body on self, simultaneously with the action and reaction of world on self, world on part of body and self, and part of body on world—is seen. (This last sentence is, I am aware, seemingly complicated. However, it is as far as I can make it, an exact, undecorated description of what actually happens in every self.) Disease is lack of wholeness. It is an interference in the accurate functioning of the self as to what isn't the self.

The stomach, from one point of view, is the self just as much as an attitude of the self is. Since a thing is *all that without which it could not be;* and since a self, humanly speaking, cannot be supposed with the absence of a stomach (or its equivalent), a stomach is the self, likewise. However, it should be seen that where a stomach is fully functioning, there must be a self present; for a stomach could not exist unless it were accompanied by other organs, feelings, life: and this implies the presence of self.

The interdependence is complete, it is inseparable. We can divide 5 into a pair of halves—$2\frac{1}{2}$'s—and we can work on each $2\frac{1}{2}$ separately; but we know and we should know that $2\frac{1}{2}$, though it can be seen separately, is also inseparable from the other $2\frac{1}{2}$; or, for that matter, from $1\frac{1}{2}$ or 2 or 3, all seen as part of 5.

The upshot of the foregoing in logical terms is that just as all health is both psychical and bodily, so all disease is both psychical and bodily. By "psychical" I mean that aspect of a person which would correspond to the shape of a spoon in a spoon. By "bodily" I mean that aspect of a person which would correspond to the weight or material of a spoon, say silver. A spoon *is* its shape; it is also the material it has. A spoon cannot function as that, unless it has a certain shape; for the silver in a spoon can exist in just that weight without there being a spoon. When the shape of a spoon is changed, something happens to the material. When the material is changed, something happens to the shape. This change in shape is in proportion to the change in material. If a person is seen as having form in the full sense of the term, with form seen as energy—just as the shape of a spoon or a wheel is part of its energy—that person is seen as having something which, though *like nothing*, has energy, does something to the material with which it *is*. The psychical aspect of a person is the form of that person seen as energy. In man, as in other things, this form and its energy can be understood only in terms of aesthetics.

The problem of the psychical and somatic in self is an aspect of that larger problem, which, in art, is expressed by the terms form and substance. The psychosomatic solution is basically the aesthetic solution. What is necessary is to see that our thought is the same as our body; but that just as *how* an artist painted a deer can be seen as different from the deer, so thought can usefully be *considered* as different from body. We know that we are the same as we were a year ago, but it is useful to see ourselves as different, too. The logic of reality itself is at this point desperately indispensable.

A drop of dew, which also has form and substance, has its perils; and a self has its ailments. These ailments arising from the mishaps of self, in its full sense, as it deals with reality, are various. Some are most obviously bodily, others both bodily and formal or psychical; and others more obviously psychical. It is, of course, to be recognized that each ailment is both physical and formal, or psychical. In Aesthetic Realism, wherever the word "body" is used in reference to disorders of self, this use has to do with where the *accent* seems to be on the common notion of body; and wherever the word "mental" is used, this use has to do with where the *accent* seems to be on the common notion of mind. Certain situations can be seen as both mental and bodily in a short space of time; just as in seeing Mrs. Dora Roberts, I can see her in the morning as a mother; in the evening as a daughter; and still have the same Mrs. Roberts in mind.

2. STUTTERING

There is an obvious difficulty of throat, lips, and more in stuttering. There is likewise a clear indication of some attitude of the self. Fear is an attitude of the self; shyness is an attitude of the self; uncertainty is an attitude of the self. There is, then, in stuttering an interaction of the organism as a whole (the self) and a phase of the organism,—throat, lips, or if one wishes, the brain as physical, or a thing of weight. It, of course, is likewise evident that the fear is a response or an attitude to objects representing the world as a whole. So in stuttering we have an unfortunate relation of self, bodily phases of the self, and the world as a whole. This relation, as I have implied, is present in all disease.

One can surmise a malformation, or physical maladjustment of tongue and lips and nerves and throat, as present in stuttering. One can say that, in stuttering, the tongue, the lips, the throat, and the nerves do not function as a good physical team. The question then arises, Why the dysfunction? Does the crucial cause lie in a malformation of any or all of the mentioned phases of the organism? Aesthetic Realism sees the important cause of stuttering as the attitude of the stuttering self as a whole to what it meets. However, the presence of what are termed "physical factors" can willingly be granted. Coal, for example, may not reach a cellar because the window of the cellar was not open; because the chute refused to work; or because there was labor trouble—a strike, for example. The effect in each instance would be the same: coal would not reach the cellar. There can be, quite clearly, an interrelation of causes. Yet in the instance of stuttering the decisive cause is most often a conflict in the self making for hesitation on the part of the self to manifest what it is. In other words, when Jim Riley stutters, he has a self which hesitates to meet what he's talking to and to have what he's talking to meet him.

All activity of the organism as a whole, considered as psychical or as an attitude, is made up of taking in, retention, giving forth. In other psychological terms, of impression, use, effect, consideration, or expression; in more physical terms, of ingestion, digestion, excretion. All this imposing language, which from one point of view is foreign to the shapely simplicity of Aesthetic Realism, means this: Jim Riley is, all through his life, taking in things, holding them, and giving them forth. If there is an unwillingness to take in from the world, hold from the world, give out to the world, Jim Riley may get into that trouble which popularly is termed stuttering.

Stuttering is like vomiting in a certain sense. There is a conflict of the desire to take in and the desire to give forth; or in this instance, reject. The self finds its satisfaction in two ways: by assimilating, taking, receiving; and by giving forth or expressing. The self, like the organism, is a point, an object intent on its affirmation, definition, survival. It also wishes to act, give forth, express.

Take the instance, in plainer terms, of William Hand who isn't Jim Riley, but who is like him. Mr. Hand has been receiving, like all of us, ever so many impressions from the outside world. He has found a good deal of his ego-satisfaction in being able to think of himself as an entity apart from the world he has been meeting. Let us look at Mr. Hand at a certain moment.—He has decided that his importance to himself comes from the fact that he can see himself as a person quite independent of other things and other people. But there is a desire on the part of Mr. Hand to affect other people. At the same time, though, that he is trying to affect other people, he wants to keep, unconsciously, certain things to himself. His friends think he is the "close type." It is quite evident, then, that if a desire to express is simultaneous with a desire to keep back, hold, there will be some difficulty. That difficulty is related to the phenomenon of stuttering. Stuttering is a collision of the desire to express the self and the desire to maintain the self as an immune entity.

However, this conflict in the self of the desire to express and the desire to withhold may have other causes. One quite evident cause of stuttering is the wish to say something and the being afraid to say it. But this situation, in its less recondite fashion, also has in it a conflict of two fundamental attitudes of self. Lester Rudd would like his words to have a certain effect; but he is also afraid that he may get into trouble. There is, therefore, a desire of the self of Lester Rudd to expand and, simultaneously, a desire to contract. Lester Rudd does not stutter as often as William Hand; but when he wishes to be bold and yet wishes to be secure, stuttering ensues. The conflict in the attitude of his organism as a whole towards what it is, is manifested in the region of lips, mouth, tongue and throat.

But there is a young lady, Hester Jackson, who stutters

constantly. She has, deeply, an "against" feeling towards people and a "friendly" feeling all the time. She needs people, but she fears them. She wants very much for herself to take in more territory; but she wants just as eagerly, unconsciously, to maintain the security of her self-kingdom. She constantly "wants to get away from it all." So, in talking, Miss Jackson looks on giving herself to others as an indignity and at the same time as a thing of fear. But she wants also to influence others and to have them like her. She is afraid that people will come close to her; nevertheless she wants them to like her. Her words, with all their mishaps, are manifestations of that basic civil war.

Whenever the self is going forward and at the same time wants to remain where it is, since words are staple, constant manifestations of the self, they and the mechanism by which they come will be affected. So Hester Jackson can't get away with having her lonely duchy. Could Hester look upon the world as friendly to her while she wishes to conquer it with one phase of her mind, could she see it as something she respected, even while she could be contemptuous of things in it, without the respect and the contempt colliding—the stuttering would not be. Furthermore, Hester Jackson, in keeping with principles stated elsewhere, has an attitude to herself that is at once too exalted and too depreciating. She finds it hard to be a princess and also a "good mixer." She has a superior and an inferior feeling at once. When she talks, these inferiority and superiority feelings meet in a clash; and mouth, throat, and words reveal the clash. The unconscious desire to hold back and the conscious desire to let go in Miss Jackson, staging a battle, use the oral regions as a battle ground. Silly, sad, and could-be-happy Miss Jackson.

As elsewhere, in the instance of stuttering, an adequate notion of causality must be had. It is quite true that a person may begin stuttering because he has undergone a shock of some kind, an unsettling, sharp experience, a sudden fright; that is, a "trauma." This does not mean, however, that the entire cause of the stuttering is the unsettling event. A "trauma," or shock, puts into a new arrangement possibilities that existed before. There is a disposition in everyone to be afraid, to hate, to withdraw. When the world presents itself to us suddenly as dreadful, as inimical, or as painfully strange, we can at that moment affirm a tendency hitherto implicit. Traumas, in so far as they affect the general attitude of a person, may simply bring the finishing, expediting touch to a process before then existent, but subterranean. A shock will disorganize our relations with reality. We close our eyes in retreat, we fear, we strike back, perhaps; and in doing these things we accentuate a likelihood already present of feeling that there is a big something we don't like, and here are ourselves who must be protected. A trauma is an instance of swift mutation within an evolution of attitude going on before slowly and with greater opposition. A person could not be completely unsettled by a specific incident were there not the seeds of unsettlement in him previously.

Eldridge Colby is a little boy of eight who stutters. He had been nervous before, but he began stuttering a week after his Aunt Geraldine had given him a severe spanking and general beating while he was playing in the cellar. His aunt had taken him to a corner of the cellar, where the electric light was dim, and there had cuffed his ears, slapped his face, called him a "no-good brat," pinched him, and said he would end in the station house, all right. Eldridge didn't like his aunt and had done the quite awful thing of pouring his father's fountain pen ink into a valise carrying her clothes. He had gone off then to the cellar and there pretended to play. His aunt remembered that Eldridge had done quite unrighteous things before. She knew that he did not like her. And therefore in a high fit of anger, without telling his parents, she had gone seeking him.

She found him in the cellar and asked him whether he had poured ink on her clothes. The boy said, after being silent to her first questioning, explosively: "Yes, and I'll do it again." Aunt Geraldine was infuriated and there in the corner of the cellar started beating him till the boy screamed. The boy, in his way, struck back. No one besides these two was present in the house and the parents did not find out what happened until dinner time that summer evening. The boy did not want to come down to dinner. He locked himself in his room. The aunt was a little ashamed by this time and finally said to her brother: "Elly and I had a quarrel this afternoon in the cellar. I gave him some good licks. The boy poured ink all over my clothes in the valise I have in my room. Most of the clothes are ruined. I got angry and I went looking for him. I found him, we had a fight, and I gave it to him good." The boy didn't come out all that night. At midnight he let his mother in but he did not want to talk much then. He whimpered: "I guess grown-ups don't like me. Maybe I don't like them either." A week later, a fairly clear stutter began.

The parents tried to tell Eldridge he hadn't been such a bad boy, the clothes had been sent to the cleaner's, his aunt had forgiven him; and the boy, at times, would stop stuttering. At other times, hardly distinguishable from the immune periods, he would stutter badly. The question is whether it was only the "trauma" that made for the stuttering. The boy had been moody before, he had been afraid of the dark, would run out of a room, and at times had had nightmares. He had dreamed of his aunt as trying to stick him with an umbrella. He had at times not wanted to talk at all when his mother asked him a question. It is, therefore, most likely that the incident in the cellar, though it immediately preceded the stuttering, was not the basic cause of Eldridge's speech difficulty.

The incident completed a murky chain of causation already in motion. Long before Eldridge began concentrating frantically on the first syllable of a word, forgetting the others, and catching his breath in between words at times, he had taken to himself that organic outlook towards things which earlier had manifested itself in other forms of nervousness. Eldridge was coming to look on what was around him as an opponent. Like many other little boys, he had triumphed in the fact that he could evade that opponent by saying it did not exist, and that he could conceal himself from it. The scene with his aunt, Mrs. Rudge, when he saw a grown-up with hate in her eyes, furiously grab and strike him, pinch him and cuff him and scold him and curse him —that incident added a culminating nervous expression to the divided, warring structure built in previous years. The trauma was really, as I have implied, an accelerated, compact period in an evolutionary process.

In order to understand stuttering as caused by traumas of various kinds, it is, therefore, important to align three phases of the history of the self. The phases, simply put, can be described as: One, all that has existed in the person's life which might give the trauma unusual symbolic significance; Two, the trauma itself, its extent and why it affected the person as it did; Three, the way in which the combination of past life and trauma shows itself in the general history of the person later. I must protest against an emphasis on particular unusual situations as causing "neurosis," and in this instance, stuttering. One of the big reasons for a shock's having a large effect, is the field ready to receive and exploit the shock. That field must be studied.

A child, as I have stated before this, undergoes many

impressions, participates in many experiences, has to meet many problems which leave his self in a state of confusion, antagonism, bewilderment. The things that please him also pain him. That which he wants to respect can often act as if it were silly, unjust, ugly. All this makes for a duality of approach, a waveringness of approach. Children are wavering, we all are. The wavering becomes steep at times and the steepness is shown.

Alicia Rowland is a child of three given to stuttering and some other minor difficulties of speech. She has already lived an opulent life in terms of fors and againsts, hopes and fears, sunniness and storm. It can be expected, therefore, that when Alicia shows herself to other people, she do not do so with mellifluous assurance. In terms of her own life, she has lived unconscious epics of acceptance and rejection, of progress and hesitation. The words that she uses mean something to her; they are her visiting cards to the reality she is trying to meet rightly. She wants to run away while she wants to be accepted with all the honors befitting an instance of humanity. Alicia, in her fashion, is going through the misgivings that a person suddenly presented with a watch at a big meeting would go through when asked to make a speech.

Alicia, like the recipient of the watch, wants to say things but is afraid she may get into trouble, or at least bring some discomfort to herself. Our basic organic attitude in all its subtleties—that is, the unconscious as a whole and the conscious—decides on what is uncomfortable. We don't know why we decide; Alicia doesn't; neither does, wholly, the man who has to make a speech, tell what he thinks to a friend, express himself about his work, and so on.

Comforts and discomforts are in hidden ambush. The self of Alicia Rowland feeling suns and bushes at one time, shows the rushing of bushes on suns, and organic retreat upon advance, in her rather cute but distressing stuttering. In her instance, a sudden fright may cause her to talk without stuttering because "traumas" may not only disarrange, they may arrange, even, for a while. A great fear, for example, may make for decision.

The fact that stuttering is related to conflicts in the basic attitude is supported by the presence of stuttering most frequently with other nervous manifestations. I know a stuttering person, for example, who is given very much to drink; but does not stutter when he drinks. He is seemingly at ease then.

Stuttering is often present with disturbed sleep, uncertain appetite, digestive complaint. It need not be, but it often is. Alfred Carr increased his stuttering simultaneously with a deterioration in hemorrhoids and sleep. He stuttered when he had the greatest hesitation in getting to the depths of himself. Strangely—if strangely—he stuttered when he was with his closest friends, the people to whom most he had a likelihood of revealing himself deeply.

Expression, which, in the fullest sense, is the acting of ourselves so that our well-being, our growth, our completion is attained, is something which goes on all the time. In certain people, for reasons to be considered elsewhere, fundamental difficulties in expression—and this implies impression likewise—may take the form of a breathing habit, a tic, yelling, a mannerism of tone, a headache, and so on. The same basic condition may manifest itself variously. Stuttering is one of the most conspicuous manifestations of the antagonistic impact of a desire to express with a desire to withhold. It is the embodiment of inhibition and forwardness; it is the explosive, excessively energetic, excessively repetitious, and excessively denying, bodily symbol of the sudden battle between the centrifugal and centripetal selves.

One self wishes to be other, to be related; and one wishes to be a snug, perfect point, capable of dismissing anything and everything. Aesthetic Realism sees stuttering as a manifestation of the self, and sees this speech mishap as a concomitant of an incomplete personality. However, since Aesthetic Realism is chiefly interested in the self as a complete, instantaneous thing, it points out that stuttering can be used to *explain* the self. A misfortune can be used to see what would be good fortune, more clearly. If we understood stuttering adequately, we would understand that antagonism in self, constantly hungering for joyous aesthetic resolution.

3. SLEEPLESSNESS

Sleep, like other physiological states, takes in the whole self. We don't know how much the self feels. There is a feeling in every quarter inch of our body which we are not aware of most of the hours of our lives. It can be said that there is feeling in every drop of blood, in every cell, in every bone, in every bit of tissue, because where there is life there is feeling.

It can readily be seen how little feeling is seen by us as an object, if every part of our organism is alive and if there is feeling in every part. One constant procedure that can be found in all motion and in all phases of life is the motion of going forward and of coming back, of widening and contracting, of expansion and concentration. This motion is to be seen in mind; and it is to be seen in every physiological procedure and in every physiological organ. The self dilates and contracts, the stomach dilates and contracts, tissue dilates and contracts; and the unity of dilation and contraction, their going for the same purpose, is health, good sense, aesthetics.

One great instance of widening and contraction in terms

of the self as a whole has to do with waking and sleeping. In waking we go towards what we see as the outside world, in sleeping apparently we go away from what we see as the outside world. If there is a disjunction between the two, a conflict without togetherness of the two, in keeping with the principles stated in Chapter 3, "The Aesthetic Method in Self-Conflict," there will be disorganization, ill-health, inaccuracy of the organism. This disjunction is very common. The disjunction can take the form of stuttering; it also can take the form of insomnia.

A child will, as I have pointed out, feel that in bed he is avoiding the confusion, the unsettledness, the pain of the hurly-burly and lack of understanding he finds in his family and elsewhere. He will, in order to rehabilitate his disturbed ego, look upon the being snug in bed with everyone else away and himself a world, as a kind of security and supremacy making up for his insufficiencies and his fears in the ups and downs of waking life. And there may come a feeling that sleep is where he has his own way and waking life is where he doesn't; or at least he can't be sure that he does.

Sleep is therefore associated with the self as alone and without relation; the self that we hug, preserve, and most often hug and preserve by trying to keep other things away. Sleep we see as the best, the most prolonged time for doing such a seemingly necessary thing. We therefore use sleep to dismiss the otherness of self as represented by objects as a whole.

For example, there is Ruth Darnton. She was, as a child, made much of by her mother, caressed, yielded to, pampered. Still, as in the lives of all children, there were times when Ruth's mother seemed not to be so sweet, not so yielding to the desires of the child. Besides, there were other children.

Ruth's mother, Sarina, once left the child's father for another man; and Ruth felt fearfully unsettled. Her mother wrote to her through Mrs. Darnton's sister; and Sarina came back; and things seemed quite peaceful again between her mother and father. But Ruth was never sure of her mother from then on. Her world had become shaky and wobbly. Even before this it had been somewhat painful, unpredictable. By now Ruth felt that only within the purlieus of her bed could she find stability, and peace, desired by a doubtful, agitated self.

Ruth took to her bed a picture of a constant mother; she took also a sweet paternal picture, and other representations of manageable calm. She imagined herself in bed as roaming sunny green fields entirely hers. She was a queen of the kingdom extending from her bed, but the kingdom was somehow still in the bed and somehow still within Ruth herself.

At the age of twelve Ruth decided she would go to bed at 9:30 every night. She looked upon 9:30 as a somewhat holy time, a time not to be interfered with, displaced by anything else. A few years later Ruth studied stenography and went to work. She found herself wanting to get home as soon as possible after work. If a friend came to dinner or to visit, she was restless until the friend left and she could go to bed. In other words, by this time there was a fight, a profound fight, in Ruth's mind: she was expansive when waking and concentrated when in sleep. And Ruth as wide and Ruth as narrow made for two people. Ruth came to see sleep as *her* time as against *that* time of waking. Yet Ruth did her work well; was quite precise and neat.

At about nineteen Miss Darnton met a young man. He came to her home for dinner a few times. Towards 9:30 P.M. Ruth found herself stating to him hintingly and otherwise, that it was best for him to go. She was in a conflict about that, because it happened that now and then she did not want him to go. As she saw more of the young man, she became more exacting of him. Once she insisted that he buy a certain kind of overcoat and no other. Though this seemed a small matter, the young man flared up for the first time and said: "You're not going to run my life. I'll get the kind of overcoat I want." Ruth was surprised: she saw the young man again, but phone calls and visits grew fewer; and once when Tom was supposed to call, he didn't and Ruth had too much dignity to complain about it.

Ruth Darnton thought to herself: "Well, I guess he could never be what I wanted him to be anyway"; and she decided that whatever else happened, no man was to put her life out of joint. She thought of her bedtime with more solicitude than ever before; Tom had interfered with that bedtime, now there was no reason for its precision to be attacked. One Thursday some months later, Ruth found it quite hard to sleep. She had been promoted at her work, was visiting quite a few people, and was "kidding" quite a few young men at the office and elsewhere. However, that Thursday night she couldn't sleep. About six in the morning she did fall asleep. Sleeping Friday night was a little easier but there were interruptions. Saturday she slept as she used to and she thought: "Well, that new restaurant must have done things to me."

A week later, however, after seemingly better sleep Ruth found herself pretty wide-eyed at two in the morning. "Well, I guess," she said to herself, "I've been working too hard. I'll drink warm milk before bedtime and keep away from coffee no matter how much I like it." Nevertheless, sleep continued to be uncertain. Ruth told her doctor and he gave her some sleeping pills. In all this difficulty, every night at 9:30, Ruth Darnton went through her ritual of bed. She closed the windows, saw that the covers were precisely placed, saw that her shoes were at the same angle in the same corner each night, saw that her nightgown was unrumpled when she put it on and was placed in the same spot each morning and folded in the same way. She tried, while in bed, to feel that the whole outside world was shut out and that she was wrapped snugly against opposition. In her tossings she attempted to maintain the symmetry of the bed and bedclothes. This was hard. But Ruth tried with all her might.

Once Ruth thought of herself as Queen Ruthianna of Ruthania. This high-sounding word jingle had come to her mind quite early in her life. The phrase still went through her mind. Ruth, when she began taking phenobarbital pills, felt at the beginning it was an indignity to her sleep ritual. But later she included the pills as a kind of wonderful adjunct to dismissing the world. She found, as the months went on, that the dose had to be increased. She became quite grumpy at the office. Previously her smile had been quick, frequent, and conspicuous. This smile persisted, but it lost some of its energy.

The pills continued to be indispensable; the dose had to be increased. The effects on Ruth could no longer be seen as triumphant. She began to worry, she began to ask: "Could it be I'm nervous? What does all this mean?" Yes, the question is, What did it all mean?

What Ruth did not see when she went to bed so blindly and so haughtily, was that one self in her did not want her to go to bed on the terms she had chosen. These terms Aesthetic Realism describes as 2-A terms. The self opposed to narrow, 2-A procedures could not earlier make itself felt. The wide self was there, but the triumphs of Ruth in being able to dismiss the world were too fresh, too desirable, to permit 1-A objection to be noticeable. It was true though, all the while, that Miss Darnton, in setting one aspect of herself—the contracting, point self—against the widening self, was welcoming civil war. Here civil war is another term for what has been called neurosis.

Insomnia is a manifestation of the pitting of the hidden, center self against the expanding, external self. When Ruth was nineteen and her insomnia began, what was happening in her mind was this.

2-A Self: "I can have a wonderful time thinking that there are no street cars, no relatives, no people who won't listen to you, no bosses who can tell you to work overtime, no mother who can make you wash dishes, no teacher who can say you don't know something, no people who can be so strange they can bother you like anything, no pieces of wood you can trip over, no children who can give you backtalk, no fellows who can beat you at cards or not ask you for dates, no strange countries which can make you think how unimportant you are, nothing at all which can act like chewing gum under your feet, a wall before your nose, a gag around your mouth, a stone before your toes, a policeman before your step. Here is where I, unobstructed, dismissing everything, have my innings. I am I and nothing else but."

(The other self or 1-A self at this time was becoming articulate. It can now be thought of as speaking.)

1-A Self: "Look, you narrow aspect of me, you have been running me up till now. You have made Ruth want to feel that her glory was in being able to see other people and other things as unimportant. You have made Ruth go to sleep as if sleep were a leaving of the whole world and everything from which she came, and everything with which she has to do. You wanted to make Ruth feel that sleep was the only time she could be victorious. You, in your controlling Ruth, have made her feel that everything she met which could really make her freer, make her realize who she was—that this everything was an interference with freedom. I now, though I was not so strong before, am quite strong now; and you and I have to fight for Ruth. I don't want her to sleep any more on the old terms. It's wrong. She doesn't want to listen to me entirely; and I suppose I'll have to bother her. It's too bad but Ruth can't sink into a being who thinks that sleep is a time to put aside the very world on whose existence she depends; which represents her; and which is *she*. Yes, it is too bad, but Ruth has to decide."

(And the debate made for Ruth's inability to sleep. The pills muffled the debate, but did not annul it.)

In insomnia, one aspect of the self wants to feel that sleep is the complacent dismissing of the world; the other aspect of the self wants to feel that sleep is a welcoming of the world, though the manner of welcoming is different from that of waking. The welcoming and dismissing processes of the self are a rhythm, a rhythm in the mightiest sense of expansion and concentration, of divergence and convergence. Where rhythm is lopsided, where rhythm is changed into conflict, there will be protest.

When Ruth didn't sleep, it was because her *whole* self could not sleep on the old terms. She felt she wanted to, but the 1-A part of her unconscious was protesting; and this means that Ruth herself was protesting. However, though she did not want to sleep on the old terms any longer, her comfortable self, her vanity or 2-A self, still wanted the triumphs of the past. We have found that in stuttering there is a desire of the recoiling self to win and a desire of the expressive self to win. In insomnia there is a similar fight between that aspect of the personality which wants to use sleep as a means of dismissing externalities, and that self which wants proudly to recognize these externalities and to grow through them.

The painful drama under the skin which I have described, goes on every night in a person whose insomnia is caused by himself. The drama went on in the organism and self of Ruth Darnton; and it goes on in other possessors of insomnia; it is a drama in which attitudes fight, swirl, and pain.

Insomnia then is one of the major indications of personality-and-world disruption. Insomnia is an ethical indication. The general ethical cause of insomnia may make for other manifestations of an undesirable kind.

Various procedures have been advocated for coping with insomnia. These procedures may be somewhat efficacious; but if, as it seems, insomnia is an intimation of a fundamental perceptive rift, then whatever merely abates the insomnia does not banish the central ethical error leading to it; a transitory abatement simply redistributes or rearranges the results of the ethical error. A study of the mishaps of self must begin where the self begins. Various professional persons have not seen that to be thorough, one must be profound.

The approach of Aesthetic Realism to insomnia is, quite clearly, different from other approaches. Aesthetic Realism sees sleeplessness as arising from an injustice to self and all its surroundings. Too often insomnia has been seen as arising from casual situations. Aesthetic Realism sees the wellbeing of a person as inseparable from the willingness of that person to see all that is not the person as friendly and useful. So a decision, unconscious or otherwise, that makes what surrounds a person unfriendly, is deeply stupid and unethical; and furthermore may lead to uncomfortable vicissitudes in sleep. Where persons have approached sleeplessness with ethics not considered, these persons it is proper to regard as insufficiently equipped.

For example, Joe Rubin was told that he had a desire to

kill his mother, and that therefore he could not sleep. What was not made clear to Joe was that his feeling towards his mother was part of a general antagonistic feeling to *all* people, to existence in general. So while it could be truly said that a feeling towards his mother was involved in his sleeplessness, the fact persists that had Mr. Rubin not felt that the world beyond himself was something to be eschewed, despised, forgotten in sleep, the long-term, painful wakefulness annoying Joe Rubin would not have taken place.

Insomnia dramatizes more clearly perhaps than anything else a fight existing in the past and contemporary personality. In sleep every self makes a decision. The unaccompanied, unobstructed personality is on its own. Every self then has been tempted to feel that since the world is not seen and can easily be thought of as not present, it need not be respected and can be complacently manipulated or dismissed.

Therefore, such anti-sleeplessness measures as counting sheep jumping over a stile, listening to soft music, drinking warm milk, being told on records that everything is peaceful and all right, making oneself like driven snow, ridding oneself of all thoughts by one means or another, and taking sedatives, are at best preliminaries to comprehensive understanding, and at worst these measures are muddlers and hindrances. The self wishes to be at ease for some hours, but it wishes most to be at ease, deeply and widely. The quiet that may ensue from soft music or counting sheep or a specially made pillow, is a trivial, miniature makeshift for the substantial, constant, *dynamic* quiet which the self hopes for. The ethical unconscious cannot be bribed. It does not know half-measures or quarter-measures. It is a neighbor of all that is true, and it must be on good terms with that neighbor.

Take Dr. Frederick Major mentioned in Chapter 10, "Psychiatry, Economics, Aesthetics." This physician took, unconsciously, the position that the world was not a friend and need not be respected entirely. In doing this he welcomed an ethical inaccuracy which made for difficult, precarious sleep. In sleep, as elsewhere, the self must approve of what it is. There are many ways in which the self shows its own discomfort; and insomnia is one of the most conspicuous and significant. It is clear that if a self is uncomfortable about a job, or a theft, or bad food, or a physical fear, or an injustice done to it, or done by it, this self might have a hard time attaining repose. The situations mentioned can all make for temporary sleeplessness; they can all make for a disorganization of the personality and a time of disturbed questioning. But if a casual disorganization of the self and a displeasure by the self with what it is, can give rise to casual sleeplessness, is it not just to suppose that a longstanding, basic disorganization and criticism by the self of what it is can give rise to longstanding, constant sleeplessness?

I have, in Chapter 5, "Imagination, Reality, and Aesthetics," dealt with Julius Harris. I showed that Mr. Harris tended to make a disruption between unity and diversity in himself, what was immediate and what was strange in his life, what was factual and what was "imaginative." When a person like Mr. Harris unwisely divides aspects of his life, it is because he has divided his intimate being from being in general. Therefore, the disruptions in Mr. Harris, because of their source, could likewise make the night difficult. Aesthetic Realism believes that the self is always criticizing what it is, and does definitely do so in sleep. Nightmares, sweats, talking in sleep, and events of even more severe import, can take place because the organism of man is affected by his ethics. The ethics of Julius Harris affected his nocturnal life; and ethics is everywhere. It behooves us to study most dili-

gently the philosophic protests of a self, which can be physi-
ological-psychological protests also.

A leading question, then, is how critical the self or organism is, and how does it *show* its disapproval?—The self of
Julius Harris, with whom I have dealt, was critical of what
the personality of Julius Harris was doing. The self of Julius
Harris did not like what he was doing and what he was not
doing. Mr. Harris, in accepting a fundamental disorganization, also accepted an unhealthful separation between the
personality seemingly under the skin of Mr. Harris, and the
world that extended beyond the skin. In other words, since
Julius Harris felt he was limiting himself, he felt guilty.

It is good to see that the acceptance of any mistake or
disproportion whatsoever, worsens, however slightly, the
constantly mobile relation between personality and existence. In the same way as an ailment of the foot, however
slight, has some effect on the heart, so the acceptance of a
psychological point of view which is incorrect and incomplete, has a deleterious effect on that possibility of equilibrium between self and world, which is perceptive health.

Julius Harris, therefore, in making too much of a war in
his mind between the immediate facts of his own existence
and what he saw as his imagination, accentuated a possibility
of division between his intimate self and externalities. In his
fashion he accepted the condition also accepted by Ruth
Darnton and Frederick Major. These three persons interfered with or neglected reality in different ways, but the
upshot was similar. Perceptive disproportion, disorganization, injustice, disturbs the accuracy wished by the self in its
dealings with things. Where the disproportion is strong
enough, and of a certain kind, sleeplessness will take place.

Earth, in its manner, is just. It has made it so that a person
unfair to it cannot sleep well in it. If we knew that a person
in the next room had been dealt with unfairly by us, had

been seen with unhandsome contempt, had been arranged badly in our minds, we could not very well be reposeful. And so, if we play unseemly perceptive tricks with the magnitude, might, and existence of earth in its immediacy and strangeness, we shall be uncomfortable, too. Our discomfort may not be seen by us, as a cellar may not be; but it is there, and it functions to our, perhaps deserved, restlessness.

4. SELF AND DIGESTIVE TROUBLES

Digestion, as I have implied before, is in its physiological way, a manner the body, as self, has of dealing with objects. The taking of food is more than nutrition alone; it is also a profound homage of the self to its surroundings. We are saying when we eat, and with humility, too, that we need the world from which our food comes. We say, unconsciously, when we eat well: Bless reality which gives us our daily nutriment.—If we can't logically bless, our daily bread will be a daily peril.

In digestion, it is clear that what was once not ourselves, was outside of ourselves, becomes *ourselves*. This is a tremendous, indispensable, biological fact, but it is also a philosophic and ethical fact. How important it is that our intimate, unexplainable Me should need that anonymous assemblage, coming every which way, called food. Nutrition is inevitable and terrifically romantic.

When a grapefruit, let us say, is assimilated by a human body what occurs, putting aside for the moment the alimentary aspects, is the taking to itself, by an organism with feeling, of something which may have come from hundreds and even thousands of miles away. There is a wonder to digestion when one thinks of how the most intimate physiological constituents of ourselves are related to such things as grapefruit from the South, meat from Argentina or Texas, pepper from the Indies, and sweets from France. Every time a person eats he is saying that his body has something to do with earth, remotely and closely; and that how his body is made is akin to how things he may never have heard of yesterday are also made. Physiology, as always, is psychological, philosophical, and inexorably miraculous.

The disturbed or divided self, in so far as it is disturbed or divided, does not look upon objects with accurate approval. If an organism is against the world, it must be, by inevitable and beautiful logic, against that phase of the world which is food. A nervous person, meaning a divided person, is divided not only towards his wife or child or mother-in-law or friend; but also towards vegetables, salads, spices and bread. All our activity, from talking to a relative to assimilating within our blood the chemistry of something edible, is continuous. The mind of man has, in its fashion, integrated an impression of a sister and an impression of something bought at the grocery—which may have come to that grocery from afar.

Digestion has many aspects. Every physiological procedure, to the unconscious, is a source of power; and so is digestion. We feel when we eat that we are using the world our way. That is why, at times, nervous people can have an inordinate desire for food. Chewing, swallowing, eliminating, all have their unconscious self-exaltation aspect. A profound cause of ever so many digestive troubles is the disproportionate feeling of power the unconscious of a person may have towards the taking in of food and the dismissal of it as waste.

I have dealt with a little boy in "Joe Johnson, Very Young American"—"The Child," Chapter 9. Joe Johnson, as a little boy, had to see himself as important, had to feel that he was a definite personality who belonged and was. His ability to chew food, take it into his body, gave him a feeling of ego strength. However, the critical aspect of Joe Johnson's attitude to digestion as a whole concerned the dismissal of food.

Once the world seems against us we try to retaliate—by aloofness, contempt, or aggressiveness. When Joe Johnson felt that his father and mother, making up the world for him, were not for him, that meant, by a kind of logical equivalence, that the world was not on his side, either. He felt, however, that this world which was against him was being managed when he ate. He honored food, it is true, when he put it into his mouth; but in being able to make it part of his body and then to dismiss it, there was a feeling of successful contempt for the world.

There are two times in the average person's life when the self is given clear opportunity to disdain the universe about it: one is in sleep; the other is in elimination. Sleep, as I have pointed out, many, many people see as a time when the besetting, oppressive, puzzling earth about them can be put in its place—which is away from their minds. There is dismissal there and very often contempt.

What goes on in the unconscious of a boy like Joe Johnson as his environment seems cruel to him, against him, is this: "I have taken the world into my body, I have used it for my own purposes, I have had my way with it, I have conquered it. I conquer it and also despise it when, after having used it, I see it come forth from my body and I am able to see how I have dealt with it."

This may seem portentous, yet, I believe, it is a fairly accurate description of the unknown processes of the mind or self in the lives of many children and older persons. A child will run to the bathroom and sit on the toilet seat because, having been oppressed by objects, he can now regain some kind of superiority. Mothers have not understood why many children, even without physiological necessity, have complacently put themselves on a toilet seat. A vast, intricate psychoanalytical literature exists on the subject. Toilet training is an extensive territory within psychoanalysis and child guidance. The essence, however, of a child's feelings as to bowel movement, I believe, has been missed. A child, like everyone else, even when he doesn't know it, is governed primarily by an attitude to all of existence. He is following an unconscious logic when he says that everything he meets, in so far as it is not himself, is something else. And that "something else," in its entirety, is the world.

It follows, therefore, that a child can feel it has come into its own when it can say, "This was in my body; I put it once into my mouth; my body did things to it; I have used it; I now send it off; I look at it; it is my work; I have shaped the world the way I wanted to." And since children usually feel themselves hunted, not fairly seen, manipulated, mismanaged, they will find tranquillity for a harassed ego in this fundamental procedure of expelling food from their bodies after it has been used by these bodies. This, in the daytime, can be the chief ego triumph for a puzzled child, vaguely yet deeply feeling injustice has been done to him.

It comes to be that a bowel movement is associated with the ego's stability. The feeling is that if the body can clearly dismiss something seen as an invader, yet conquered, the same thing is possible in other matters. When a person gets a sudden diarrhea it isn't the fear alone that causes the diarrhea. There is the unconscious connection of bowel movement with equilibrium.

In fear we seek equilibrium: we can do this in various ways. The well known fact that nervousness, apprehension, sudden anxiety, or other forms of fear can make for diarrhea, has to be considered more deeply. Is there a motive—an organic, unconscious motive—in meeting a situation of fear with diarrhea? Is the diarrhea just a casualty, or does it have

something positive to it? It is my belief that every unconscious process, no matter how seemingly absurd, silly, or
unnecessary, has positive, logical motive to it. No gesture or
manifestation is *merely* inane or superfluous.

Let us take, then, the situation of Jethro Tolson who has
suddenly heard that a person is coming to see him whom he
doesn't wish to meet. Tolson is afraid to meet this person,
for something may come from the meeting against Jethro's
comfort and position. Mr. Tolson receives a telegram; the
feared person is coming to his town. He is agitated by the
unlooked for news. At noon the telegram arrives. At 3:30 a
sudden desire for a bowel movement occurs in the body of
Mr. Tolson. Did the fear alone cause the diarrhea? No, the
diarrhea was an unconscious, logical way of conquering the
situation. There is a logic to our crying when a bit of dust
gets into our eye. Our crying is an efficient way of dealing
with the dust invader. To have diarrhea when a situation we
don't like is with us, may not be the last thing in efficiency,
but it is logical for that part of us which wants to have a
victory over an enemy. We curse and despise a condition
with a digestive disturbance of our own. This digestive disturbance, from one point of view, is a cunning triumph;
from another, it is an undesirable physiological mishap.

Mr. Tolson, as a child, had things happen to him which
displeased him. However, he could have a feeling that all
was going his way while he was seated in the bathroom. A
successful bowel movement meant accomplishment not
only for the body of Jethro Tolson, but for his ego. The
world could be puzzling, not so benign; but Jethro found a
kind of pleasing pattern in it when he dismissed food. Is it
not likely, considering the logic of the organism, the prudence of the unconscious, that when Mr. Tolson meets a
tough, sudden, fearsome situation he try to regain symmetry

through his body? In the same way as a person will laugh when he is disturbed, so a person will get diarrhea, not only as a result of the disturbance, but as a means of meeting it.

Diarrhea, as an implication of nervousness, like all nervousness, has its purposive aspect: there is an object to this visceral acceleration and this disturbance. In fact, it can be said that every uneasiness, distress and catastrophe within the body has its purpose. The unconscious is made up of aims: aims and counter-aims. Purpose is implicit in the general motion of the self. In every specific motion, there is purpose, too. It is necessary, to understand the mishaps of the organism which is man, to see how every motion, known or unknown, *is* purpose.

Digestion, like physiology in general, goes on because a direction of the self is helped. The activities of the body have a complexity equal to the complexities of mind. There is not one bodily situation which does not have a mental correlate; and nothing happens in mind which does not have a bodily correlate. Strictly speaking, when we are thinking of rain there is a bodily situation different from when we are thinking of a suspected brother, or a war, or some economic condition of the past. Body is atomic and atomically interacting; and mind is like that. Whatever organic situation a self undergoes there is its mental side; and the evaluation of that organic condition from the mental side is something that cannot be done by chemical tubes and microscopes and stethoscopes and such things, alone. The seeing of form and the possibilities of form, in a subtle, exact, and complete fashion, is also necessary. Aesthetics explains physiology. Without aesthetics, we cannot understand physiology.

It has long been known that the stomach is sensitive. The intestines have also been regarded as indicators of mental happenings. Physiology, as a complete study, includes the meaning of the form and reality behind all the vicissitudes of stomach or intestines or liver or spleen—vicissitudes occurring each day in the human being.

Every bodily happening takes along with it an attitude of the self towards that bodily happening. The failure of a bodily happening would also be accompanied by an attitude of the self. If the meaning of this bodily happening is not seen entirely, or if it is seen distortedly or excessively, what ensues is an opposition of the self as a whole to this bodily happening. Ignorance in the self, distortion in the self, is so much opposition of the self to what it is. The self wants to be known; and where it isn't, that self protests. All physiology is an affirmation of the interaction between organism and that from which the organism comes. All physiology has purpose to it. Physiology is complete when the purpose is known.

I have pointed out that where sleep is used as a means of disparaging exterior existence, the self is against sleep because the self, in its completeness, cannot disparage its cause. Where, also, another fundamental physiological procedure, elimination, is used to make for the separateness of self as against togetherness, the self also, in its completeness, is against that. Sleep and defecation are similar in unconscious significance. If an organism cannot have triumph of a just kind, it will have triumph of an unjust kind.

It occurs, consequently, that the ego, bent on its exaltation, can use bowel movement not as a means of honoring things without, but as a means of being contemptuous of them. Where a child has used his going to the bathroom to say that he is a king there and can have his own way, disregarding or making small or despising what isn't himself, there may later be a deep unconscious protest. One aspect of the organism does want this unmerited exaltation; the other, which represents the whole being, may be quiescent for a while but later, owing to the fact that the child has lived through more, will make its objections felt.

The person with insomnia is afraid, deeply, of using sleep as a means of despising what isn't himself. A person with constipation may also be afraid to have a bowel movement when, in the past, he has misused the meaning of the bowel movement to curtail the outside form of himself. This person must punish himself before this basic physiological procedure can take place.

The relation between insomnia and constipation definitely exists. Juanita Vickers was constantly dreaming of sleeping in public or approaching a toilet in public. She had used being in bed or in the bathroom to think of herself as alone, and majestically alone. The body is, however strange it may sound, essentially ethical. Even physiologically, it is deeply true that we cannot do a thing unless we feel we deserve to do it. The deserving can be described as a situation where all in us necessary for an occurrence is working accurately together: accuracy here is ethics.

When gratification occurs wrongly, that much true gratification is difficult. Physiology, too, has purpose; and if that purpose is dealt with untruly, it becomes harder to reach our true purpose. Punishment ensues. The question that medical persons should ask, though to be sure they have kept away from asking it, is: What is the relation of physiology to purpose? Because, once a relation of physiology to mind and the unconscious is granted, then relation of physiology to purpose must also be sought: for where there is unconscious there is mind, and where there is mind there is purpose.

Related to the problem of digestion is the significance of the most hidden part of the human body: the anus. A great deal—much of it questionable—has been written of the symbolism of the anus and of "anal eroticism." The anus is critical in the life of the self because (like finger tips and toes) it is a decisive point between the self as *here* and the self, or world, as *there:* the ego in its envelopment and the ego in its expansion.

A child feels its anus as the place where something else begins and which still he has, in a certain sense, within his own body. A delicate, shuddering apprehension of triumph has to do with this part of the body. The child expels the world; and yet that by which he does so is *within* him. Contrary to what psychoanalysts have written, I think it will be found that the existence of "erogenous zones" comes from the fact that these zones are richer, more critical signs of the togetherness of a living self and that which it meets. The physiological sensitivity arises from the form or the function rather than the function from the physiological make-up of these parts of the body. Anyway, the anus is connected exceedingly with the feeling of ego triumph. There is mystery and there is power in this part of the body. The desire to touch it, therefore, the desire of the ego or 2-A to honor it, is to be expected.

One ailment regarded by most physicians, dermatologists, allergists, as of psychic or nervous causation, is *pruritus ani.* This ailment, of a most intimate physiological kind, has a relation, however, to the self in its largest and most concentrated meaning. The sordid, if one wishes to see it as such, meets the abstract. *Pruritus ani,* quite common among women and often to be met with in men, arises from the desire in a person to seek comfort from the onset of a puzzling, discomfiting, unsettling, foreign reality. We touch ourselves where we are most secretly ourselves; and when we do this, a bleak, immeasurable invader is warmly defied.

Pruritus ani is akin to thumbsucking by a child. "If what is not ourselves seems not to soothe us, honor us, please us, why then, let's go to ourselves," the unconscious as physiology says. We make of our bodies an external, reassuring world; and yet we know it is ourselves. The thumb and mouth are used by the child; the anus by the troubled person looking in a bad way for reassurance; and the whole body is used by a schizophrenic who puts his arms tightly around his trunk and brings his knees as close to his nose as he can. If we don't like the universe, we can make of our bodies a substitute, scornful universe. Picking one's nose and putting a finger in an ear are also examples of this frequent desire.

In *pruritus ani*, therefore, as in digestive troubles, we can find the use of ourself as body as against what is outside. Once a person is unconsciously disposed to scorn and hate and fear what is not himself, physiology can become versatile in disturbance. All of physiology can be enlisted to show the scornful and fearful disruption of a self from all else. The body as talking can show this disruption in stuttering; the body as sleeping, in insomnia; and the body as eating and digesting, in constipation, diarrhea, nausea, *pruritus ani*, and so on. These are but examples. Heart, blood cells, genitals, liver, eyes, joints, muscles, and other aspects of the body are not exempt. This is why that rather contemporary manifestation of medicine called psychosomatics is so much on the move, every year getting into new physiological territory.

5. CONCLUSION

In this chapter, I have dealt with physiology as *ethics*. Terms most often to be heard from professional medical people have been used. Nevertheless, since these medical terms are contemporary ways of describing an occurrence of ethical import in persons, it is right to ask: What does stuttering have to do with a good life and a bad life? What has insomnia to do with ethics as Aristotle saw it, or the Bible, or Thomas Aquinas, or Thomas à Kempis, or Spinoza, or a troubled child in Philadelphia? Do the Ten Commandments and the

ethics of David Hume or Adam Smith or John Stuart Mill
have to do with infelicities of digestion? Are occurrences on
the surface of our bodies related to the ponderings of Confu-
cius, of Maimonides, of Herbert Spencer, of G. E. Moore
and of A. N. Whitehead?

We do not see Dr. Sigmund Freud as quite adequate on
the subject of ethics. Regretfully, we must also say that
many persons who have become engrossed, in one way or
another, with ailments, have not taken ethics or form with
sufficient seriousness. Aesthetic Realism does not separate
the physiology of Tom Jones from his attitude to good and
evil. Aesthetic Realism is insistently, pervasively ethical. It
sees ethics as a pervasive, unavoidable force, akin to gravity.

We should like to teach professional and lay persons the
meaning of ethics in relation to the ups and downs of cor-
poreality. This, to us, is a logical subject. We should like to
see whether a child can encourage infantile paralysis by
wanting to get away from the world and using its muscles
to do so. (We know of dreams where children are much
taken by beings in stone and beings who, while sleeping,
seem to be unable to move, even dead. We know that people
may have a desire to be rigid. It is likely that a tendency of
children to a basic immobility has a relation to infantile
paralysis.) Aesthetic Realism would like to join forces with
courageous medicine in an effort to find out what ethical or
unethical state, what condition of unconscious fear and triumph, may make for muscular disability in infancy and
childhood.

The psychosomatic people so far have been insufficiently
aware of ethics as energy. Terms have been used like "disturbed," "upset," "in conflict"; but these terms are not used
in an organized, sharp fashion. To understand the meaning
of a term like "upset," an efficient grounding in ethics must
exist. Ethics is not spurned these days as it was by the

psychoanalysts of the 1920's; but still, good and bad are not seen clearly. There is a welcoming of the moral, but the fuzziness persists.

We feel that philosophy has to do with infantile paralysis. We feel that cancer, multiple sclerosis, heart ailments, are connected with a just life and an unjust life. Aesthetic Realism has much to say about just and unjust; for a sick body is inseparable from an incomplete, that is, an unjust existence. Honest people, not necessarily ecclesiastic, have known this, however dimly, all through history. Their honesty should be organized today.

Appendix I
2-A Pleasure Described

2-A Pleasure Described

It is to be presumed that every self has two sides. What one side likes, the other side doesn't. The "bad" side has been talked about a great deal but has not been permitted heretofore to talk adequately in its own behalf. Here it is permitted to talk in the first person and show how "wonderful" it is. To be sure, there is also the rebuttal by the whole self.

The Self:

Like every other human being, I am in a fight between two kinds of pleasure. In order to decide between the two, I must see both for what they are. I have in the past accented the pains (very great) which have come with my having the pleasure which Aesthetic Realism calls "ego" or 2-A pleasure. If this pleasure is greater than the other, it would be unwise to give it up. It would be sanity, good sense to continue it. Let me try to make this pleasure as attractive as possible.

2-A Self:

1. It seems to give me a feeling of pure individuality where I don't have to undergo the "humdrum" competition with other persons that seems to make up such a great part of the present world.

2. I can endlessly despise, and the more I despise the more, apparently logically, my own ego is glorified.

3. I get a sense of triumph from being "invisible" from humans. I can hide with great unconscious glee.

4. I am in touch with perfection; the boring and imperfect have been nullified.

5. I can make fun of everything I want.

6. Matter, objects no longer seem obstructions. I have done away with pavements, walls, furniture, stone. I am in nothing, and free.

7. I can make expeditions into the other world, which I still see as shadows, and at my leisure pretend I am part of it. This gives an added fillip to my triumph.

8. I can talk of my pains eloquently, and fool people as to their cause and meaning.

9. I can be a deceptive emperor; be present and not present in a room; know the time and not know the time; exist and not exist; and have myself, myself, myself while I fool everything and am not affected by anything. (I can pretend I am affected.)

10. I (sometimes called Ego) know this pleasure. It is what I want, and I'll use pain, pain, pain from the world to get it; pretend I haven't got it; and justify my continuing to have it under opposition.

The Whole Self:

I should know this (the above); I know it. But I, the whole self, want the other pleasure. It is greater, it is honest and it has *more* than this. And I don't have to use pain to get it. It does not make guilt. It is the really indescribable pleasure from seeing things wholly, honestly, wonderfully, humorously, excitingly, truly as they are. This pleasure would take the rest of time to describe. It is infinite. It is 1-A pleasure, Real Pleasure.

Appendix II
The Frances Sanders Lesson

Second Preface, April 1974

In April 1945, one could, in carefully reading the transcript of *The Frances Sanders Lesson,* see that the main thing in the life of Frances Sanders was how she saw the world. The definition Aesthetic Realism has of the world is: All that different from ourselves by which we can be affected. If we look at a finger of ours as if it were an object like any other object, we are making ourselves like the world, for the self that is looking is different from the self looked at.

The word *situation* in the very first sentence of the transcript deals with the self as if it were a landscape—the word *site* is in the word *situation;* yet the word *situation* is about something within. Aesthetic Realism is much concerned with the geography of self. The word *environment,* now so much used, implies that the self carries with it a geography seemingly outside, which may do all kinds of things to the land within.

The world is nearer to seeing that the large problem of self is how it sees what is different from self; and, again, What is different from self—is a useful definition of world. All literature, all painting, all music is about the effort of man to see the world in a way that pleases him, in a way that is valid, and in a way of which he can be proud. The world can be called man's inexhaustible, mysterious, and dazzling material.

The crucial thing which may be observed in *The Frances*

Sanders Lesson is that the possibility has been given to man of not liking the world. This possibility is a beginning presence in man's freedom. If man could not object, disparage, say no, be disgusted with, run away from, be superior to, he would not be wholly free. Man has been given an unlimited ability to dislike, forget, despise—in general, an unlimited ability to have contempt. Furthermore, we all use this ability.

The possibility of contempt and the exercise of this possibility are at once the haughtiest and the dreariest aspects of man's life. It is clear that as we say something is a mistake, is not so good, is not to our liking, is imperfect, we are reaching heights of affirmed individuality. How could one be an individual if he did not have the unfettered privilege of disliking?

This individuality, or aspect of individuality, is in Aristophanes, Ibsen, Nietzsche, Camus, and many other persons noted in literature. However, individuality is not confined to the memorable persons in literature. To live is to have the likelihood of asserting oneself contemptuously against all that is not the self. A bourgeois, a proletarian can despise as much as Molière, Emerson, Dostoevsky, Sartre. It is the quality of the despising that matters. Contempt is a fine thing if felt in behalf of the world as possibility; however, as it usually is, if it is a means of enhancing the vain, secret distinction of self, it is hurtful.

That Frances Sanders used her power of contempt to enhance herself is clear. And we are nearer to the beginning drama of contempt. It is that which distinguishes a self secretly and that which makes that self ashamed and weaker. Frances Sanders, it can be observed, was triumphantly disabled. She found the world not much good; but in finding the world not much good, she endowed herself with disaster.

The study of how the self, surmising triumph, abets disaster, will be, as Aesthetic Realism sees it, the future study of mind as a means of encouraging persons to be more the way they would like to be. Since 1945 and earlier, the purpose of Aesthetic Realism has been largely to have one see the felt triumph and the actual disaster of self, brought about by the having of contempt, secret or expressed.

The recent great effect of *The Exorcist,* which is about a girl's yielding victoriously to contempt, has made Aesthetic Realism more current; more in the midst of things. It has also made contemporary psychiatry, with its nubbin of psychoanalysis, less regarded. Persons are coming to see that sex, in all its mastery, is yet something which self has, which self does; and if sex is of self, it is quite clear that the beginning, large thing is self. Here, as we have said often, Freud was elaborately immature.

The Frances Sanders Lesson has been enacted at the Terrain Gallery with fine, deep effect by Marilyn Enderby, Sheldon Kranz, and Anne Fielding. This is a good sign. It means that in 1974 people are asking at last: What can Aesthetic Realism mean to oneself? What can Aesthetic Realism mean to another?

This, then, is a Second Preface, inspired by useful and happy circumstance, though the circumstance is much concerned with inward, darksome calamity. So we are nearer to the annotated edition we talked of in 1945. The annotations will be observed by ourselves and fetched by future happenings and attitudes.

ELI SIEGEL

April 1974

Preface, 1945

The present document is a transcript of one decidedly important Aesthetic Realism lesson. What most acutely troubled Frances Sanders no longer did so after one lesson. There were no other lessons.

Frances Sanders was recommended to Aesthetic Realism by her sister (mentioned as Hazel London in the transcript). Frances came unwillingly, as is quite evident from the document itself.

When Frances came, Aesthetic Realism was in a hurry. For Frances wanted to leave her world. She thought she was going to die; she was not interested in what was about her; she thought she was going to have hemorrhages; and that the doctors were against her. They had said nothing was wrong with her.

Aesthetic Realism felt that what was really troubling Frances was the fact that she felt she could be important—a queen—if, after disappointments and puzzlement and pain, she could despise the world, hate it, and leave it. Something in her wanted to. (This something is called 2-A in Aesthetic Realism.)

After the lesson now presented, the thing in Frances which was ready to be interested in the world, to like it by seeing it as it is, came into the majority. And so, a deep condition troubling Frances no longer troubled her that way.—Frances was provided with a transcript of her lesson: the present document.

It is important to know what was going on in Frances Sanders' mind. For the interior events and procedures and attitudes of her mind are like those of most people in the Federal census, in city directories, in telephone books, and in private address books.

It is possible that the depths of a mind in interior trouble were never made so clear, in some organized, everyday fashion, as they are in the report of this lesson. I had to be in a hurry with Frances Sanders. Decisions were in the making: decisions as to the basis of a life or mind. It was not the time to go into corridors, to ask innocuous questions, to gossip learnedly. The situation had to be attacked in its midst from the first moment. I think it was.

A different approach to sex can be seen in this document from that customary elsewhere. Mrs. Sanders' problems about sex are seen as a phase of, subsidiary to, her problems about the reality within and about her.

Anyway, the lesson worked eminently, and has kept on working. From latest reports—about seven months after—Frances no longer talks of hemorrhages. She is more interested in her child. She's interested in things generally. Her tight melancholy is gone. She was stopped from being a queen of the world she herself made, as against the world of other people; and this is equivalent to her being stopped from leaving her home, to be, most likely, a resident of some institution or sanatorium.

I believe this lesson should be studied. The lesson is literal except for a change of names. The facts I have stated, and others, should be checked. There are means of checking them.

There will be a fully annotated presentation of the Frances Sanders lesson. Meanwhile, for the understanding of the lesson it is perhaps necessary to state here that: Sam is Frances' husband, Jeanie is Frances' young daughter, Hazel is Frances' sister.

Blanche Hoffman, an Aesthetic Realism Associate who was present at the lesson, took a stenographic transcript of it. Frances had never seen her before.

ELI SIEGEL

November 1945

The Frances Sanders Lesson

Mr. Siegel. The situation you are in you don't want. There is something in you which you don't like. If you let me help you see it, and don't hide it from me, you will be happy.

Frances. I'm losing my memory.

Mr. Siegel. You want to lose your memory.

Frances. No, I don't.

Mr. Siegel. When we are unhappy it is because something in ourselves or something outside of ourselves makes us unhappy. Which is it?

Frances. Inside.

Mr. Siegel. Are you ashamed of yourself?

Frances. No.

Mr. Siegel. Are you ashamed of your husband?

Frances. No.

Mr. Siegel. You have to find out what you have against yourself. You think if you saw that, such terrible things would happen the world would fall. I want you to feel the deepest things in your mind are like the sunlight outside. —Do you think you have been fair to people you know?

Frances. I have been to so many doctors.

Mr. Siegel. I'm not a doctor. I know you will be annoyed by my questions. Do you think sometimes you hide from people? *(Frances doesn't answer.)* Did you hide from your husband?

Frances. No.

Mr. Siegel. If you weren't hiding you would feel good. That is what you are trying to do in being ill.

Frances. I'm not trying to make myself sick.

Mr. Siegel. Frances, you have been leading two kinds of life: one for yourself and another for somebody else. You have to make them play the same melody. You haven't shown yourself to your sister, your husband, or Jeanie. I'm not saying you want to get sick; but you want to hang on to something in yourself. When do you have a better opinion of yourself, when you are sick or well?

Frances. When I'm well.

Mr. Siegel. Do you know all your thoughts?

Frances. Yes.

Mr. Siegel. Can you look at them and like them? I want you to say things here you have never said before—and like saying them. You are embarrassed, but you are coming here to feel better.

Frances. The only time I enjoy something is when I have my periods.

Mr. Siegel. That is good. When you are having your periods, some force outside yourself is reaching you. The first thing in being happy is to feel you deserve to be happy. If you don't want to enjoy things, you feel you don't deserve to. If you enjoy things, it means they are affecting you. You are so troubled, the only way you can get a solution is by saying other things don't exist. You can feel freer by seeing things exactly as they are. I say that you would welcome the fact that there is good weather, people, and would smile if you didn't have things against yourself.—I don't think your problem is essentially your husband and Jeanie: it is only a phase of the problem. Your problem is to feel that what begins where your finger tips end and goes out into space, is on your side, is not against you. You came from that, didn't you?

Frances. Yes.

Mr. Siegel. You, yourself, right now, came from the world. Are you welcoming it?

Frances. No, let me be, I don't remember things.

Mr. Siegel. You don't want to remember. The ego in you is afraid to remember. You think the one way to have yourself is to separate yourself from everything. It is conceit. I have to tell you these things because you don't like that part of yourself, either. You don't like the fact that the one way you do have a kind of life is where you don't want to have anything to do with outside things. Is that true?

Frances. Yes.

Mr. Siegel. You have a motive for forgetting.

Frances. I'm not bashful, it's—

Mr. Siegel. I know, I'm coming at you all of a sudden. I want you to, and you will in time, understand the motives. I don't want you to agree to anything I say. Unless you see why it is so, it won't do you any good. I want you to see this problem as between you and what isn't you.

Frances. I know, but I killed myself already.

Mr. Siegel. You want to kill yourself because it is a phase of conceit.

Frances. My heart is beating so fast. Everybody thinks I'm trying to make myself sick.

Mr. Siegel. You are sick, I know you are. *(Mr. Siegel now begins to give words for sentences: giving words embodying conflict is part of Aesthetic Realism method.)* Give me a sentence with "Frances" and "smile."

Frances. (Giving sentence) "Frances should smile."

Mr. Siegel. (Commenting on sentence) Why do you think you should smile?

Frances. To make myself feel better.

Mr. Siegel. Is there anything in the world you now like?

Frances. Now?

Mr. Siegel. Do you think you could like the smile of a newborn baby?

Frances. No.

Mr. Siegel. Could you like the blue sky?

Frances. I don't know.

Mr. Siegel. Do you feel mad at me now?

Frances. I feel mad at Hazel for bringing me.

Mr. Siegel. If you are mad at Hazel, we'll take that up. There is something in you, you don't like. You are mad because it is being attacked. You are sick because you welcomed something which doesn't represent you. That has to go. At the same time, don't you think you could smile at anything sincerely? You used good grammar now. Grammar, you know, has order to it and even beauty.—Do you think you are against the number seven?

Frances. No.

Mr. Siegel. Then there is something you are not against. Do you think you are fair to things when you don't like them? Are you fair to the world when you are this way?

Frances. No.

Mr. Siegel. But something in you makes you unfair?

Frances. Yes.

Mr. Siegel. Don't you think you want to work with me to make something in you stronger? I should like you to feel you can have a good time here, because you can hear things you have always wanted to. You think you are important when you keep to yourself.

Frances. That's what I think.

Mr. Siegel. Do you think the only way to be important is to keep to yourself? *(Frances doesn't answer.)*—Do you think you have a memory of a mountain you once saw, in you?

Frances. I might have.

Mr. Siegel. Where did you get the words you use? They came from people you never heard of. You are also what isn't you. Aren't you ashamed of wanting to keep to yourself? *(Frances doesn't answer.)* Well, you are. When you say the world which made you is now to be separate, that is guilt. In so far as you haven't seen the guilt coming when you separate from things, it has taken the form of these symptoms. What you have done essentially is to say that the world which made you, you want to put aside as if it were ugly.

Frances. I understand you.

Mr. Siegel. Don't you see that is what is making you suffer? *(Frances doesn't answer.)* You don't like it, do you?

Frances. No, I don't remember what's been happening. Right now, I feel I'm going to drop.

Mr. Siegel. Go ahead. I know we are going to have fights. You haven't liked Jeanie, Sam, Hazel, and you think the only way to have yourself is to put everything aside. What's in you makes people not want to eat: they think they would destroy their individuality by eating. This has been going on a long time in you. This is the culmination. You put on a very good show to yourself. It was too good. *(Proceeding with words for sentences.)* Give me a sentence with "Frances" and "Blanche."

Frances. I can't concentrate.

Mr. Siegel. Say anything in your mind. Do you think you would feel better if you knew her?

Frances. Maybe.

Mr. Siegel. (To Hazel) Frances has said maybe she'll feel better if she knows Blanche.—What was the happiest moment in your life?

Frances. When I met my husband.

Mr. Siegel. Do you think that happiness is still in you, or is it out?

Frances. Right now, it's out. I worked myself into something physical now.

Mr. Siegel. You just said you remembered it, didn't you?

Frances. Yes.

Mr. Siegel. You are not completely apart from it then. Do you think you know Sam?

Frances. Yes.

Mr. Siegel. Do you think it is fair not to know anybody else? You made Sam your world. In making Sam your world you were unfair to love. The reason for liking a person is to accept the world. You said: "I have Sam, I love him, he loves me, let the world go by."—Do you love Jeanie?

Frances. Yes.

Mr. Siegel. Did you ever hate her?

Frances. When she's not good, I don't like her.

Mr. Siegel. Did you ever hate Sam?

Frances. Yes, when he's not good.

Mr. Siegel. Did you ever have any bad feelings? Did you ever think of hurting Jeanie or Sam?

Frances. No.

Mr. Siegel. Did you ever think you didn't want to see Sam?

Frances. No.

Mr. Siegel. When you were against him what did you think?

Frances. I don't know.

Mr. Siegel. You had some very bad thoughts, but you don't want to see them. You have separated from Sam. In a certain sense you have "killed" him, you have "killed" people. If you "kill" people, you will feel guilty, won't you? Your motive for doing this is, you think in making yourself the only thing in the world, you will be something like God. That is false. Your real glory comes from how many things you are related to, not how many things you can destroy. Don't you think that is possible? *(Frances doesn't answer.)* I know this makes you uncomfortable.

Frances. I don't feel good.

Mr. Siegel. Do you feel proud when you don't feel good? *(Frances doesn't answer.)* Frances, you are fooling yourself. If you say, "I don't know what is going on in my mind," we'll fight it out.—Do you have any dreams?

Frances. I have been dreaming that I didn't see my husband, and it just worked on me.

Mr. Siegel. Do you know why you dreamed you didn't see him? Because you got rid of him in your mind. You are punishing yourself. I'll tell you the thoughts that make you feel the most ashamed; and if you look on them as you would on the New York streets, butter, a coat, you will feel good. If you want to feel good, you will have to give up the conceit. *(To Hazel)* The problem in Frances' life is whether she wants to be happy by giving up fake conceit. *(To Frances)* You will either give up your secret life, or you are not going to enjoy things. If you can give that up by meeting each thing as it comes, you won't feel that you can't enjoy anything. If you want to be nothing but yourself you will have to pay the price. Do you understand me?

Frances. I'm not putting on any act. I don't remember anything.

Mr. Siegel. You are trying to forget everything so you can have yourself "pure." You are trying not to remember. If you check on yourself you will see that you can remember. You are intelligent, but you have come to feel the only way to be important is to put things aside.—Can you think of one beautiful thing in the world?

Frances. No, I don't feel good.

Mr. Siegel. Would you say the multiplication table existed even if you felt bad or good? *(Frances doesn't answer.)* If you had ulcers, ice cream could still taste good, couldn't it? *(She doesn't answer.)*—You remember the happy moment when you met Sam. The reason you don't want to remember pleasant things is, you don't want these things to feel good because if they did you couldn't be yourself alone. You have made Sam the world, which you didn't have any right to do. You feel guilty because you wanted to swallow him up.

Frances. I know.

Mr. Siegel. Don't look upon your sister as an enemy. Talk about what you were doing when asleep in bed. You put aside Jeanie and Sam. Don't talk about hemorrhages; talk about whether you are fair to the world, which is the same as God. When Hazel came here she had that trouble, too. The reason you are sick now is because you have tried to be alone, glorifying yourself.—Give me nine numbers.

Frances. 2, 4, 6, 3, 1, 8, 7, 5, 6.

Mr. Siegel. Two hundred forty-six million, three hundred eighteen thousand, seven hundred fifty-six. 246, 318, 756. Did you ever use that number in your life before?

Frances. I don't know.

Mr. Siegel. That number is unique. Do you think that number could exist if there weren't other numbers?—You have been collecting this for years and you sprang a couple of days ago.

Frances. I sprang long ago.

Mr. Siegel. You can glare at me if you want to.

Frances. It is my condition.

Mr. Siegel. You are related to everything. If you didn't have air you couldn't breathe. That number is unique, you are unique but also related. Just like the earth which goes around on itself and at the same time goes around the sun: both things at once. You can be yourself and still feel you

have to do with everything. You have come to think
uniqueness means how many things you can forget, and
how many you can despise.—Another sentence. "Maybe"
and "certainly."

Frances. You won't get anything from me: my heart is beating fast.

Mr. Siegel. You are just as intelligent as you ever were. You
don't want to use your intelligence on obstructions in
your life. You feel I'm taking something away from you.
You are doing away with yourself by saying you are the
only person that exists. I want you to get rid of that.

Frances. If I say my heart won't stand anything, nobody will
listen to me.

Mr. Siegel. Aren't you having a good time?

Frances. I'm not.

Mr. Siegel. You didn't think anybody would tell you this?

Frances. No.

Mr. Siegel. You should be so glad.

Frances. Oh, God . . .

Mr. Siegel. You feel very thankful.

Frances. I'm not trying to be difficult.

Mr. Siegel. I understand. I'm fighting something in you. I
know you have to be this way, but I'm trying to tell you
what you really feel. The phony self is running you. I
want you to change your life from hiding into knowing.
I can do things even now.

Frances. We went to a doctor . . . then there was a rabbi, I
ran away . . .

Mr. Siegel. A rabbi married you, didn't he?

Frances. Yes.

Mr. Siegel. Don't you think rabbis can be nice people?—The
big thing, Frances, is what you have to tell yourself. Tell
Hazel what you think of Jeanie, Sam, your mother. *(To
Hazel)* She is compelled to think she is ill. Frances, you

have a symbol about menstruation and pills. The outside force takes you by the belly, you want to have a hemorrhage; because you want to issue blood. *(To Hazel)* Frances wants to be in relation to the whole world. In sending forth blood she feels she is punishing herself. The whole cause is that she has separated herself from the world.—Now, the sentence.

(Frances can't give sentence with both words.)

Mr. Siegel. (After a pause) All right, with "maybe."
Frances. (Giving sentence) "Maybe I'll go home."
Mr. Siegel. Yes, you'll go home. Now with "certainly."
Frances. (Giving sentence) "Certainly I'll go home."
Mr. Siegel. A sentence with "Dr. Burke" and "unhappy."
Frances. (Giving sentence) "Dr. Burke examined me and chased me out of the office and I'm unhappy."
Mr. Siegel. Look, Frances, the things you have been doing the last twenty years I can't change in one day. You are going to hate me maybe. I'm sure you won't want to come again. You'll give logical reasons but you won't fool me. —Do you think Dr. Burke could be unhappy, too?
Frances. Could be.
Mr. Siegel. Do you think Dr. Burke also feels lonely sometimes?
Frances. Most likely.
Mr. Siegel. A sentence with "Dr. Landman" and "Fanny." *(A friend of Frances' in childhood.)*
Frances. (Giving sentence) "Dr. Landman is older than Fanny."
Mr. Siegel. Whom do you like better?
Frances. Neither one.
Mr. Siegel. Why do you dislike me?
Frances. Because Hazel made me come here today.
Mr. Siegel. That is not my fault. Why do you like me?

Frances. I can't even answer. I have nothing against you.

Mr. Siegel. Do you think something in you agrees with me?

Frances. How do I know?

Mr. Siegel. You do know. Do you think something in you has agreed with me? *(Frances doesn't answer.)*—Do you want to give up being queen of the world?

Frances. I'm too far gone physically.

Mr. Siegel. If you stop being queen of the world in your own mind, you are not going to be physically sick. Are you queen of the world now?

Frances. I am now because of how I feel.

Mr. Siegel. Frances, you want to feel this, don't you?

Frances. My heart hurts.

Mr. Siegel. I know, I sympathize with you. Are you willing to give up being queen of the world? In order to feel better you have to give up a secret life in your own mind. Are you willing to pay that price?

Frances. I can't answer you.

Mr. Siegel. If you stopped being queen of the world would you feel good?

Frances. Yes.

Mr. Siegel. *(To Hazel)* Frances has been so disappointed in her life that she has made a separate world for herself. She's been punished by God and the world because she has done that.—A sentence with "Dr. X" and "queen."

("Dr. X" has been chosen because Frances can't remember name of third doctor. The purpose of using the doctors' names in sentences is to relate an external thing like a doctor's office to Frances' real feelings. Frances complains of heart, doesn't write sentence.)

Mr. Siegel. Your heart is acting that way because you want to hear what I'm saying and you are afraid to hear it. You are frightened.

Frances. It's no use. It's all physical now with me.

Mr. Siegel. It isn't.—Frances, do you want to keep on feeling this way?

Frances. No.

Mr. Siegel. What do you have to do?

Frances. I want to go home.

Mr. Siegel. No, that's not the answer. Do you think you will feel good by doing nothing? What price do you want to pay for feeling good? *(Frances doesn't answer.)* "Prescription" for Frances London: To feel things are, to stop having a secret life.

Frances. The minute I get down I'm going to pass out.

Mr. Siegel. What are you ready to do to feel good? You want to feel good and be queen of the world at the same time.

Frances. I don't know how I feel.

Mr. Siegel. Frances, you know very well what I'm saying. When a condition like this goes on, I know what has occurred.—A sentence with "true" and "afraid."

Frances. I can't write.

Mr. Siegel. You can't write a sentence with "true" and "afraid" because you are afraid of what's true. You shouldn't be, Frances.

Appendix III
Aesthetic Realism and Dreams

Aesthetic Realism and Dreams

The meaning of dreams is not the thing that Dr. Freud said it was. It is not the thing that many people, who think that dreams come because you have eaten too much, say it is. It is not the thing which the dream books say it is. It isn't something, either, which is going to tell you what is to happen. But dreams represent something we are doing all the time. Aesthetic Realism says that a person, whether he knows it or not, is criticizing himself all the time. The purpose of Aesthetic Realism is for that person to be able to put, happily, his criticism into words: as accurate and as beautiful and as efficient words as possible. If he cannot put his criticism of himself into words, he will criticize himself with his body, or with thoughts he doesn't understand.

Dreams Are a Criticism and a Hope

Now, all dreams are a criticism. All dreams are also a hope, because when we criticize ourselves, we have a purpose for the criticism. We hope that the criticism can be annulled and its object reached. Every time we go to bed we are looking at ourselves, and that never stops. The way we hope and the way we criticize ourselves, the way we say this is what we can be, and the way we warn ourselves—all this is to be seen in dreams, which take place in the theatre of our minds.

Aesthetic Realism says that dreams are not about sex, as

such; nor are they merely disorderly and a hiding of what we truly want to do. In every dream whatsoever there is a logic. Hopes and warnings can come together, and when they do, there may be a jumble; but there is not a dream I ever looked at carefully—and I have heard and dealt with some thousands of dreams—that didn't make sense. I cannot this evening deal with lengthy dreams, but I wish to show how dreams are always about something: the way a self wants to be, and the way a self can stop itself from being what it can be.

Nearly everybody has had dreams about teeth. Perhaps a hundred dreams about teeth have been told me, perhaps more. Dr. Freud, with his customary lack of imagination *Dreams of* on the subject, has said (though his proponents *Teeth* have coyly denied it later), that a dream about the falling out of teeth has to do with sex, principally. The dream about the falling out of teeth is frequent. Teeth are used as a private means of power: when we take food into our mouths, we think we are conquering the world. Certain of us also can use teeth to show off with. Teeth are a private way, and also an arrogant way at times, of showing our importance in not so beautiful a fashion.

When we have dreams of teeth falling out, or teeth being loose, or something going on in the back of our mouths which we don't like, and when we have dreams of dentists unable to help us, as people have had—all these dreams are a way of saying: The private way you have of getting power is not what you like. There are many variations on the teeth dream, but in all instances something about power is present.

Take another dream, which many women have had: the dream of losing a purse. Now, a purse is like teeth in a way. On the one hand you have private things in it, very private; and on the other you show it in public, this purse. You also may have public documents in it. A purse represents a way of being secret and public at once. And many women, as many men have, have tried to separate their private lives from their public lives. When they do try to do *Dreams of* this, something in them says, through a dream: *Losing a Purse* "Look here, Madge, you may lose your purse." So the Madges of New York and elsewhere have dreams about losing purses. The self says: The private-public relation— the way you see yourself when alone and the way you show yourself—is in a bad situation, and you are losing the solution, here somewhat represented by a purse.—Very often this dream has a stranger finding the purse.

If we look at these dreams, we see them as criticism. All criticism is a wish. When a person playing the piano says, "Jerome, will you please criticize me?" he also wishes to be a better piano player. The idea of criticism goes along with the idea of wish. But that very assiduous Dr. Freud certainly whipped the idea of wish fulfilment into meaninglessness.

Another kind of dream, very frequent, is the examination dream. There are many persons who, when they take an examination and when they sign a questionnaire, go through lots of things, including visceral disturbance. An examination dream is a common *Examination* inward mental happening during the nocturnal *Dreams* hours. The examination is always something like this: You are supposed to write something on the blackboard, but you can't; you are supposed to write down an answer on the paper, but the paper seems to slip over the desk; you are supposed to give an answer to something, but you're tongue-tied; you are supposed to do something, but it's so complicated that you get all wound up, and time is going on, and you feel awful.

These dreams are a way of saying that when you examine yourself in terms of the way you see other people, you don't like it. You are saying that if people asked you a question that involved them and yourself, you wouldn't be able to meet it gracefully.

Take another dream which is fundamental, a dream which very often takes a partly wakeful form: the dream of falling. This dream with its many forms, of sometimes falling from a window, sometimes down a chasm, sometimes *Dreams of* into a ditch, sometimes sinking into the water *Falling* —this dream is a beautiful, symbolic representation of the fact that as we lie down, there is a tendency to sink into ourselves, and hide. All falling dreams are hiding dreams. They have no more to do with sex than the fact that Abraham Lincoln signed the Emancipation Proclamation.

These falling dreams are a representation of a common desire in sleep. A person is said to fall into himself, to sink into himself; we say, "my spirits sank." Whenever we go into ourselves, we do sink, and we want to have a self underneath the one we show. That is why many people wake up in the night with a feeling of having fallen.

And then there is the dream, quite common, which is accompanied by breathlessness: the chase dream. Children *Dreams of* have dreams in which policemen chase them; *Being Chased* adults have, too. Chasing goes on in the night hours very much. And if chasing goes on tonight—we'll be chasing ourselves. We'll be chasing ourselves because we don't like ourselves, and one part of ourselves is trying to catch up with the other. Sometimes the chase is so furious that our hearts begin palpitating.

To show what I mean, I read a stanza from a famous English poem by Francis Thompson. The poem is about the chase that goes on in dreams. And though in Francis Thompson's poem, God is chasing someone, all through the poem we can get the feeling that the self is chasing itself. So

I read this beautiful, breathless first stanza of "The Hound of Heaven":

> I fled Him, down the nights and down the days;
> I fled Him, down the arches of the years;
> I fled Him, down the labyrinthine ways
> Of my own mind; and in the midst of tears
> I hid from Him, and under running laughter.
> Up vistaed hopes, I sped;
> And shot, precipitated,
> Adown Titanic glooms of chasmèd fears,
> From those strong Feet that followed, followed after.
> But with unhurrying chase,
> And unperturbèd pace,
> Deliberate speed, majestic instancy,
> They beat—and a Voice beat
> More instant than the Feet—
> "All things betray thee, who betrayest Me."[1]

Outside of religion, there is a possibility of the self betraying itself. That possibility is a constant factor in dreams. How we can betray ourselves, and how we can allow ourselves to be what we can be, is what dreams are about. It is interesting to see that the falling idea is in this stanza too, in the line, "Adown Titanic glooms of chasmèd fears."

Also in dreams there can be the feeling that we're dead and we can't move. In a story like "The Pit and the Pendulum" of Edgar Allan Poe, in a story like "The Fall of the House of Usher," or for that matter, "The Tell-Tale Heart," the desire of a person to use *Not Being Able to Move* sleep as a means of death can be seen. Many people have nightmares because they do try to get away from everything; they even try to get away from the air, and in the process they dream that they are in a place from which they cannot get out, and they cannot breathe, and they feel as if they are being stifled. That is a nightmare. There is also the nightmare of not being able to run or walk or talk; because once we use sleep as a means of being immobile, we can punish ourselves by thinking that we cannot move from a point, that we cannot talk, that we cannot get up. We can also have a feeling that a big weight is on us, pushing us down, and we cannot move the weight.

Now, we dream this way because we are interested in our progress. We are interested in two things: we are interested in what is intimately ourselves, and we are interested in the world around us. This is shown in dreams.

Sometimes a person has a lovely dream, of seeing the whole world in color, and there is a sense of space, and *Lovely Dreams* for a while a person feels free. The person doesn't have to fly, there is just the feeling that there is more light and color in the world. This eulogistic dream is a way of saying: This is the kind of world you want to have, a world in which there is space and also intimacy.

We should see that dreams are always good, with the accent either on criticizing what is bad or on praising *Dreams Are* what we want and what we may not be *Always Good* faithful to. If it seems that something is praised, we say the dream is "good"—that is fine. But even a dream in which there is terror is good, because dreams are friends of ours. Every time we dream, something in ourselves is saying: "Look here, Lizzie; look here, Lloyd; look here, Larry; look here, Lucy, this is what you want. I know in the night I can't speak a clear language, but I still speak a language." And that language can be seen as making for sense.

In order to show what, in a good way, dreams can be about, I read a little known poem (I am translating it from the French), by Sully Prudhomme, who lived from 1839 to

1907. This poem is called "A Dream." It is likely that the
poet really had it.

> The laborer told me in a dream: Make your own bread,
> I won't nourish you any longer, sow the earth, plow
>   it yourself.
> The weaver told me: Make your clothes yourself.
> And the builder told me: Take the trowel in your
>   own hand.
>
> And alone, abandoned by the whole human race,
> From which I carried in me everywhere the
>   implacable curse,
> When I asked of God a great pity,
> I found lions standing in my road.
>
> I opened my eyes, doubting if the dawn were real:
> I found strong companions whistling on their ladder,
> All trades and work buzzed, the fields were being sown;
>
> And then I knew my happiness and that in the world
>   where we are
> No one can say arrogantly he can do without other
>   people;
> And from this day on, I have loved all people.[2]

This dream ends pretty well. But the lonely dream, the
dream where a person goes into a room and cannot find a
chair—that dream is a punishment for saying, "At a certain
time, I want to have nothing to do with nobody." (That is
2-A talking from the side of its mouth.) Sully Prudhomme,
in this dream, opposes the temptation of thinking we can
arrange the facts for ourselves and go on being esteemed.
Aesthetic Realism says all the facts are our best friends.

Another common dream is of somebody coming into a
room, and pointing a gun, or looking at you, *Dreams of an*
and saying, "Give up your money" or, "I want *Antagonist*
to stay here." This dream is one which says that if you

cannot take the other side of yourself while sleeping, in a friendly manner, that side will take the form of an opponent, one who attacks you. This dream has many, many variations. The antagonist can fight you in a restaurant, can fight you on the street, sometimes the antagonist seems to be a spy; but the point is that this antagonist of ours is ourselves in another form. Since we have not been able to make a friend of that part of ourselves, the neglected possible friend acts like an enemy. It is interesting to see that sometimes there is a satire: the great enemy seems to be really harmless.

I have mentioned in other talks the common dream of war time. You're in a city, you may be in a cellar, and bombs begin falling. One dream runs this way: the bomb is going to get to the cellar where you are, *Dreams of War Time* and you try to run out of the cellar, but you can't. This is a way of saying that from somewhere, something is going to come at you, wherever you may hide. Dreamers use the Nazis and the Japanese, and some few play tricks with the Russians, as a means of punishing themselves. In one way, bombs are like rain: rain can be seen as an opponent coming from a strange place, and so can bombs. These war dreams were a new way of saying that the strange outside world is close to you, and you might as well see it, and don't think that any time you can get away from it.

Then there are many dreams, in these days of the 20th century, about telephones. Many times in a dream a person wants to call somebody up and he or she can't. The dial *Telephone Dreams* won't work, you think it's this number but it's really another number, and somebody is already in the telephone booth, and the telephone is too high, and you can't talk, and it seems a different person at the end of the wire. Such dreams are saying: "You haven't wanted to communicate with things distant from you. You have wanted to live under your skin. You have made a pretense of living outside of yourself, but you don't fool *you.*" Dreams are a way of saying always: "You don't fool yourself, even under the covers you don't."

Then there is the common dream of just not being able to talk; you feel as if sand had choked you. This has to do with the problem of stuttering, the problem of difficulties of speech, swiftness of speech, inability to talk at ordinary times. However, it is a way of saying: "You don't have a right to communicate, because you *Not Being Able* don't want to show yourself. And if you don't *to Talk* want to show yourself, why do you pretend that you do want to show yourself?"

Quite a few dreams have occurred too on the subject of death. I have said that dreaming someone has died is not a wish fulfillment. We dream that someone has died because we haven't wanted to give full individuality to that person. A daughter will dream that a mother has died, *Dreams about* a wife will dream that a husband has died, a *Death* friend will dream that another friend has died. But in all instances there is a saying: "Your purpose is to make this person only part of yourself, and you want to care for this person because you can see this person as an annex of yourself." Not wanting to give a specific individuality to a person, is equivalent to not giving him life; and therefore we punish ourselves by thinking that the person to whom we have denied a separate, independent life is dead.

I am dealing with some of the general ideas in dreams, but dreams can be so subtly charming. I remember a dream told me which got in a house, and then a garden which at the same time was a wilderness. There was a *Some Charming* feeling of intimacy and wilderness. All of us *Dreams* want to feel cozy, tidy, just close to ourselves, and this desire is represented by the neat house. The garden is an in be-

tween step; it is still tidy, it is the outside become symmetri-
cally likable. But as the garden merges with the wilderness,
we feel that the things we don't know, the things that are
disorderly and spacious and mysterious, are also connected
with tidiness.

And dreams can be so beautiful. For example, only last
week a dream was told me in the following words, except
for a change of name:

> Harry Winston, wearing the cap of a conductor, with his
> back to the lunch counter, was slicing boiled potatoes. He
> looked younger than when I knew him twenty years ago,
> his face was ruddy and full. And at the other end of the
> counter he faced forward and was counting money.

This is a beautiful dream. It is a way a person has of
saying that twenty years ago he could have been better
than he was. The dreamer liked this person, Harry Win-
ston, and he now sees that he could have used him honestly and perceptively in his mind. But what is important
in the dream is that he feels he can face forward and
backward; that is, what he shows and what he doesn't
show can exist at the same time. There is a disruption
between front and back deep in our unconscious, and
what we have here is the same person seeming to be in
front and also in back. Furthermore, this person is dealing with a problem quite important to the dreamer: the
boiled potato represents heat and neatness. You feel a
boiled potato is warm, but at the same time it seems to
be pretty trim; it has symmetry. He is putting this boiled
potato into parts. You may say he is analyzing it, but in
the slicing, though there is heat, there is also accuracy.
And then while there is the narrowness of the slicing,
the face seems round; and this is a way of putting together wideness and narrowness. But what do we find
further? We find that while he's putting something into

parts, dividing it, he's also adding something; that is, counting money.

So the meaning of this dream was: You can integrate yourself. You can divide things and you can add them; you can be narrow and you can be wide. You can be hot and you can be neat; you can look this way and that way. In other words, you can have profile and full face. And the tendency on the part of this person was to make separate people of himself. This dream, I say definitely—and in this instance the dreamer agreed—is a road to felicitous integration.

And of course there is a wish. We all have a wish; we want to be better than we are. Why do we stop ourselves?

The dream I have just discussed has in it aesthetics; there was also a dream which deals with the problem of the self as center and the problem of the self as circum- *Dreams of* ference—which two problems are, of course, *Center and* *Circumference* one problem. A young man got a record of Beethoven, and as the record went whirling around he felt the needle would never reach the inner edge of the record, but somehow, with the nice music, it did. The young man at this time felt that there was no real relation between the center of himself, deep inside, and the outer world; but as he saw the needle going around on the record making music, something in himself said: "Look, Ludwig" (his name is not Ludwig), "Look, Ludwig, if the needle can, with lovely music, go from the circumference to the center, why can't you—and have Beethoven, too?"

A similar dream was had by a girl recurrently: she dreamed of being in the center of a big ring with children dancing around her. She wanted to be in the center, she felt gorgeous and regal there; she felt like a mingling of Queen Elizabeth and the Empress Catherine; but as she was in the center of this large ring and the children danced around her, she felt lonely, and she wanted to be where the other children were even if it meant giving up her regal central position. But the children didn't seem to be interested in that; they just kept on dancing.

Another dream about center and circumference was the following: A young man dreamed that his father, instead of separating the seed inside a grape from the outside of the grape, sees the grape as a whole, and takes it in his mouth, seed, flesh, and circumference—that is, skin. And the son wonders about that. Through the dream he could see himself as having a seed within, a flesh, and an outside skin; and he was trying to integrate himself by looking at this happening in terms of his father, about whom he had many feelings.

We have had the idea of the center and circumference in three ways: one, the record, with the outer edge of the record going towards the center with music; two, the girl in the dancing ring of other children; three, the grape with the seed in it being seen as a complete thing. These dreams have a deep aesthetic and a deep ethical purpose, and they should be seen that way.

Coming to some of the more unpleasant dreams. How often people have had dreams in which they want to go somewhere or they want to find an address, *Dreams of Wandering* and they can't. They are in a city; they are supposed to know where a house is, and they wander around; they go up and down, this way and that, and they can't find it. We use this kind of dream to punish ourselves because we haven't wanted to see something exactly, and we have wanted to feel that we are not at home in things.

The idea of not being at home in things is related to the dream of a girl who, in a movie, saw a wolf caught in *Dream of Being a Wolf* a trap, and the wolf had a fur that was her own fur coat. I asked her, "Did you ever feel you were prowling among people? Did you ever feel that you were visiting people and you really weren't visiting, that you were elsewhere, that you were just making the rounds?" And she said, "Yes." And then I said, "Don't you think that a wolf does something like that?" And she in time agreed. We can be prowlers; and this girl chose to describe herself as a wolf caught in a trap. That was her business. My job was to explain it.

Then there was the dream of a person about a turkey. This turkey seemed to be a strange invader of his nocturnal experiences. However, I said, "Did you ever talk suddenly and then feel that you wanted to be silent *Dream of Being* again? Did you ever say something and want to *a Turkey* take it back?" And I asked him, "Did you ever see a turkey put its head forward and then back, when it went a little into the world and then retreated, as a turkey with its gobbling does?"—"Yes."—And that was the reason he dreamed of himself as a turkey. We have here a very deep and lovely logic. It is not the logic of mathematics in the collegiate sense, but it is a logic and can be talked about.

There are many dreams where one is in a train, or on a subway. A train is a way of being in a room and *Dreams of* being in motion at the same time. We want to *Trains* feel that we are at rest and also on the move. A train is a means of our feeling this.

There is also the dream which has to do with covering. One girl told me a dream in which she felt that something came off her skin, and there was another skin underneath; and she felt that if she took off the *Dreams of* second skin she would have a further skin. *Covering* Children have told me that when they went to bed they took off a skin. And Balzac mentions a phrase in the slang of France for going to bed that meant taking off a skin. Dreams of covering are quite frequent.

An interesting and very simple dream was told me by a person who, like others, said he never dreamed. And then he told me he had had "a very simple dream—wasn't worth mentioning." I asked him what it was, and he said that just before getting up, around eight o'clock, he dreamed that he shaved and that he liked it. Yes, this was an idyllic dream, a nice dream, no awful complications, no getting in of the catacombs of Paris. However, it meant something. In taking off the cover of his face and liking it, he was saying that if he took off other covers, he could also like it. And that was very important for him.

A frequent dream that women have—and occasionally even men, in a strange way—is of having a baby. *Dreams of Having a Baby* Women dream themselves pregnant often. And they often find themselves with a baby in their arms; sometimes they don't know what to do with it. The having of a baby means that they want to present themselves in an outward fashion; they want to feel that they have an external existence. And the chief reason mothers should like having babies is that through this process they take the form of the outside world. When a woman is disposed to narrow herself, to contract, to say that she has nothing at all to do with things, up comes a dream—or in comes a dream—and says to the woman: "See here, Veronica, you want to get away from the world, but you really don't, so I'll give you a baby." This kind of dream has many variations, but the essential notion in it is that a woman is tempted to say, "Down with everything; go away, Everything"; but she has a more beautiful temptation to say, "Come, Everything; if I knew you I might like you." And this is what 1-A in us says.

Difficulty in dreams can take the form of difficult sex. A man feels he has a woman in a lonely hut, and everything *Sex in Dreams* seems to be all right, but for some reason carnality is not successful. This has to do with why men can be impotent actually, when they think they are carnally in a most successful fury. Women can have this dream, too. It isn't really so much about sex, though obviously sex is around: it is a saying that one cannot enjoy a person, standing for the outside world, with thoroughness.

And then there are the sex dreams themselves. These, strangely enough, are not only about sex. There was a man who was pretty pompous, pretty selfish, in the bad sense of the word. He told me that when he went to work he would think of when he could get back home and have the right to sleep, and he said he hoped he could make it by 9:30 though sometimes his friends kept him up till 10, poor thing. Later, he wasn't able to sleep. This man had a dream, and he was somewhat shy about it. He said, "It's unimportant." And I said, "You haven't been having so many dreams, so let's have it." So he said, "It's a bad dream." I asked why was it bad, and he said it was a "wet dream." I said the ceiling could stand the phrase, and we should have it. He told me that there was a woman in his office who seemed to be interested in him. He didn't have much respect for her, but in the dream she was being sought for by him. He sought rather successfully, and there was an orgasm. I had been telling this man that the reason he couldn't sleep was because he looked on sleep as too important: sleeping was the time he felt he could be contemptuous of everybody. And I had told him that if he welcomed the world in his sleep, he would have an easier time sleeping. So he dreams that he goes after something. I had told him he despised the world. He had despised this woman. I had told him he'd have to give himself to the world he wanted to be contemptuous of. He gives himself to this woman, in fact he runs after her. He has an orgasm. And the orgasm here means the successful giving of oneself.

An orgasm is delightful, as humanity has known; but the reason it is delightful is that it represents the giving of oneself. 2-A can spoil it, but sex is the greatest tribute to the

outside world there is. The reason there is so much trouble
about sex is not because sex is physiological or because it has
so many puritanical associations (the youth in the schools
now, who have had lots of sex education, still have lots of
trouble about sex)—the reason is that sex means a giving of
oneself to the outside world. An orgasm is the loss of oneself.
Aesthetic Realism says if you can lose yourself and have
such a good time physiologically, why not try to do it logically?

This man was saying in his dream that if he went after
something he hadn't wanted to respect, and gave up something of himself, it would be what he wanted. The sex dream
wasn't about sex: that's the funny thing.

Now I am going to read some sentences from a book
called *The Language of the Dream* (1939), by Dr. Emil Gutheil, who sometimes says he doesn't follow Freud in every
point, and that persons who think psychoanalysis explains
things in terms of sex have an insufficient knowledge of the
subtlety and comprehensiveness of present day psychoanalysis. I regard Dr. Gutheil as superficial, but in his book he
has some interesting dreams. Gutheil writes:

> A woman who complained that her husband never spoke
> a word to her while being intimate dreamed: "My hus-
> band kept handing me pitchers of food without speak-
> ing." The patient's drawing of the "pitcher" indicates a
> distinct phallic symbol.[3]

Well, this is interesting. First of all, there is no "censor-
ship," because the woman definitely knows that she's been
having sex with her husband and that she hasn't liked his not
talking. But what does she do? She changes sex *that she
knows about* into handing of pitchers—that is what Gutheil
says. The question is, if the woman knows that she and her
husband have sex, why does she have to conceal it in a
dream? The sex is a well known fact; it is in keeping with

the marital morality of America. We really have not a dream about sex. The woman feels that her husband though he gives her things in general, including sex, is not giving himself.

Gutheil has some statements as to the impropriety of seeing all kinds of things as meaning sex, and still he writes as follows (this is from page 58):

> *Coitus symbols.*—Symbols expressing contact: To telephone, to dance, to write a letter, to eat a meal together (see above: satisfying a desire), to give a party, to travel together, to walk together, to heat the stove, to sew, to weave, to rescue a person, to ride in a car or on a horse.

This is *revised* psychoanalysis! Now we have the masturbation symbols:

> Symbols for masturbation: Riding a bicycle, picking flowers, riding in an auto, pouring liquids, squeezing fruits, swimming, washing with soap, shaving, pumping water, etc. [p. 59]

And I say, Nonsense—especially to the "etc." Persons, first of all, *know* they have masturbation. And then in dreams they have all these symbols to hide from themselves the fact that they have something they know about? I could go on.

One thing that can be seen in dreams and also in life is that on the one hand we want to go ahead, and on the other hand we want to check ourselves. This desire takes many forms, and one of these days I am going *Abandon* *and* to talk more about these forms. We should see, *Restraint* however, that the desire to be wild and abandoned and the desire to be self-restricting are common desires, and are present all the time, both when we sleep and when we are awake. We are the same person whether we're awake or whether we're asleep.

I have mentioned the dreams of being stifled. There

are dreams which are accompanied by coughing, are accompanied by all sorts of respiratory discomforts, dreams where breath is gone. These dreams are witness to the fact that we *Dreams of* would like to stifle ourselves. They are horri-
Being Stifled ble, and they are related to things that happen to people in the way of asthma and so on; they are related to the fact that when we sleep we even try to say we don't "breathe" the outside world.

Among the interesting phenomena of dreams is the using of print and handwriting. A dream was told me of a person copying Beaumont and Fletcher's *The Maid's Tragedy*. He was changing print into handwriting. He was trying to see something happening in his own life in relation to literature. But besides that he was putting together the private feeling *Print and* that handwriting gives and the public feeling *Handwriting* that print stands for. Quite a few dreams are of this kind. In another dream, a woman got a letter from President Roosevelt. It was printed, but it was a personal letter. In this dream she was trying to put together her political activities, her political feelings, with something very personal. As I said last week in the talk on "Aesthetic Realism and Economics," people cannot put together their economic or political lives and their "psychological" lives. A desire to put them together was shown in this dream.

Then we have the using of geography. In dreams people are sometimes on a trip and they stop in the Midwest, maybe *Geography* in Chicago, and they think of California. The *Directions* reason is that the East represents one part of oneself and the West another. The Pacific Coast would represent the opposite of New York, and Chicago the in-between. All sorts of dreams having to do with geography have been told me.

Further, we have dreams that have direction in them: for example, going south, which is concerned a good deal with the unconscious. South represents down, and north represents up, as can be seen on a map.

To show how the problem of loneliness takes place in a person, I present a dream given to me some *Dream of* years ago which has satire in it, and which *Loneliness* shows that a person wants to be lonely and at *with Satire* the same time wants people to stop him.

I dreamt that I was in the navy. I was sleeping in the fore part of the ship and was dimly aware that we were traveling all over the ocean. Finally the prow pushed up into a lot of other ships. I was surprised that they didn't secure the fore part of the ship to the ships with rope. I came on deck and looked to the rear and felt satisfied that the ship was secured well there. I noticed a great number of ships all around. It was a secret rendezvous in the Pacific Ocean. I walked further on deck and noticed a few other sailors in blue uniforms sitting around leisurely and casually looking opposite to my direction. One slightly but politely inched over to let me pass.

This person wants to have a rendezvous with himself. He did have thoughts, as he told me, of being on a ship by himself, or sometimes people would be around, but he could dismiss them if he wanted to. He did use sleep to be satirical about persons, and he would go into the bathroom to do that. In doing so, he felt bad. In this dream he is on a ship, and he bumps into something. He has a feeling of great secrecy. But what does he find? He finds that other sailors are there; they are polite to him, they greet him. Though this person wanted to be magnificently and dismally alone, he saw this as pretty funny at the time of the dream. Even if he got into mid-Pacific he'd bump into something, and furthermore, the sailors would just take it for granted.

There was also a dream of a person who got himself into a closet with a tiger, and he thought he'd have an awful time.

He ran out and he told people about the tiger. And they *The Peaceful Tiger* came back and saw the tiger on a board, looking very peaceful. This person was trying to make an enemy out of something he should understand better.

An important set of dreams is the kind that have to do with the bathroom. I have mentioned a woman who had dreams constantly of going to the bathroom in public and sleeping in public. Well, the bathroom is a place which, like the bed, is used to dismiss the world. So people, when they're troubled, go into the bathroom. Very often people dream of wanting to go to the bathroom, but somebody else *Bathroom Dreams and Dreams of Sleeping* is there; and then the bathroom is dirty, and sometimes they have to go to a public place and everything is dirty, and things are too high and too low, and too small. There's all kinds of trouble as to the bathroom. The message of these dreams is: When you go to the bathroom, don't use it to despise people. (The psychoanalysts have said going to the bathroom is another way of having sex.) The point is that there are two situations of essential importance, somewhat similar, in which we can say to the world, haughtily: Good-bye. One is the bathroom, and the other is sleep. So people will have all sorts of bathroom dreams. I should say that millions are had in a year. I have heard ever so many.

I also have heard dreams where people know that they are not sleeping well, or think that they are not—with complications. These dreams are likewise saying: "Yes, you have two opportunities to forget and despise the world. One is the bathroom, the other is what you are taking advantage of now. If you yield to these opportunities, your best friends, your queer friends, your complicated friends will try to stop you by having you go to the bathroom or go to sleep and not have an easy time of it, in your dreams."

And the dreams are right. Dreams are always right. They always are.

I close this talk by saying that the essential problem of life, as seen by Aesthetic Realism, is in dreams. We have to protect ourselves, we have to be snug, we have to feel that we're somebody; we also have to meet a swirl- *Dreams and* ing world, a confused world. We have to see *Ourselves Have to Do with* general things, we have to see specific things. *Everything* Everything that we do look at—a dish, a floor, a train, a book, a person, a dress, a shoe—all these things, without our knowing, we see as about ourselves. So in our dreams, we say everything has to do with ourselves. And we warn ourselves: "Look, what you're not doing"; and we give ourselves hopes: "Look, what you could be doing." We should welcome the understanding of our dreams because they are our friends, trying to have us like ourselves and the world we are in, together.

NOTES

1. From Francis Thompson, "The Hound of Heaven."
The complete poem is accessible in the Modern Library
edition of Thompson's poems; also in various anthologies.

2. Sully Prudhomme, "Un Songe." The poem is here
translated from *Pages de Littérature Française,* by Ch.-M. des
Granges (Paris: 1926). It is also to be found in *Les Épreuves*
of Prudhomme, 1866.

Un Songe

Le laboureur m'a dit en songe: Fais ton pain,
Je ne te nourris plus, gratte la terre et sème.
Le tisserand m'a dit: Fais tes habits toi-même.
Et le maçon m'a dit: Prends la truelle en main.

Et, seul, abandonné de tout le genre humain
Dont je traînais partout l'implacable anathème,
Quand j'implorais du ciel une pitié suprême,
Je trouvais des lions debout dans mon chemin.

J'ouvris les yeux, doutant si l'aube était réelle:
De hardis compagnons sifflaient sur leur échelle,
Les métiers bourdonnaient, les champs étaient
semés.

Je connus mon bonheur et qu'au monde où nous
sommes

Nul ne peut se vanter de se passer des hommes;
Et depuis ce jour-là je les ai tous aimés.

3. Emil A. Gutheil, M.D., *The Language of the Dream* (New York: The Macmillan Company, 1939), p. 54.

Index